Marketing Today

SECOND EDITION

R. W. Chapman

Senior Lecturer in Marketing, School of
Management Studies, St. Helens
College of Technology

INTERTEXT BOOKS

Published by
International Textbook Company Ltd.,
24 Market Square, Aylesbury,
Bucks, HP20 1TL

First edition published 1969
Students' edition published 1971
This edition published 1973

ISBN hardback 0 7002 0202 1
limp 0 7002 0203 x

Printed in Great Britain by
Billing & Sons Limited, Guildford and London

Preface

When I moved from the world of business, where I had spent many years in the marketing of both consumer and industrial products, to the semi-academic sphere of the School of Management Studies, I had much reading to do to catch up with what had been written whilst I was concerned only with doing. Like many others, after my original academic training I had learned almost entirely by doing, although I had occasionally read a book and usually followed the papers in management publications to pick up something of what was happening beyond my immediate sphere of operations. I soon discovered that books on management subjects were legion, and that, whereas books on marketing (except perhaps technical books on advertising and selling) had not been very numerous a while back, they had suddenly become as common as daisies on a lawn.

Two things stood out for me. One, that writers in the U.S.A. had produced the vast majority of marketing books in English. They covered every aspect, often in great detail, if only one could locate the right book and (probably) wade through a great deal of unwanted material. Two, that there was developing a new jargon of marketing phraseology which seemed to go beyond what I consider to be the usefulness of jargon, i.e. to express ideas germane to a particular subject briefly and clearly. I cannot avoid all jargon, but I have tried to limit it to a reasonable level.

There seemed to me to be a job of work for a further book in a U.K. setting which would cover the main areas without going too widely or too deeply; a book moreover which could be a useful background without trying to lay down a pattern to fit any particular operation.

This book has no claims to contain new fundamental thinking. The subject is in any case ecological, and because of this it must also be coloured by my own experience. It is bound to be eclectic, yet by its very nature it does not lend itself very obviously to the acknowledgement of specific influences. It has been written because I hope it will help bridge the gap between massive tomes and surface descriptions. It contains some description, some analysis, some management, some conceptualisation.

I hope it may be of use to those for whom it is written—the mid-way manager (such as comes to us at St. Helens) who wishes to know more about marketing than his own immediate experience has shown him and the student of marketing, struggling to grasp the fundamentals of the subject from a limited amount of time spent with lecturers like myself (mostly practitioners) and with never enough time for "wider reading".

It is, I repeat, difficult to specify all the influences affecting a book such as this. I have tried to indicate particular references in the text, but I would like especially to thank Mr. J. H. Parfitt of Attwood Statistics (Great Britain) Ltd. and Mr. R. E. Thomas of Lancaster University, both former colleagues in very different operations. Each has allowed me to use material and also helped with advice in dealing with brand loyalty and the analysis of brand switching. I must of course accept full responsibility for the book as it now stands.

Preface to Second Edition

Since this book first appeared, the most important single change in the marketing world has been the entry of the United Kingdom and Eire into the European Common Market. This puts yet more emphasis on the importance of marketing overseas apart from affecting the lives and personal habits of each one of us.

In the first edition, after the most careful consideration, I did not treat overseas operations separately because I felt that the basic factors involved were essentially the same as those in any other marketing operation. It now seems to me not only appropriate but necessary to examine the export situation in its new context, therefore I have added a chapter on exporting and international marketing.

For the rest, I have up-dated information and examples and have added a number of references to some of the latest texts. For the most part these references amplify material in the book for those seeking more detailed analysis or description. I hope the reader will not assume that they are the only marketing books worth reading.

Contents

vii

"Consumption is the sole end and purpose of all production and the interest of the producer ought to be attended to only so far as it may be necessary for promoting that of the consumer. The maxim is so perfectly self-evident that it would be absurd to attempt to prove it."

Adam Smith

PART ONE

Marketing and the Product

In Part One we discuss the modern conception of marketing. The function itself is rapidly becoming better known and understood. What is new is the bringing together of a number of activities, previously scattered throughout the company or ignored, as an integrated function with the borrowed title MARKETING. We also examine the broader aspects of the strategy of developing and managing the company's products as this is the base from which to attain the company's objectives by means of successful business operations.

CHAPTER I

The Meaning of Marketing

What is business about?

Although there may be other objectives, the fundamental objective of "business" is to make money. Nationalised undertakings or non-profit-making institutions (which are only questionably "in business") may have other objectives. The owners and/or the management of companies may have yet other objectives, such as a desire for power, a wish to provide employment, a desire to let the majority enjoy what was once the privilege of the few. Yet few if any of these other objectives can be attained if the company does not make money. Profits are the sole means by which a company can, in the ultimate analysis, expand. From profits only can the company have the means to command the necessary resources until the return from the product these help to make starts flowing in. This is, in essence, what investment is all about. Investment consists of acquiring resources *now* to produce something in the future. The resources acquired will have to be paid for at once (especially the manpower element), but only after the product is made and sold does cash begin to flow inwards.

True, you can borrow money for this—but only if the lenders consider you are running a successful business. One of the prime criteria of this is whether you are currently making a profit. Lenders are not usually impressed by the argument "I could make a profit instead of a loss if you lent me some more capital", but are usually sympathetic if you are already profitable and can show how you plan to become more so.

If you do not believe this to be fundamentally true ask yourself two questions:

"Would I prefer to work for, and put my lifetime career in the hands of, a company making profits or a company making losses?"

"If I have a little money from which I hope to augment my eventual pension shall I invest it in a company consistently making profits or one making losses?"

It is unfortunate that the word "profits" has become associated with moral censure but perhaps there are already signs of the pendulum returning so that profit may regain a place of understanding and appreciation among the majority of people.

What is marketing?

Most of us would agree with Adam Smith on seeing his words (see page viii) yet for two centuries we seem to have ignored them. "Marketing" has been brought into the everyday language of business since about the mid-1950's as though it were a new word describing a new business concept, moreover a new word of which Alice might have said "it means what I want it to mean".

Broadly from the time of the Industrial Revolution until about the time of the First World War business men were able to set themselves up to make things they knew about or invented. They competed vigorously with each other to sell what they then made. By and large they succeeded and they learned by trial and error as the world struggled painfully along from a rural economy towards our modern industrialised society. For those manufacturers who succeeded and therefore survived it seems fairly clear that they made quite considerable profits in the process. They were also criticised by economists in later years for the unfortunate side-effects often produced by their laissez-faire profit-motivated actions.

As the 20th century advanced it became clear to most manufacturing companies in the Western world that competition was increasing; sometimes the situation was quite painful. Other manufacturers were joining in almost everywhere and customers no longer came to buy so that the manufacturer had to develop a sales organisation to go out and *find* customers for his wares.

Between the wars the whole world seemed in the grip of inescapable industrial depression and under-employment. Some few economists, led by J. M. Keynes (later Lord Keynes), devoted considerable thought to the fact that the economic system as a whole did not necessarily produce an equilibrium where all resources were fully employed. They considered the ebb and flow of consumption and investment but they did not go further into the situation of the individual firm than to consider that actions could on occasion be taken to create an element of monopoly or semi-monopoly. These actions could indeed enable an individual company to put itself in a more favourable situation than competing companies which did not take similar action. Even so, the focus of interest remained largely on the industry rather than the manufacturer, and on what government might do to create a favourable economic situation.

This period soon ended, for manufacturing techniques had been stimulated by the needs of the armed Services and very soon there existed the capacity to produce more of many products than "the market could consume". About this time, the keener or more clear-headed business men really began to sort out their thoughts. "What does the market want?" they said. "Let us find out; let us make it; we can then be sure of being able to sell it." And this became known as "marketing". The world had come full circle once more. The village craftsmen years ago made their wagons or saddlery by hand to the requirements of their customers, *whom they knew* personally. The new factory manufacturers of the 19th century made textiles or nails for people they never met, but who they *knew* (instinctively) would want them. Their successors sent out salesmen to get orders for products the manufacturers *felt* that people *ought* to want—but latterly did not seem to want in such quantities as expected. Finally the fourth generation is going out *to find out first* what is wanted and then coming back to convert these needs into products which can be sold to the satisfaction of the user and also to the profit of the maker.

We must not take this to mean that literally every manufacturing operation is now preceded by elaborate market investigation, or that every product is the result of such an investigation. There are still people and firms who can somehow sense the market. There are still inventors —or plain ordinary people—who have an idea and from it produce a product. Either way, before a lot of money and time is put into it the prudent business man wants to know more about the prospects of success and the risks of failure. How can one find out if people *want* a product that has never been made before? Can markets be created *de novo?* The answers surely come from within the concept of marketing as being that function responsible for the bringing together of a company's resources and the needs of the market so that the latter may be satisfied—with profit to the company. Let us not forget, of course, that there are times when a firm has to go out and sell what it is equipped to make, or even has already made (what sales manager has never had to deal with that situation?). Yet clearly these circumstances cannot be tolerated for long, if the business is to prosper, for the time must come when even the least knowledgeable buyer just will not put up with it.

So we may now perhaps agree that marketing is a business function and that it exists in a real world of live people going about their normal business. This is a simple but important starting point.

Economists once saw business men as passive individuals operating in and responding to economic events beyond their control and uninfluenced by their actions. Now, the business man is no longer seen as operating in and responding to economic events outside his control and uninfluenced by his actions. Drucker says in *The Practice of Management* that business management "implies responsibility for attempting to shape the economic environment . . . pushing back the limitations of economic circumstances upon the enterprise's freedom of action". Even this does not seem to go far enough for there is here an implication of material environment only.[Marketing goes further in that it is also concerned with the psychological environment and the fact that the consumer may have wants and needs which lie within him often unrecognised and certainly not formally expressed. This concern for the consumer's needs and the realisation that profit should be earned by satisfying these needs is now also bringing the economist round to have more sympathy with the business man, whom he formerly saw as being merely concerned with profit regardless of the consequences.

We see therefore that the marketing concept really insists on "making the consumer king". It recognises that we start with the consumer and his needs, continue with finding a product or service to satisfy these needs, and arrange for this product to be made and sold to the consumer, so that the whole operation is to the mutual benefit (profit) of both consumer and company.

The acceptance of this view implies that marketing action needs definition, direction and distance—that is, the setting of objectives. These objectives will then be seen as reference points or yardsticks which management can use for planning, action, review and re-checking. Our purpose, then, is to outline some of the approaches to the setting of marketing objectives and their attainment.

Awareness of marketing

Whilst we may smile at the idea that "marketing" was born in the 1950's (it will become more and more apparent that "marketing" has always been carried out to a greater or lesser degree by every man ever "in business") it is worthwhile looking at some of the reasons why the *awareness* of the subject has increased so markedly in the last decade.

First of all must come, as already mentioned, the appreciation by business men of the need to push back the limitations apparently forced on them by the economic surroundings. We will outline instances where this has been successfully carried through, but the crystallising of the idea that the environment has to be seized by the throat and pushed back, or aside, if the business is to develop, is important. Business today takes the world as it is seen to exist or expected to develop and in that world creates its markets. After all, once there was no steam power, no railways, no motor cars . . . the Duke of Bridgewater nearly ruined himself building canals for a trade that he knew was there but which could not be developed until after the canals were built. No one could accuse the pioneers of accepting the status quo and not pushing aside the constraints of environment.

Next, perhaps, we should consider the increase in real wealth, not only of countries but of social groups and individuals, especially after the Second World War. Disposable, discretionary income—what we can voluntarily spend on items other than shelter, food and warmth—has vastly increased in real terms as well as monetary units. Even a cursory glance at expenditures in almost any range of consumer goods shows how true it is that yesterday's luxuries are today's necessities. Today there are more people able to buy more things than ever before in our history.

This increasing ability to buy has been matched by increasing numbers of manufacturers making the requisite items and being ready to sell. In their eagerness to keep their plant fully occupied they have spread to right and left of their normal paths (the grass is always greener on the other side of the fence) and tried to get business from those who were not even in the same business field. So competition has grown and intensified. Never was such a wooing of the customer by such ardent grooms!

The tendency towards more intense competition has also been strengthened by the growing size of companies (in all size groups); by the increasingly large numbers of people employed; by the need to keep them fully employed lest they go to another employer; and by the increasingly large amount of capital employed in the business and hence the ever increasing amount of turnover and profits required. All these factors have influenced companies to look for new fields to conquer, new sources of cash and profit to enable them to go on growing and, if their growth impinged on another company or industry, "competition is a good thing" was always an acceptable answer.

At the same time that the need to influence the environment has been becoming more urgent the appreciation of the true function of market-ing has become clearer and more compelling in the eyes of progressive managements. This has manifested itself in a need to define, with some precision, the business area in which the firm will operate. That in turn leads to the determination of the needs of the customer and how to fulfil them. Finally, management has to ensure that the company makes at least enough profit to stay in business—and this clearly implies that the risks inherent in its operations must be minimised as one important step towards making a profit; by starting with knowledge of what is wanted before ever it is made, much of the risk element is so minimised.

Making markets

How far can it be literally true that marketing can "create" a market? Later we will look a little closer at some of the reasons why people behave as they do but for the moment it may be acceptable to suggest that it is difficult, if not entirely impossible, to persuade anyone to do anything that is *entirely* against his general character and make-up. To persuade a person to do something can only be possible if somewhere, consciously or subconsciously, he would like to do that. This is even more true when it comes to evoking a voluntary action such as buying a product, especially if the product is a type which the consumer may buy quite frequently and know quite well. However we start with an assumption that very often there *is* a further need lurking below the surface. If we can locate it and provide a product to satisfy it—at a profit—we are in a new business!

Let us look at some examples where it has happened in this country.

There is a very popular alcoholic beverage which in its early years enjoyed but little success. The marketing people examined the situation and came up with a reasonable hypothesis in the mid-1950's:

(*a*) The product is a good one and compares favourably with similar light alcoholic beverages.

(*b*) There is a young adult female sector of the population which is unaccustomed to hard liquor but which wants a sociable drink, not full-bodied beer.

(*c*) These people want to participate in a social life which has excite-ment and glamour in it.

(*d*) The product we have is fairly innocuous and could well fit the needs of these people if it were presented in a new setting.

Market research both in public houses and among people at their homes showed that the hypothesis was almost uncannily accurate. The product was therefore re-launched with a co-ordinated (marketing) plan designed to attract and satisfy the now clearly defined market of young female social drinkers. The basis of the plan was:

(*i*) Product—as before.

(*ii*) Theme—excitement and luxury sustained by glamorous settings for all illustrations; innocuousness emphasised by always illustrating wholesomely happy and healthy young women.

(*iii*) Packaging—a small bottle, emphasising innocuousness and limiting volume; luxury emphasised by gold foil on bottle (champagne association).

(*iv*) Price—fairly high to support luxury image.

The resultant operation was a resounding and profitable success for the new glamorous Baby Cham against the former rather dreary product record.

There is a similar case with a new wild bird food launched in 1960. Here it was hypothesised that people feed wild birds regularly with table scraps as an act of "nature-loving". Why not, therefore, give them a special food to make their action easier and indeed more effective?

Here, too, market research in a wide door-to-door check confirmed the broad hypothesis, which was really hunch-based on a wide experience in preparing pet foods of all kinds. The nutritional experts were consulted and the formulation of a satisfactory wild bird food was not too difficult. The proposed product was, however, most carefully developed, tested and test-marketed.

As a result Swoop appears now to be still a quite unique product— and one which assuredly benefits from the spate of (inspired?) editorial articles appearing each winter on our duty towards supporting the wild-life of the country.

A similar approach in a different field was that followed by the Gillette company in the 1960's. Gillette then built up a diversification strategy based on two of their own specialist resources—deep knowledge of the making of sharp cutting edges and great experience in making small plastic pressings such as razor and blade cases. A wide range of possible fields was narrowed down to examining the possibilities of disposable needles for hypodermic syringes.

The company followed up this intuitive approach with intensive market research. This disclosed that many hospitals were dissatisfied with their sterilisation methods on grounds of fallibility, cost, or human error; many did not know the cost of sterilisation; hospital staff usually found the sterilising of equipment an unpopular chore; some hospitals were already considering the use of disposable items, where available. The information obtained allowed Gillette to formulate clear directives on the product required: the needle must be positively sterile, securely packed against damage or contamination, easy to use, and cheap. Further, supply must be guaranteed, once begun, as once the old methods were abandoned it would be difficult to return to them.

Product development was guided by these needs. Help was enlisted from many disciplines ranging from production engineering to bacteriology; original work was done on the mechanics of puncturing the skin (this gave the company an additional advantage in expertise). Yet one particular difficulty was met largely by fortunate coincidence. Gillette needed a sterilising technique suitable for mass production and packing. About this time the government was encouraging the use of nuclear energy in industrial activity. It had been found that cobalt 60, available from the nuclear programme, could sterilise by radiation. The company were able to adapt this method in a new plant answering their product need and giving them a further technological advantage. The packaging requirement was solved by using a snap-off-end type of plastic container.

Similar approaches led to the development of a range of other disposable surgical instruments.

These examples of the successful development of products to meet identified customer needs should not, of course, be taken to mean that the process is easy. Customers do not necessarily rush to buy products, largely because so many of them (doctors in this last instance) are very conservative, and so they have to be persuaded to buy the new and leave the old. However, once they do change they often become formidable protagonists of the new!

Making marketing policy

These illustrations highlight a number of questions which the marketing management of a company should be able to answer.

(1) *What is our business?* The importance of thoroughly understanding what we are endeavouring to do can hardly be over-emphasised. Yet all too often management does not know the answer. Levitt pointed out almost ten years ago in his paper "Marketing Myopia" (reprinted in *Harvard Business Review,* July/August 1960) the dangers of companies seeing themselves as manufacturers of this and that rather than suppliers of the means to enable the consumer to satisfy a need (e.g. to supply transportation, not run a railway; to entertain people, not make films). The idea is simple enough, but all too often manufacturers, once they become encased in their buildings with machinery and people all around, say "our business is making metal goods" or whatever it is. Surely

there is a lesson here from the failure of Meccano, who continued to supply old-established metal construction kits when boys wanted space-age plastics (or at least parts to build rockets), as compared with the continued existence of the former coal-mining company Powell Duffryn as an industrial company with wide interests long after it ceased, because of nationalisation, to own any coal-mines. So the first step must be to define the area in which the company will operate in terms of the needs of consumers, or customers (the case is precisely the same for industrial as for consumer operations) which they will satisfy.

(2) *Should our business be different from what it now is?* Here we should be looking to the future to determine whether or not we shall be able to advance within the area we have given ourselves. If we confine ourselves too much we shall obviously fail to reach our optimum. On the other hand we should not be wild and woolly and seriously believe that we should cover all the areas often included in the Articles of Association of a company. Legally we may have to be authorised to act as publishers to enable us to use advertising brochures—but we do not seriously intend to rival Odhams or Penguin Books!

(3) *Can we say who are our customers?* Here we mean the firms or people to whom we should now be selling our products. If we don't know who they are, where they are, what kind of people (firms) they are, how can we hope to satisfy their needs?

(4) *What product, group or range, forms a proper part of our business and will meet the requirements of our customers?* We cannot generalise very easily here but the man *in* business will have little difficulty. For example we may be providing clothing to keep people warm or dry and underwear may be considered quite separately from outerwear. On the other hand, whilst stockings and lingerie may once have been considered quite separate markets, a stocking manufacturer may now consider lingerie fair game for his expansion.

Then there are some further questions, rather more technical.

(5) *How shall we get our products from our factory to the consumer?* This is concerned with the physical channel of distribution and selling and revolves around using shops, wholesalers, factors, selling at the house door, the use of advertising and so on. Often the answer may seem clear—use the traditional means, yet the non-traditional approach may be very attractive. It was not the door-to-door selling methods of Bloom which caused the collapse of his washing machine empire, in fact this unorthodoxy was the main reason why he was within an ace of quite fantastic success. Avon Cosmetics have captured a leading share of the cosmetic market by selling door-to-door rather than via the normal

shopping facilities. Ask the question again!

(6) *What price structure shall we adopt?* Another basic need but one which can best be covered as a separate subject later in the book.

(7) *What reasons shall we put forward as to why our consumers should buy our product?* This determination of the basic selling platform is a fundamental part of marketing in action. The example of the alcoholic beverage given earlier (page 8) indicates how the presentation and sales story can be vital.

(8) *Depending on the answers to these questions, what kind of organisation do we need?* There can be no question of one organisation for all types of operation for obvious reasons. Nor can there be any denial that in many companies the chief executive is also the chief marketing man. However in a company which is really marketing-minded and honestly customer-orientated a basic functional approach might be that shown in Figure 1.

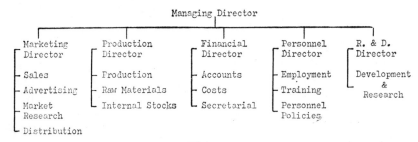

Figure 1

There will always be argument. The marketing director should at least have parity with the other functional heads, though many would say he *must* be "primus inter pares" and be designated deputy to the managing director. We recommend also that the relationship between marketing and R. & D. should facilitate the direction of R. & D. effort towards those areas which are fully in line with the company's marketing policies and that any activity outside of this should be specifically agreed and financed from "hope money" rather than "investment money".

There is one last question to be asked.

(9) *Are our answers to the other questions up-to-date?* Clearly companies cannot go through a major soul-searching operation four times a year. Nevertheless the danger at the other end of the scale must be guarded against and it is essential that a regular and frequent re-appraisal should be made.

Marketing—the dynamic function

From our definition of marketing and our outline of the policy-forming questions involved in arriving at a policy, the marketing function seems naturally to become the true dynamic function of the business. It is responsible for the collection and the interpretation of information about the market; it is responsible for adapting the company's operation to the market or creating a market for the company (in this sense environment and market may be considered as synonymous); it decides what is needed and hence what shall be made and in what quantities; it affects, often controls (or at least governs) most of the other activities of the company.

Clearly marketing is a top-management function and clearly top-management must agree the fundamentals of the company's marketing policy for these are identical with the company's overall policy. But the first job of the top marketing man must be to ensure that the whole of his top-management looks outwards and realises that a company lives on the income obtained by supplying satisfactory answers to the *needs of its customers.*

Suggested Reading

BARKSDALE, H. C. *Marketing in Progress,* Holt, Rinehart & Winston Ltd., 1964. (A series of papers giving landmarks in the history of marketing, indications of current developments and thoughts on what is to come.)

DRUCKER, P. F. *The Practice of Management,* 3rd edn., Pan, 1968.

HOLMES, P. M. *Marketing Research: Principles and Readings,* Edward Arnold, 1966. (Despite its title this very readable book has a short piece about, and references to illustrate, almost every facet of marketing.)

LAWRENCE, R. J., & THOMAS, M. J. (Eds.). *Modern Marketing Management (Readings),* Penguin, 1971.

LEVITT, T., 'Marketing Myopia', *Harvard Business Review,* July/Aug. 1960.

CHAPTER 2

Product Management

Consumer satisfaction

Before looking at the kernel of the management aspect of marketing we must consider for a moment what a product (or service) means to the consumer (or user).

Let us start, as always, with the consumer—an ordinary person with an ordinary person's likes, dislikes, prejudices and attitudes. Scarcely any one of us is quite like any other of us. Yet one thing is common to us all—we all have both an objective and a subjective reaction to almost everything. Sometimes we see both equally clearly, sometimes one or other side is to the forefront. But the two facets are still there, that which is outside our own being, that which is inside and part of our being.

Every product we buy performs two services, one an objective physical performance which is factual and can usually be measured with some accuracy, the other a subjective psychological or emotional satisfaction. The latter stems from the psychological aura which surrounds everything. This is a compound of our own experience with it and what we have come to know about it by conversation with friends, advertising and so on. As a result, when we use a product we get the benefit of both the physical performance and the emotional satisfaction of using that particular thing.

Should any reader doubt this, consider for a moment whether the only difference between a 1st and a 2nd class seat in a train is the degree of comfort of the seating. Or, in a quite different sphere, try to persuade any confirmed user of a liquid dish-washing product that, by going to the chemist, buying certain chemicals, mixing them and diluting them with water, you can save her a sizeable sum of money each year. She will take some convincing as she "knows" her regular brand is safer, better for her hands, more efficient, more economical or different in a dozen other ways. In recent months (1967–8) the author discovered in casual conversation that at least three of his course members had tried this experiment independently and had achieved these precise results.

The reader who is intelligent, sensible, rational, may not like this situation. But it exists. There may be occasions when we consider such prejudices irrational and wrong—but to forbid the exercising of them, to set up as knowing better than the other man what is good for him, leads into a political argument outside the scope of this book. Let us accept that the situation exists.

The consumer, then, buys a product and gets from it both a physical and an emotional satisfaction. The latter derives from the presentation of the product, its packing, its maker's name and reputation, its own name, the advertising of it, what other people say. It may also come from the method of selling: who can doubt why hairdressing and beauty salons are normally more luxurious and sensuous in their appointments than the greengrocer's shop? Nor should we consider that this is entirely a phenomenon of consumer product operations. Even in industrial operations where goods and services are bought for use in the business of the buyer, both buying and selling organisations are made up of people. These are the same people at work as they are at home with their families, when they are called "consumers". Apart from their business duties they still have their normal human reactions which include, for example, the sense of pleasure in dealing with "nice" people, or a "nice" company or a "reliable" concern. Are these not emotional satisfactions to those concerned? Do they not influence events, especially, in the last analysis, when all other things are equal?

The marketing doctrine

In moving on to operational marketing let us repeat our doctrine.

(*i*) Fundamentally a business depends for its continued existence on its customers rather than its production facilities.

(*ii*) The basic function of marketing is to define the need of the customer and find a way to satisfy it at a profit.

(*iii*) This implies that marketing decides what is wanted and how much should be made, and also controls the operations necessary to get the product to the consumer because until the product is "consumed" the need of the consumer is *not* satisfied.

(*iv*) This concept firmly places marketing in the centre of the business as the energising force from which all else is driven.

A mere mental nod in approval here is not enough. It will probably occur to the reader that most people will agree about the marketing concept but that too few have really embraced it and practise it. Lip service is *not* enough and it may help to repeat with Drucker (from *The Practice of Management*) "The purpose of business is to create a customer" for this makes good sense.

The company, then, makes its products because of the satisfaction they afford to the customer. This satisfaction derives both from the psychological aura surrounding it and from its physical performance.

Product planning

In setting about the task of handling his products the marketing manager uses:

Quantitative market research,
Motivational market research, and
Intuition.

The idea of consciously planning products implies both having an objective and also realising that the business situation is never really stable. Even when the objective is known and a plan is made to achieve it, another objective may rapidly replace the old one. We have already seen the need for an overall long-range objective and will later consider it in more detail.

In the immediate operation, however, whether he wishes it or not, the marketing manager finds that a number of factors are constantly tending to promote the development of new (or improved) products. Some of these arise in the market; some within the company itself. The following are some of the basic marketing pressures concerned.

(*a*) A new consumer need is discovered by market research.

(*b*) Consumer complaints indicate that the present product is inadequate.

(*c*) Complementary or associated products are needed to round out the range and thus give a more complete service or coverage to the consumer.

(*d*) Change in the availability or price of raw materials makes a change of product unavoidable.

(*e*) A technological change or invention makes possible a product which will now fill a known and hitherto unsatisfied need of the consumer.

The environmental conditions in the market may also produce similar pressures:

(*i*) A competitor produces a better or cheaper product.

(*ii*) Economic or social circumstances change.

(*iii*) Trade and/or consumer custom requires the frequent remodelling of the product.

Finally, from the factory itself come other pressures towards the same end:

(1) A desire to utilise plant to the full (e.g. to even out a heavy seasonal variation in output).

(2) A desire to use waste products profitably (e.g. making dog biscuits from waste cereals or cork insulation from cork chippings).

(3) A desire to reduce costs by producing products which are easier or more convenient to make.

(4) A desire to make use of the findings of R. & D. (e.g. X-rays and insecticides which originally were by-products of other scientific research).

Developing a product policy

Whatever the pressures tending to hasten the development of new products the marketing manager must have some organised method of approach and we will first look at factors over which he can exercise some control and later at those where he cannot do this.

It is clearly desirable that there should be screening and filtering processes to eliminate time-wasting, unnecessary excursions into unprofitable ventures. Further than this, however, positive criteria should be agreed for deciding, before a project is investigated at all, whether it will fall into the category of likely worthwhile projects. V. P. Buell lists eight such criteria in his book *Marketing Management in Action*:

(1) The idea should be in the company's specified field of endeavour (or a closely related one).

(2) It should utilise three or more of the following company strengths —design ability, production expertise, reputation with customers, channels of distribution, selling or advertising skills.

(3) The product should have a selling price in a specified range.

(4) The product should be capable of reaching a pre-determined minimum volume in three years.

(5) The product must reach a pre-determined ratio of profit/turnover and profit/capital employed.

(6) If similar products already exist any new one must have a demonstrable advantage in use, or lower cost, or the company's sales/distributing organisation must be better—or all three.

(7) If a similar product already exists it must be in the early stages of its life cycle.

(8) There should be a minimum capital investment required to

prevent small low-overhead competitors coming into the market too easily.

Not all these criteria need be applicable to every case but the desirability of screening ideas even at the discussion stage is clearly sensible.

The standards set by the criteria will vary from industry to industry and firm to firm. It is seldom, if ever, possible to apply the norms of incremental profit and incremental cost* as these can rarely be pinned down in practice. What can be done, however, is to ensure that profits are calculated over the full estimated life of the product. Standards for return on investment must be influenced by the industry's normal achievements and the firm's own history. Both should clearly be considered in the light of market rates of interest and, above all, in the light of alternative opportunities for using the company's time and resources. Should there ever be an element of "the shareholders would do better to put their money in the Post Office" then indeed the project would look doubtful.

Even before the strategy of the development of a new product is fully worked out some issues which affect its implementation must be considered because they react back on the original strategy. Timing, for example, is of the greatest importance when fashion or attitude trend is involved. A new idea can be so far ahead of the market that people will not accept it at once. This actually happened with both the use of rear-engined and front-wheel-drive cars and also with the spread of central heating in the U.K.

When rear-engined and front-wheel-drive cars appeared on the U.K. market in recent years, despite the fact that both techniques had been used even before the war, the car-driving public were slow to embrace them with enthusiasm. They were too different, too unfamiliar. When, however, a number of them had been seen on the roads, when car owners had been able to talk to owners or garage men who had experience of them, the new types soon became very popular.

In the same way many large houses had central heating well before the 1939–45 war. In the later 1950's, however, manufacturers began to try to develop central heating installations using gas, oil, electricity or solid fuel and gradually house owners became aware that this amenity was not just for the rich who lived in large houses. In the mid-1960's central heating became, in a matter of two or three years, very much a popular project because a large segment of the population were now

---

* This is the economics concept that maximum profit is achieved when the level of production is expanded until the extra profit from selling the last unit made is equal to the extra cost of producing that unit.

"ready and willing". In all three instances the manufacturers who were too early had to wait until the time was right, although their product conception was perfectly sound.

Frequently indications of the possible situation can be seen in the life cycles of other similar products, where these exist. Even then, there is always the successful case of the marketing manager who carves out a substantial share of a declining or obsolescent market, as witness the success of Ajax scouring powder in the U.K. since the war.

In the U.K., Procter and Gamble is both a leading and a well-informed company in the soap and allied products market. It considered that the household scouring powder market was obsolescent and withdrew from it altogether after the late war in order to concentrate its energies on more worthwhile sectors. Despite this assessment (which may or may not have been known to them at the time) Colgate–Palmolive launched their candidate Ajax in this field in 1947–8. Since then Ajax has prospered; it is one of the leaders in its market and has been a most successful venture. Nevertheless any marketing manager should consider whether he should normally devote his resources to an expanding market and what the conditions are for the exceptions.

Clearly allied to the factor of timing is the question of promoting obsolescence. This has been successfully done by Ronson in England, where new up-to-date models of cigarette lighters are frequently produced and where a high proportion of the products are sold for the buyer to give as a gift. In some consumer durables, such as cars, there may even be a deliberate development of a secondhand market with the idea both of freeing the original buyer to buy another new car and also of getting the secondhand buyer accustomed to the make, in what is a secondary and cheaper market, before becoming a new car buyer.

A third factor is whether the marketing manager wishes to promote a policy of diversification or simplification of the range of products. There are always arguments in support of extending the company's range of products and we will look at some of these shortly. The other side, the case for reducing the range, is not so frequently discussed. Yet it must often happen that the consumer becomes embarrassed or confused by a wide choice of overlapping products even from one company. Within the company the position may be even worse, it may be positively harmful.

Simplifying the range

There are many reasons why products should be dropped from the current range. Sometimes products which are candidates for elimination are sheer mistakes and should never have been introduced in the first place; others may have been obtained fortuitously in the purchase of another company with some good and some poor products. From time to time competitors may produce something which renders a product out-of-date; sometimes it is the market's needs which have turned in another direction. A typical example of this last came to the author's notice in 1964. He met a manufacturer in a Lancashire town who claimed to be the last of the old clog-iron makers. Clog-irons are metal bars fixed to the soles of the old wooden clogs once so popular in the mill towns. As clogs declined in popularity and finally became almost non-existent this manufacturer had turned to making heel and toe

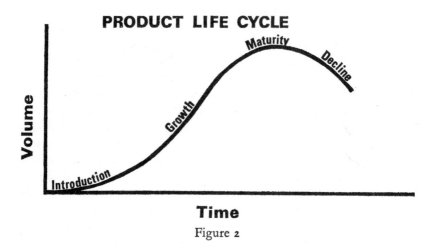

Figure 2

plates for heavy boots to keep up his business. Finally, the army authorities decided to put a composite rubber heel on army boots instead of the traditional leather one with steel plate. The manufacturer's last major source of business was gone. He was elderly and decided to close down.

Whatever may be the reason, the marketing man must be realistic about the harm done by ailing products and the hidden costs they trail along with them. Most products and many services (the local cinema in the entertainment world is now a Bingo Palace) go through a fairly clear life cycle. They start slowly through an introductory phase, then they go through a development stage and finally, unless there is some way of rejuvenating them, they go through a phase of maturity and then decline. They do not die quickly and painlessly—indeed one can still find "clog-iron makers", but more often than not they should be making something else.

The time factor varies greatly from, say, a few weeks in the case of a toy fad to many years in the case of heavy capital equipment.

When the possibility of dropping certain products is raised there is usually a great deal of internal opposition. They may include old favourites, proven leaders in former times and sentiment is often expressed in terms of attempted justification. "Look at the overheads they carry! How shall we replace this loss of contribution?"

Yet there are a number of positive reasons why it is better to take the plunge and eliminate ailing products firmly and quickly. The first of these is that in fact resuscitatory action is very seldom successful for a product which is in genuine decline. Attempts at revival all too often lead to a long and dreary fight which uses up resources which were better applied elsewhere. Secondly, when products are firmly dropped the search for new products is prosecuted more vigorously, for the need is greater. At the same time efforts to increase the sales of the other products in the range are also pursued more enthusiastically, again partly because of the greater need to keep up turnover but also because the distractions of the declining products are no longer there to hinder other effort.

Fourthly, obsolete products may damage the company's overall reputation and cause it to be connected with older out-of-date thinking. Building a good reputation is a long and difficult job but repairing a damaged reputation may often be even harder.

Finally, ailing products tend to use up a disproportionate amount of time and effort in both marketing and production. Frequent price changes, more advertising and more selling effort are often required in marketing whilst there are often shorter runs and more changing of production schedules for products which never quite come up to expectations. The result of all this is that there are always hidden additional costs incurred by declining products.

Despite these considerations simplification and rationalisation of the range of a company's products is often carried out piecemeal or at a time of crisis. This is quite unnecessary for a much more sensible way is for the marketing manager to fix criteria for the performance of existing products in the same way as he fixes them for the necessary performance to be achieved by the introduction of new products. Then a periodic review, say once a year, will reveal the products which have failed to reach the necessary criteria levels for retention. Automatically this will lead either to positive efforts for reviving declining products or their removal from the range. The implications of this action and the machinery for phasing out declining products must of course be worked out in detail when the standards for retention are set. It is sad that such a procedure is so seldom adopted for it would save much trouble.

Before leaving this subject we must make two further observations. The first is a truism that the smaller the range of products the more necessary it is to ensure that each one is exactly right and in a healthy state. Secondly, there may always be a case—which must be allowed for in the criteria set up—for retaining a product which, whilst not in itself fully profitable, is truly necessary to complete the range and thus offer complete service to the customer. If this case is genuine, the product is not really failing to meet the (correct) criteria. If a false case is put forward, resting merely on an accountancy argument concerning the methods used for calculating costs and overheads, then the right criteria will certainly separate the healthy products from the ailing ones.

Diversifying the range

The basic reason for wishing to diversify is to increase the level of profit by adding turnover from new business and by spreading the costs of distribution and selling over more products. Diversifying includes not just the making of new (or improved) products but also the extending of geographical coverage; for example to export when previously all sales were in the U.K. This is not merely a theoretical concept but one of particular importance, especially where the developing countries are concerned. A product which has been outmoded in an older industrial country may well be still a growth product in a developing country. The market overseas for unsophisticated agricultural equipment is a case in point, as bicycles have also been in the post-war years. Territorial expansion is also an obvious early choice for the smaller company which has not yet developed to a national scale of distribution.

The possibilities provided by technological developments should clearly be examined very early in the process of arriving at a product policy. Can improved, or similar but cheaper, products be made? Recent years have seen great advances in this field such as transistorised equipment, ready-prepared meals and new fabrics for clothing. Alongside technological possibilities the marketing manager should also consider possibilities identified by research into and knowledge of the market. Customers do on occasion request new products. Whilst this may be a phenomenon largely of the industrial sphere the author remembers some years ago a growing clamour from users of the then new packeted dry soups for larger packs suitable for the catering trade.

Finally these were produced although previously the manufacturer had not considered them worthwhile. In very many cases, however, diversification follows because marketing research has identified a need or a new segmentation of the market where a closely tailored new product can offer real scope.

There are two other important factors to be considered when approaching the marketing of a new product. Firstly, if there is a competitor already in existence will the cost of establishing the new item with a reasonable volume of business be greater than the cost of buying the company with an already established product? Secondly, what will be the effect of the new product on the company's general reputation? Will it help develop it in the desired direction or will it do positive harm and react adversely on other products? This factor may not always be important but when it is it can be vital.

Market segmentation

Market segmentation is the splitting of a larger, more heterogeneous market into smaller more homogeneous segments. It is carried out in order to satisfy the needs of the segment with a more precisely fitting product. A typical illustration is the breaking up of the overall soap market, once served by the universal block of soap cut up in the grocer's shop, into separate markets with specialist products—hard soap, toilet soap, soap flakes, light and heavy duty soap powders, light and heavy duty synthetic detergents, washing-up liquids, shampoos and so on. Each product group is now bought and valued for its particular qualities in a much narrower field of use.

Segmentation may be based on one of several approaches. It may be geographic, for example, based perhaps in the case of soap on the hardness of the local water supply, or in the case of food on a tradition of eating porridge or soup more in Scotland and the North than in the South of England.

It can also be based on demographic factors, for example the tendency of younger people to have a sweeter tooth so that they buy more sugar and chocolate confectionery than older age groups—hence the very many products specially designed to appeal to the young and the rather less numerous ones designed for the more mature palate.

In recent years another school has taken a more sophisticated approach altogether. This is based on the *attitude* of people towards an activity, and how they think about products. In marketing a cold cure one manufacturer fashioned his approach to take account of three different attitudes (Skelly and Nelson: *Scientific Business*, Summer 1966).

Some people believe in taking medicine to overcome colds and are not concerned about possible side-effects. They are normally healthy and will try almost anything—and hope. Others feel there is no way of overcoming a cold save to retire to bed with a hot water bottle and a hot drink. They won't normally try any sort of a "cure". A third group would like to feel that they are actively trying to overcome a cold when they get one, but they are against taking anything "strong" or which might have side-effects. The manufacturer looked on each group as a separate segment to be treated in a different way from the others. In a later chapter we will discuss some of the implications and practical problems arising from this kind of segmentation which, from the behavioural side, seems to offer a great deal of assistance to the marketer.

Segmentation is often considered to be a cost of growth. It is thought to be the necessary accompaniment of a drive to get more business. In reality it is designed to enable the marketing man to get a firmer hold on the entire market essentially by obtaining a closer "fit" between his product(s) and different sections of his total market.

Market leadership

The last of the factors over which some control may be exercised in arriving at a basic product policy is the strategic approach to market leadership. Do we wish to lead the market or to follow it? Drucker, in *Managing for Results*, defines market leadership as *a status conferred on a product by the market* which, because of a specific advantage gained by using the product, is either prepared to pay more for it or to wait for it when it is not immediately available. Leadership, he says, carries with it profitability. It is not the same thing as possessing the largest *share* of the market but it does mean that the market leader may have to take risks with a new product concept and not be a mere follower of others. The concept is equally applicable to consumer products although Drucker writes of industrial products. Following behind may be easier in many ways but it carries in its wake its own dangers. It may be safer to let someone else pave the way—which may also be a good deal less rewarding. The decision (often burked in practice by Messrs. Facing Bothways) is not just a matter of desire. It is also a question of whether the resources available, the scale of operation of the company, its ability to obtain and pay for the necessary information, will permit of the size and quality of operation to ensure success as a market leader. One large operator in the soap world seems to pin his faith on his ability to research the market, find a segment where there is a need which is not being adequately covered, devise a product and mount a campaign, regardless of whether he is first or not, which will ensure him a leading position in the market. An equally large company in a different field clearly believes that success and eminence in the world of prepared foods means being first with the idea and its introduction, even if the product (though good) is not quite perfect. It is largely such different recipes for success that make marketing so fascinating.

Factors beyond marketing control

In arriving at his product policy the marketing manager must also take account of factors over which he can exercise little or no control. Their influence can hardly be described or evaluated as one general case but in each specific instance he should not ignore them.

Firstly, in the technological field, there is no certainty of how techniques may develop. A judgment or assumption about the technology of the future may nevertheless be inescapable and it is normally better to make it explicitly than ignore the factor altogether. Next come changes in productivity. Efficiency in administrative and distribution operations is improving. What was impossible yesterday is child's play today and the vast increase in frozen food consumption in recent years is certainly due in part to the use made of improved distribution techniques.

Another factor is the change in the total of, and distribution of, the real wealth of the country bringing with it great increases in the amount of disposable income allied perhaps to equally great social changes. Modern social and industrial organisation and the universally shorter working week have led to more leisure time for most people. Modern communications, particularly T.V. in the realm of ideas and easier travel in the realm of physical movement, have led to an upgrading of taste and a desire to translate higher incomes into an enormously improved general standard of living. These factors can scarcely be thought to have settled down yet into any certain and predictable groove but they have already brought about great changes in the requirements of large numbers of people.

Lastly, we should include changes in the structure of the population. Whilst the population of the U.K. is not growing quickly there are rapid changes occurring in the relative size of different age groups, in the number and size of families, in the family life cycle. These in turn are being reflected in changes in the location of people's homes and a change in the pattern of retail distributive outlets to care for their needs. In addition to all this there is also the large body of new post-war immigrants who still carry with them elements of their own ancient cultures but who may sooner or later merge into the present patterns of the indigenous population. None of these factors should be ignored by the marketing policy maker if he wants to develop a sound basic policy for developing his range.

Developing the new (or improved) product

Much has been written in an attempt to classify and formalise the actual handling of the introduction of a new product. This is not surprising in view of the small proportion of new ideas which eventually lead to a successful product. In *Mathematical Models and Methods in Marketing* (Bass *et al.*) of some 2,100 new proposals examined only 17 were found meritorious and these were subsequently classified as:

Really successful	2
Fairly successful	5
Borderline	6
Too early to say	3
Failure	1

Chorofas, in his book *Sales Engineering*, quotes Scotts (papermakers) in the U.S.A. as claiming that 6,000 new products appear in the U.S.A. each year but that only 500 survive even the first year.

Others have estimated that 80 per cent of new consumer products fail, yet 75 per cent of U.K. grocery trade turnover in 1965 was estimated by Nielsen to come from products not in existence in 1950. Let us then see if we can at least find some broad guide lines to help simplify, perhaps ease, the way.

Screening out probable failures as early as possible is the first requirement for avoiding the unnecessary waste of time and money which stems from a needless failure at a later stage. Very elaborate procedures are used for many products (especially in the consumer sphere) but simpler methods can be adopted for less complicated operations. The basic principle is to use progressively more demanding tests at each stage so that when the product finally appears on the market it has a reasonable prospect of success, the manufacturer's risks are reduced to the minimum and he is not faced with heavy losses from investing in a huge failure.

In the earliest stages the development personnel themselves use their own judgment in accepting for further development, or rejecting, the outcome of their attempts to produce the product desired. When they believe they have a possible answer, this is then checked with an informal panel of people within the company who have not been concerned in making it. When this panel is satisfied a more formal check is made.

This stage is a procedure called a "blind test" which consists of taking prototype samples to consumers, of the type who will eventually buy the product, and obtaining their opinions about its performance. At this stage there is no presentation, packaging or maker's or product's name involved so the reaction is purely on the physical performance.

When any product amendments found desirable have been made the product is now "test-marketed". Here the manufacturer arranges to try the product in a limited section of the market only. The product now appears for the first time with its proposed price, packaging, presentation, name, with advertising support and sales effort scaled down to the size of the test market. The object is to limit the commitment and expenditure until the manufacturer has knowledge of how the trade and the consumer react; the test marketing operation will show up weaknesses in his plans, it will help him assess more closely the probable future of his project on a wider scale.

What advantages will this quite elaborate procedure give to the marketing manager? Essentially it will indicate weaknesses. It may also enable consumer research to be carried out to find how many people knew of, or bought, the product and their attitudes towards it. It will indicate the effects of *the whole plan* as a "marketing mix" and if specific elements (e.g. price) are to be checked then additional test areas will be required with all the elements the same except the one variable to be tested. The procedure should only be used with the greatest restraint for *predicting* broad scale results because of the many approximations involved in setting up the test market.

Some kind of procedure, step by step, trying to eliminate weaknesses, screening with an increasingly fine screen, does seem to be worthwhile in the larger operations. It is, however, an expensive business—though cheaper, as we have said, than a full-scale mass-market failure which is more likely to occur if such approaches are ignored.

In addition to this kind of marketing technique, other measures likely to help can also be instituted inside the company. The author's own experience is that the most important single factor is to create, at the earliest possible moment, a development team composed of all those involved in the various stages of each operation at the appropriate level. Only by involving all concerned in the creation (within a general policy framework) of those parts of the plan for which they are to be responsible can true co-operation be obtained.

Planning the operation

Test marketing is near to the end of the whole development procedure. There is a good deal more to be done than we have so far covered and most of this is more conveniently discussed in more appropriate sections of this book. Let us, therefore, summarise the procedure before passing on.

Stage 1. Screen the concept of the new product to ensure that it fulfils the criteria for new product approval.

Stage 2. Estimate the probable demand at various possible price levels.

Stage 3. Calculate the investment cost in terms of plant, materials, labour, marketing costs.

Stage 4. Determine the price and re-work costs and volume estimates to check that profit criteria are still reached.

Stage 5. Complete the plan of how the product will be put on the market showing in detail who carries out each operation and how each part fits in with the others. A detailed time-table is necessary. A network analysis can often be used with advantage.

Stage 6. Whenever possible include a test marketing operation in the overall plan showing what this test is intended to show, how this information will be obtained and what effect this information will exert on the different later stages of the original plan.

Once these plans are completed the marketing manager should check them over to make sure that his organisation is able to cope with the needs of the situation or whether changes may be necessary. As a general rule the needs of the operation should not be subordinated to the existence of a particular organisational form: again, the customer takes precedence. He is "the king" and, if his needs require it, the organisation should conform, not vice versa.

There are two general principles in product planning and development. The marketing manager must:

(*a*) show clearly to all concerned where the division of responsibility between the planning and the operations groups comes. He must make sure that everyone concerned knows this;

(*b*) bring all the functional areas concerned into the procedure at the earliest possible moment. If they can be interested and encouraged to contribute to the formation of the plan—not merely told to carry it out—many difficulties will be avoided and a real team spirit engendered.

Suggested Reading

AMES, A. C., 'The Dilemma of Product/Marketing Management', *Harvard Business Review*, Vol. 49, 1971.

DRUCKER, P. F., *Managing for Results*, 2nd edn., Pan, 1967.

FOSTER, D. W., *Planning for Products and Markets*, Longman, 1972.

Guide to Locating New Products, T.T.A. Information Services, 1971. (Has useful information on facilities and services available to help manufacturers in this area.)

KOTLER, P., *Marketing Management*: *Analysis, Planning and Control*, Prentice-Hall, 2nd edn., 1972.

OFFORD, R. H., *Product Management in Action*, Business Publications, 1967. (What a product manager actually does.)

PART TWO

Behavioural Science Approaches to Marketing

CUSTOMER BEHAVIOUR

The customer is an individual, a human individual. *This is the case whether we are considering a buyer in a company, a housewife buying food or clothes for her family, or a teenage boy buying a gramophone record for himself. As marketing is so inseparable from the customer we must at an early stage examine the behaviour of the individual to try and find out what makes him act as he does. Without some understanding of behaviour —in which there is no great unanimity among the "experts" themselves— it is not possible for us to appreciate large areas of our primary subject and the reader is strongly advised to read some of the specialist literature. He is also counselled to be chary of over-generalising and of using semi-technical words lightheartedly. The subject is a fascinating one: the author hopes the reader will not expect to learn it all in a few pages.*

CHAPTER 3

Psychology and Customer Behaviour

Let us first consider how psychology, one of the oldest of the behavioural sciences, can help us. Psychology, dealing with the working of the human mind, tends to emphasise the differences between individuals, who are all in some way unlike. At the other end of the scale, the economist tends to disregard human individuality and reduce his argument to the abstract level of figures and impersonal analysis. In late years, however, the social sciences have contributed very considerably to the development of marketing thought which is now advancing along two main lines, quantitative analysis and behavioural analysis.

Motivation

Motivation, perception and learning are three basic issues in the psychology of buying as well as that of the individual. Much of modern psychology begins with the concept of human need as the source or inspiration of human behaviour and there is considerable agreement among the experts that there are four primary drives in activating human behaviour:

HUNGER   THIRST   SEX   PAIN

Hunger is a motivating influence; a hungry person is more likely to notice food than a person who has just eaten: his objective is not food but the eating of it to remove his hunger. In psychology "motivation" is thus defined as the "energising process which impels behaviour". It does not give precise direction to that behaviour as we shall see, but motivation is what starts off the process.

There are other (derived or learned) needs which A. H. Maslow, one of the leading writers on motivation, lists (*Motivation and Personality*, Harper & Row, 1954) after the primary needs as:

> Safety
> Love and belonging
> Esteem (in one's own regard and that of others)
> Self-actualisation (to become all one is capable of becoming)

He considers that none of these latter needs has an important influence until those higher on the list have been satisfied—if the need for food has been met to about 90 per cent and that for safety to only 30 per cent then the need for safety may dominate in sensitising and energising behaviour.

Some authorities feel that drives *must* be separated into primary and secondary drives and that the physiological drives of hunger and thirst far outweigh any others. In Britain, however, we have a generally high standard of living and literal hunger and thirst are not commonly experienced. For our purposes it seems therefore to be more reasonable to expect useful guidance for practical marketing from the Maslow concept of an order of priority of needs according to the circumstances prevailing at any one moment.

To save unnecessary difficulty let us now look at a number of definitions of terms which we shall use in the next pages.

Sensation. An experience closely dependent on the stimulation of a particular sense organ—burning one's fingers; light shining on one's eyes.

Cue. A stimulus causing a sensation: this determines if the subject responds or not and a change in the intensity of a cue may be more important than its actual value—a flashing light attracts more attention than continuous light.

Perception. An experience resulting from complex stimuli plus past experience plus present attitudes—seeing a traffic light change or interpreting a round red/green object as an apple.

Drive (also *need*). A strong stimulus impelling action.

Attitude. A combination of belief, emotion and tendency to action about or towards any object or event. This can be illustrated by the child who "believes in God, loves his mother and hates his brother".

Perception

Perception is the interpretation of sensations and because of the enormous volume of cues and sensations affecting each of us at any one moment three immediate problems occur.

(*i*) How will these huge numbers of sensations be grouped to give us a few meaningful categories with which we can cope?

(*ii*) Which sensations will impinge on our awareness or behaviour?

(*iii*) When there is conflict caused by several simultaneous sensations, which sensations prevail and are perceived?

Gestalt psychology, which is based on the premise that perception is paramount in the process leading up to behaviour, has shown that humans appear to see things in patterns which are common to all humans and which are based on the principles of contrast and grouping. Things in contrast stand out, for example a melody against noise, or a moving bird against a tree; similar things are grouped, for example animals together in a field or humans and animals separately; people tend to see two-dimensional drawings in three dimensions. In all there are three or four very common bases for grouping objects together so that we may more readily perceive them when they are exposed to our view.

The creation of categories or groups may nevertheless be something we learn. Pavlov, whose dogs have been described wherever psychology has been discussed, showed this with one of his many simple experiments. A bell rang, food was produced for the dog, the dog salivated as his body prepared itself for the food. After a few repeats the dog salivated when the bell rang—even when the food was not shown. Then a buzzer was substituted for the bell and the process was repeated. The dog still salivated at the sound. He had generalised his response of salivation to a particular noise to a similar response for a similar noise because his response had always been rewarded with food. He had learned to place two different sounds in the same category or group.

However the trials were continued longer and the reward of food was once again produced only after the bell; the dog then learned to *discriminate* between the sounds of bell and buzzer. The rewards of learning discrimination thus limit the categories which are perceived and at the same time influence which of two objects are perceived when the choice is given. We can learn to make a response to a stimulus because the response brings with it a reward; we can extend this response to a wider set of stimuli (generalisation) if these, too, bring the same reward; but if the response is only rewarded when made to one particular stimulus we learn to discriminate and respond to that only.

Perception of qualities and quantities has some interesting connections which also bear on our understanding of human behaviour. If we divide objects into two classes, for example, we tend to exaggerate the differences between them as classes. Prejudiced persons are usually sensitive towards identifying members of groups they dislike but relatively insensitive towards differences inside the group. Experimental work has confirmed this by showing how those prejudiced against negroes found it very difficult to tell one from another; whilst those prejudiced against Jews were very sensitive to picking out Jews from photographic "evidence" only.

Our expectations affect our perceptions so that we see what we expect to see. These expectations may be based on years of experience, as when we see an object from an unusual position but still identify it as a round plate or a pipe, because we know that is what it is, or when we read rapidly and miss a mis-spelling so that we read "though" as "through" because that is what we expect it to read and that is what the sense demands. On other occasions our perception depends on the immediate past, for example, a character thus 13 on a blackboard following a mass of figures will be read as 13, but a very similar character among a series of letters will be read as letter B.

Some things we tend not to perceive at all. Cannell and MacDonald were able to show that a heavy smoker tends not to see newspaper stories about cigarettes and cancer ("Impact of Health News on Attitudes and Behaviour", *Journalism Quarterly*, v. 33). If he does see them he tends not to read them. If he reads them he tends to distort the message. If he understands the message he forgets it as soon as he can! This is called "perceptual defence" and is the converse of our commonly acute sensitivity to things we find interesting or enjoyable: because of perceptual defence we do not perceive things we do not want to see. There is much dispute in this area and the arguments tend to be clouded with emotional words, but the reader in this, as in many other matters in this field, must judge for himself.

Learning

Common sense suggests that learning plays an important part in buying behaviour, especially when this is concerned with the first purchase of a product or the purchase of a new product.

There are many different approaches to a theory of how we learn to do things. The study of compulsory learning (under duress) has been much neglected but it seems in any case that, since buying is a voluntary activity in so far as specific items are concerned, we should look to theories of voluntary learning if any learning theories are to give us guidance at all. Of the many theories of learning there are three general approaches which we must mention.

Stimulus–response. Learning is said to occur if these two are temporarily contiguous—e.g. touching a hot coal burns one's fingers so one learns not to do it.

Cognitive theories. Learning is said to occur under certain social or psychological stimuli. We shall look at some aspects of this later but our discussion of perception has already given some indications to follow.

Stimulus–response–reinforcement. This theory emphasises that reinforcement is an essential condition for learning to occur. It is the stimulus–response relationship which is reinforced by the action taken when this action proves to be satisfactory. When we are hungry and smell the food in the dining-room, we eat: eating satisfies our hunger and this reinforces the relationship of the smell of food and our eating of it.

What is immediately clear is that the learner is motivated by whatever lies within him and that this determines his actions. He must learn: but he cannot be taught. A boy practises on the piano after school. Does he do this to learn to play well or because he knows that when he has practised he may go out and play football? This question indeed illustrates that goals may be either extrinsic or intrinsic to the learning process. The latter are self-maintaining goals such as eating when hungry whilst the former are a means to a more distant end, such as working to get money in order to live. It is the importance of a particular goal to the individual at a particular time which governs his action and we must try to understand what lies behind his behaviour especially if his goal may not in fact be what it seems at first sight.

Our attitudes clearly affect what we learn. It is easier to learn and harder to forget information which tends to support present attitudes. Levine Gardner and Murphy have shown this experimentally (*Journal of Abnormal Psychology*, 38: 507–17). They took two groups, one with Communist attitudes the other with anti-Communist attitudes, and showed both groups Communist and anti-Communist literature. Each group, when questioned later, showed that it had assimilated more of the literature supporting their own previous attitude than it had assimilated literature supporting the opposing dogma; similarly, each group remembered more of this literature, at a later date when they had had an opportunity to forget it, than they remembered of the literature supporting the opposing view.

A number of factors affecting the learning process have immediate application to marketing practice. As the learner's goals, not those of the source (whether teacher or advertiser), determine what is learned, the advertiser should put forward the benefits which the product will confer on the buyer because the latter will only be motivated to buy if the product appears likely to satisfy one of his needs. Similarly with regard to the timing of advertising, the advertiser should offer the satisfaction of that goal (among many) in which the prospect is currently interested.

The rewards of the response it is desired to evoke determine whether that response will be learned. These rewards can be positive or negative; punishment is a negative reward and it may create learning or maintain a habit but it may also create a hostile attitude to the source of the punishment. Positive benefits will therefore be much more likely to create a favourable attitude towards a product and its maker than negative influences such as threats or punishment.

It has also been shown experimentally that the fastest learning is achieved when every "correct" response is properly rewarded. This also has a clear application in the launching of a new product. When we wish to establish quickly a new pattern of behaviour, it is essential that the buyer should find that the benefits promised by the product are in fact fully experienced when it is used. In other words, the new product must live up to its advertising claims or there will be no real reward for the buyer.

The chain of learning may of course be a long series of events with initial stimulus and final response quite widely separated, as when a product is advertised over a long period in a number of different media. Each stimulus (advertisement) is perceived perhaps a little more clearly than the last and one day ("impulse purchase"?) the prospect, noticing the product in a display, buys and the satisfaction obtained when the product is used reinforces the response (buying) to the stimulus (advertisement). But the buyer may have been almost unaware of the process and certainly may not have consciously thought of the effects of the advertising on his attitude to the product and his gradual approach to the state of being ready to buy. This raises the debatable subject of whether advertising must achieve apparent attention in order to be effective. Many students of consumer behaviour argue very strongly that so long as an unconscious impression has been made the advertisement has achieved its purpose. The argument continues—and has important implications in the field of research into advertising effectiveness where most research is still devoted to finding out if consumers are conscious of having seen an advertisement when they have been exposed to it.

Generalisation and discrimination

Before leaving learning theory let us look a little more closely at generalisation and discrimination. Again we must have definitions of technical terms.

Extinction occurs when a learned response to a stimulus is repeated without reinforcement so that the tendency to respond decreases or dies.

Forgetting occurs when a response to a stimulus is not practised.

Generalisation exists when the reinforcement of a specific response to a stimulus not only increases the tendency for the particular cue to get that response but also for *similar* cues to get that response.

Gradients of Generalisation

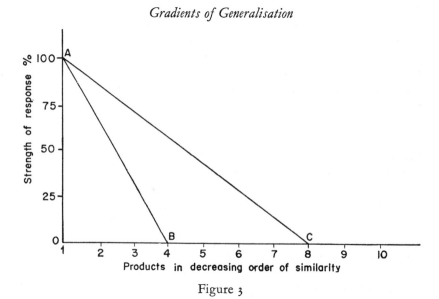

Figure 3

Discrimination occurs when learning increases the *specific* cue–response relationship so that similar cues do not get that same response.

A gradient of generalisation can be illustrated as shown in the diagram. The strength of the response of potential buyers is shown on the vertical axis and on the horizontal axis products are shown in decreasing order of similarity. The value of the "goal object" is assumed to be a constant, i.e. there is a constant drive or motivating force in any one situation.

In a garrison town under siege the line AB (Figure 3) may indicate the acceptability of various foods at the end of two weeks when no great strain has been put on the food supply. Foods 1–5 may represent say beef, chicken, mutton, pork, horse. Everyone is prepared to eat beef, most people are prepared to eat chicken and so on down to horse, which is not acceptable to anyone (AB in Figure 3). Six months later food is very scarce. All foods are more sought after (motivation has increased, line AC in Figure 3). As before, everyone will eat beef but more people will eat the intervening foods and horse (5) goat (6) and dog (7) now become acceptable to some people (AC in Figure 3). Cat (8) and rat (9) are still unacceptable to anyone but if the siege lasts long enough a higher value for the goal object (extreme hunger) could well make them acceptable too.

When drive (goal value) is increased generalisation occurs and products not previously considered are included. In the direct application of this to marketing, if advertising creates or intensifies a drive which has been learned it may create purchases not only of that product but of other, similar products. This emphasises the need for the advertiser to ensure that his product is widely available in the shops so that potential buyers do not buy something else because his product is not there. On the other hand, if the advertiser presents his product as, say, a symbol of status and the achievement of status is a dominant drive, then the prospective purchaser may in that case insist on that one product; that is, he has learned to discriminate.

Marketing makes practical use of learning theories on many occasions. In particular we may mention the following:

(*i*) The importance to the marketing manager of the "distribution" of his product in the shops. By distribution we mean the opportunities which an average shopper would have of buying the product when calling in a shop. Fifty per cent distribution means the average shopper would have one chance in two of finding the product in her shop. It does not mean 50 per cent of all shops, but that shops doing 50 per cent of the trade would have stock. If distribution is poor, extinction of learning may occur and all previous effort will be wasted.

(*ii*) If generalisation exists in a product field there will be considerable switching of purchases from one brand to another and one's competitors may obtain sales from one's own advertising effort. The practical effects of this are likely to be that a manufacturer with a dominant share of the market may gain far more from his competitors' advertising than they may gain from his. On the assumption that generalisation tends to manifest itself in proportion to the share of market controlled, the dominant manufacturer gains and the newcomer finds development of his business much more difficult.

(*iii*) Discrimination, on the other hand, demands high brand-consciousness, considerable product differentiation and, above all, that it is the brand and not the product type which is sold. Leaders like Cadbury and Heinz are careful to promote their own names and it must be clear that each of them may be the winners from any competitive advertising campaign which appears to sell only milk chocolate bars or baked beans, respectively. To break into a market characterised by discriminatory purchasing or to try and develop buyers' discrimination in favour of one's own product means strengthening and emphasising the differences between one's product and those of competitors. Many readers will remember the amusing and doubtless effective trade advertising for Messrs. Accles and Pollock a year or two ago, when they wished to impress their services on industrial buyers of steel tubing. To the onlooker this seemed a very clear instance of a determination to make a difficult name "stick" and become so associated with a quality product that discrimination would follow.

APPENDIX TO CHAPTER THREE

Simplified Hullian Learning Model

This is only one of many learning theories but Hull's theory, based on stimulus, response and reinforcement of the stimulus–response relationship is one which seems very close indeed to what we observe around us in the everyday market-place buying activities of consumers.

The factors in this theory are:

E = reaction potential, i.e. the strength of the response.
D = drive, the need or motivating force of the subject.
K = incentive potential, i.e. the value of the goal.
H = habit strength. This is a function of previous satisfactory learning procedures when a response was reinforced and thus it must have some positive value.
V = stimulus intensity dynamism, i.e. the strength of the cue.

$$E = D \times K \times H \times V$$

This is a multiplicative relationship, so that all elements must have a value greater than zero. Low habit strength and high drive can, therefore, produce the same activity as high habit strength and low drive. There is evidence to support this multiplicative relationship and we can see this in phenomena around us every day. This theory seems to fit quite closely to much marketing practice.

It is interesting also to compare this with the economists' theory $B = f(u)$.

Where B = behaviour, f = functional relation, u = expected utility and $f(u) = g(M.I.P.)$. In this latter equation

g = functional relation.
M = Motivational disposition (i.e. similar to drive).
I = Objective value of product (i.e. similar to K).
P = probability of product having actual value which chooser thinks it will have (i.e. similar to Hull's habit strength).

The model of the Hullian theory is developed by J. A. Howard in *Marketing Theory* (Columbia, 1965).

CHAPTER 4

Social Psychology and Customer Behaviour

Social psychology

So far we have been considering classical psychology in an endeavour to discover how this subject can help us to understand the customer. We must now turn to another of the social sciences to see what further light it may cast on our subject. Social psychology deals with how the individual adapts himself to his total environment. This is more than just his reactions to social influences, for in one sense it is another learning theory derived from the interaction of the individual with groups of people and their influences. In essence social psychology examines the relationship between the individual's needs (which we have already seen are the driving forces motivating him to some form of action) and his actual behaviour as evoked by his beliefs, his attitudes and his system of values.

In social psychology *motivation* is the impetus (drive) to current behaviour; *cognition* determines the form and direction of this behaviour; and *attitudes* and *beliefs* are thought to be indicators of probable future behaviour. In this field there has been less experimental work than in classical psychology and the argument may therefore be less certain. Again the reader must judge for himself, preferably after further reading.

Motivation

In social psychology, motivation is considered to begin in the individual's current psychological field as determined by the external physical and psychological environment and also his internal physiological state. The goal is seen as action not just the goal object; when hungry, eating is the goal, not food. We must be careful to appreciate that in social psychology we are concerned with the current state not past history (which is so much emphasised by psychoanalysis) and, as the various parts of the psychological field are constantly interacting, instability is likely to exist at any one moment. Instability causes tensions. Tensions plus basic needs lead to action. Action in turn leads to a reduction of the particular tensions and the process starts all over again with other tensions, either new ones or older ones which had been temporarily pushed into the background.

Because the individual's needs are heterogeneous and not homogeneous and because these needs are often incompatible, the subject has to establish his own hierarchy, or order of importance, for them. When this is clearly defined the individual is considered to have an integrated personality but this integration can only emerge from his own system of values, which is what determines his hierarchy of needs.

Cognition

Cognition is the mental process of "knowing", i.e. perceiving a thing, relating it to all that has gone before and making sense of it to oneself. For example one perceives the round red/green object as an apple. One's cognition of it is that it is an edible fruit of greater or lesser desirability as the case may be. Cognition is concerned with perceptions plus previously existing cognitive structures (the existing cognitions of all kinds).

When new information is perceived (and we have already seen that most does not "get through") it is taken in conjunction with existing cognitive structures to produce a conclusion about some object or event. This conclusion may change the existing cognitive structures themselves, so that a new situation is formed and similar information thereafter may lead to a different conclusion. For example, a new food is offered by a waiter to a diner but the recipient has doubts about eating it because on a previous occasion apparently similar foods were distasteful. He does, however, now try it and he finds he likes it. Next time he has no doubts. Most of social psychology turns on explaining this type of phenomenon. Of course the stability of cognitive structures varies. Some are very stable general reference frameworks such as "one plus one equals two". Less stable than these are cognitive structures of cultural reference including beliefs, social and moral ideals such as views on marriage, or sex, or socially desirable activities such as a code of road behaviour. Least stable of all cognitive structures are attitudes towards events or things. A brand image is an example of one person's own cognitive structure with regard to a product; in a wider context a brand image can also be the total of such structures for all the people making up the whole market.

An interesting feature of cognition is the importance of "other people". Sufficient group pressure can influence what an individual believes he perceives (as we have already seen if it is not perceived it does not get into his cognitive structure at all). A typical case is the pressure on an individual to accept the political beliefs, dogma and attitudes of the rest of his family.

Similarly, when an individual feels that he has no objective standards or accepted authority available he tends to turn to other people for advice, judgment or evaluation (see page 59). The person to whom he turns depends on the situation—and his own cognitions—but it is likely to be to a recognised authority (a doctor for drugs); a presumed informed person (an assistant in a shop); or a trusted friend; for it is information that he can rely on and accept that he wants.

Cognitive dissonance

This phrase originated with L. Festinger but his work has been followed up by a number of others. Festinger said that the individual always tries to avoid internal psychological stresses and incompatibilities because he sees himself as a rational, integrated, sensible person. He therefore tries to maintain a consistency between what he does and what he knows. He will not only try to avoid such a clash but, if one occurs, his cognitions will be dissonant (unharmonious) and he will immediately try to reduce this dissonance and so become rational and integrated once more. For example, if he has two attitudes which are inconsistent he will alter one or both to achieve consistency. On the other hand, if he acts in a way incompatible with an attitude he holds then, since he cannot undo his act, he will change his attitude. Festinger held ("Cognitive Dissonance", a paper reprinted in Barksdale (Ed.), *Marketing in Progress*, Holt, Rinehart & Winston, 1964) that dissonance was particularly felt after making a decision, especially if the decision was a choice between two almost equally desirable objects. Each has desirable characteristics and the rejection of one inevitably means dissonance because of the subject's view of himself as a rational sensible person who would not reject a desirable object. Having chosen—say between two cars—the subject then justifies his choice by finding and emphasising good points in his chosen car and at the same time emphasising the disadvantages of the rejected one. By thus making the one seem much more desirable than the other the dissonance or inconsistency is turned into consistency; he has made a good choice by buying what is clearly the better and rejecting what is clearly the worse!

Others have developed this concept to include pre-decisional events. If the individual has developed a habit of buying a particular article, say a brand of cigarettes, then the first stage in making him change is to put into his mind that another brand is more desirable. When this has been achieved, so that it has now become part of his cognition and accepted as factual, then his new situation clashes with the habit of buying his normal brand and the dissonance will be removed by changing to the new brand.

Cognitive dissonance may well be of great importance in understanding buying behaviour and a good deal of thought is currently being given to the concept. Certainly it seems a worthwhile area for further study but let us still remember that whilst cognitive dissonance may be seen in almost any decision-making activity the magnitude of the dissonance and the importance of it to the subject concerned does vary with the importance of the purchase. When buying a house, changing a job or buying a car it may have tremendous influence but it is not so likely to be prominent if the individual for one reason or another buys an unfamiliar box of matches.

Beliefs and attitudes

Social psychologists believe that an individual's beliefs and attitudes must be known before it is possible to predict his behaviour in any situation. At the same time it seems clear that, unless his beliefs and attitudes (i.e. his relevant cognitive structures) are known, what he experiences when a new stimulus is received cannot be described meaningfully.

Beliefs may be described as a pattern of meanings around an object which includes knowledge, opinion and faith. Beliefs as such are motivationally neutral, they do not impel action of any kind; on the other hand by their very nature they are more enduring than attitudes.

Attitudes are active predispositions for or against objects, events or people, because as we have already seen (page 34) they are tripartite and consist of belief, emotion and tendency to action. An individual cannot have an attitude towards an object if he does not know it exists but he can have a neutral attitude towards something he knows about but has no interest in. He can also have an antagonistic attitude towards an object that he has heard of but really knows nothing about, because people sometimes fear the unknown or what they do not understand. First-hand knowledge is not a pre-requisite for forming an attitude because reading, radio, television or discussion can influence people in almost any area.

The argument runs that if attitudes can be expected to predict behaviour (because they lead towards it), then to change present behaviour (e.g. to induce buying) requires that present attitudes must first be changed. This means creating a favourable attitude towards the object which is now to be bought. It is because of this argument that much motivational research is directed to measuring the dimensions of attitudes. Some of the most modern analysts, however, doubt the practical value of this approach, certainly with present techniques. Krech, Crutchfield and Ballachey in *Individual in Society* share these doubts and in a fascinating exposition of man's reaction to his social surroundings doubt whether attitudes can be located, identified and defined sufficiently closely to warrant the importance currently assigned to them by much market research practice.

Let us for a moment, therefore, examine the structure of attitudes and see how they are made up. An individual's attitude depends on four factors. First comes the *precision* of his perception of the object or event around which his attitude is formed. As we have already seen, without perception the object would not come into his consideration at all and the clarity or otherwise with which the object is perceived is central to whatever attitude is formed.

The second factor is the *saliency* of the attitude, that is to say the degree to which the attitude stands out from and is isolated from other attitudes. Some attitudes are closely connected with each other, such as attitudes towards politics and attitudes towards various political parties. Other attitudes, for instance those towards politics and sport, are generally unconnected and individuals may go to some lengths to try and keep them so, as has been seen in recent years when the South African apartheid policy has impinged on international sporting activities. An even clearer example is that of the all-Ireland Rugby Union teams which for years past have represented both Eire and Northern Ireland and play their home games alternatively in each country despite the political cleavage between their countries.

Thirdly comes the *strength* of the attitude. This is a measure of its resistance to change (rather than its difference from other attitudes). Those who hold particular views on religion, for example, often feel so strongly about religion that they will not even listen to anything which seems to be contrary to their own views. A characteristic description of those with the strongest attitudes towards a particular object is that they have "closed minds" in that direction.

Last of these factors is the degree to which an attitude has been *verified*. This is the relation between opinion and objective fact. When an individual holds a view, based on other positions he has taken up, such as holding that a particular political party is a bad one, he may impute all sorts of failings and inefficiencies to individual members of a government formed by that party. At the other end of the scale a man who has spent much time in a country such as Rhodesia may have an attitude in the current dispute with the United Kingdom based on much more real knowledge than a friend who has never been out of the home country. When the individual knows his attitude is based on objective fact this attitude is likely to have quite a different meaning for him than an attitude towards something else which is not based on fact.

Having considered the structure of attitudes we still have to ask if attitudes determine future action so that knowledge of the existence of an attitude will enable us to predict future action. If so, can attitudes be economically measured in the field? Many practical market researchers believe that the answer to both questions is "yes", and certainly current techniques of attitude measurement seem to be obtaining useful results even if they are not fully proven.

Attitude measurement

We shall discuss in Chapter 8 the use of depth interviews and group discussions in motivational studies. At the present time attitude measurement is approached by using either or both of these techniques to throw up indications of attitude and then following up with individual interviews aimed at quantifying the indications obtained previously. Usually the objective is to produce for each individual a recording, on a scale, of the importance of various factors which together indicate his attitude. Then the individual scales are also added to give a total value for the whole sample.

Although there are a number of different methods of measuring attitudes most of them make use of a series of statements or items related to the attitude being investigated. Respondents indicate, on a scale, their own position in relation to each statement. This scale may, for example, contain the following possible statements:

>agree very strongly
>agree
>on balance agree
>uncertain

on balance do not agree

do not agree

very strongly disagree

The respondent is asked which of these descriptions best fits his views on the statement concerned. Other scales are used for other statements. From the pattern of response to all the statements an *inference* of his attitudes can be made and, in many cases, by numbering the responses in a particular order an evaluation of the attitude which indicates the valency of the respondent's attitude towards the object is also obtained.

APPENDIX TO CHAPTER FOUR

Some methods of measuring attitudes

1. *Scale of equal intervals* (*Thurston scale*)

A great many statements and questions believed to have a bearing on the subject under investigation are assembled and classified by a large number of judges. Statements which are ambiguous or cause considerable inconsistency in the ratings of them by judges are omitted. The remainder are administered to the sample being interviewed. Judges' own attitudes do not affect the result of the study among members of the sample. Items finally selected appear to have equal value intervals between them and the number and variety of items enables deduction in considerable detail of the attitudes of respondents to the object being investigated.

2. *Summated ratings* (*Likert*)

Again a large number of items related to the subject is collected. Judges are not used and even items apparently not related to the subject are retained as experienced users have found them to be diagnostic. Respondents are shown each item and asked which category this fits into most closely, e.g. strongly approve, approve, undecided, disapprove, strongly disapprove. These responses are rated 1–5 for favourable items or 5–1 for unfavourable items. All items are analysed and the scores for each item compared with those for all items; also individuals can be compared with the average. [The difficulty with this method is that whilst it can show clearly hostile or favourable attitudes there is much doubt as to what midway scores signify.]

3. *Social distance scale* (*Bogardus*)

This produces a series of categories varying between complete acceptance of an idea to total rejection. It is based on replying to questions arranged in a similar way to the questions below relating to a foreign person:

(a) would you admit him to close relationship by marriage?
(b) would you have him in your club as a close friend?
(c) would you allow him in your street as a neighbour?
(d) would you allow him to be employed in your kind of job?
(e) would you grant him citizenship of your country?
(f) would you allow him in to your country as a visitor only?
(g) would you exclude him from your country altogether?

An examination of answers to a series of "batteries" of questions arranged in this way enables deductions to be made as to the attitudes of the respondent in the areas concerned.

4. Cumulative scaling (Guttman)

This method can measure one attitude only and is a cumulative method of evaluating statements. It is similar to a weight scale in that each category includes all those below it, e.g.:

(1) All members of the Government should be hanged (Yes/No)
(2) I hate all members of the Government (Yes/No)
(3) I dislike all members of the Government (Yes/No)

[One advantage here is that the results obtained are believed to be extremely reliable.]

5. Scale discrimination

This is an attempt to synthesise Thurstone, Likert and Guttman. It is based on a list of dichotomous items which judges rank in order of favourableness. Inconsistent pairs are rejected as ambiguous and six pairs are administered to the subjects in the sample. It is felt to be a reliable method but there are doubts as to whether this method brings out the importance of an attitude at the particular moment. Its predictive value is unknown.

The reader is recommended to read D. Krech, R. S. Crutchfield and E. L. Ballachey, *Individual in Society* (McGraw-Hill, 1962), for a more detailed account of an illustration of the use of these methods.

CHAPTER 5

Sociology and Customer Behaviour

Sociology

We now turn to a third branch of the social sciences, that which deals with the growth, development and nature of human society. Most of us are familiar with the concept of man as a gregarious animal, a *social* animal in fact. Let us see how sociology also can help us towards understanding our customer. Again let us define our terms:

Group: a body of people with common goals and a measure of inter-action.

Status: the position of the individual in the group.

Role: the pattern of behaviour which a group attributes to and expects from a position.

Status set: all the statuses of the individual.

Role set: all the roles of the individual.

Status sequence: the process of changing status (e.g. undergraduate, medical student, G.P., specialist).

Groups

Man gets together with his own kind, that is, he and his fellows join in groups, formal or informal, for countless purposes. He has family groups, neighbourhood groups, cultural groups, sporting groups, business groups, almost groups without number. These groups together make up our social structure; sociology, in studying the development of society, regards this structure as a fundamental feature of the subject. We are all aware of groups and all belong to many, but most of us have never thought very deeply about the differences between groups although there are quite clear distinguishing features which can help us to evaluate them.

The first of these features is the *frequency* with which interaction between the members of the group occurs. This interaction depends substantially on the quality and effectiveness of intercommunication within the group, but it also depends on the size of the group and the motivation of members to communicate. In turn, both the size of the group and the motivation of members to communicate with each other are determined by the group's objectives or goals and the importance of these goals in relation to other activities of the group members. All the groups of which an individual is a member do not rank equally at any one time. For example, a housewife may be a member of a local informal group with her neighbours based substantially on their motherhood and all living near to each other. She may also join the tennis club. The two groups are quite different and their relative importance depends on the situation at any one moment. Groups where members are in frequent communication are likely to be more active than others, but this is obviously not the only criterion and it would be misleading to assume that groups where the members might only meet, or communicate, occasionally are weak. A parents/teachers association or an old school association may only hold occasional meetings but when the occasion arises each might be a very strong group. In the former case this was shown in the affair of the Enfield Grammar School. In 1967 there were proposals in Enfield to alter the organisation of local schools and introduce the comprehensive system. This involved a material change in the traditional intake of pupils by Enfield Grammar School. Many of the staff of the school and many parents of pupils disagreed with this. There already was in existence a parents/teachers association, and this group actually raised funds and resisted the proposed changes to the extent of challenging the authorities and the responsible political minister in the law courts.

The latter case is seen whenever old school reunions are held and members take up old associations which have been dormant for long periods.

A second feature of groups is that most of them have *norms of behaviour*, patterns of interaction which are binding upon the members but do not affect outsiders. It is this pattern of behaviour which, especially in informal, social groups, tends to set one group apart from others, whether the group be a few youngsters wishing to flaunt their freedom from the "squares" of the outside world or a group of well-to-do people touring the horseracing meetings and holidaying in winter in the Mediterranean. In many instances, as we know, a non-member who wishes to be a group member copies the behaviour of the group in order to become identified with it and from this we get the phenomenon of status-seeking, or "keeping up with the Joneses" which is a very old social activity indeed.

This leads us to two further features of groups: the extent to which a member *defines himself as belonging to a group* and the extent to which *outsiders consider him to be a member of a group*. When an individual is a member of a group, such as a specific cultural group, a choral society perhaps, or a business group, such as a company which employs him, he may or may not identify himself closely with this group and he may or may not make it clear to non-members that he is such a member. But whatever he does in this respect indicates, at least in part, his own attitude to the group and the importance of the group to him.

Similarly, outsiders observe a group member and from his behaviour may deduce that he is a member of a particular group. The extent to which they do this depends upon the group norms of behaviour, how closely the member follows these norms and the degree of knowledge of, interest in, sympathy with, or antipathy towards, the group which the observer possesses. The outcome for each observer depends on the importance of the group in his scale of values and of course on the acuteness of his own perception of the group's behaviour and the behaviour of the individual members.

Groups can be quite formal, even possess a legal entity such as a company or a college, or can be very informal, perhaps be just a group of men who habitually gather for a drink in a particular corner of a particular room in a particular public house. Nevertheless in very many groups members have allocated to them (or assume) different tasks in order that the group's objectives or goals may be achieved more effectively. These tasks result in different members having different roles in the group such as leaders, organisers, administrators, managers or workers. Their positions in the group, as a result of these roles, confer on them different statuses according to the importance of their roles in the group (i.e. as leaders or followers, planners or "doers"). These status differences can be very subtle indeed, according to the group concerned, and we should note that the role and status which a person holds in one group may have no bearing on his status in another group. The captain of the works football team may well be a rank and file worker on the factory floor.

We have spent some time describing the features of groups and we might well ask: "Why do groups exist?" Basically there are three reasons underlying all group existence. The first is to *achieve the goal* or objective for which the group was formed by carrying out the various tasks which together form the means of doing this. In a company, different tasks are performed by different people at different levels in order to produce goods or services to sell and thus make a profit. In a choral society, some members are arrangers and planners, some administrators, some singers, some instrumentalists; all are working towards the common goal of enjoying musical activity.

The second reason is to *ensure the continuation* of the group. This is done by some system, formal or informal, of policing and applying sanctions to those who do not conform to the group norms of behaviour. According to how tightly organised the group is, so is the policing likely to be strict or lax. By all accounts the standards of policing of the old-established Ku Klux Klan have been very strict indeed; certainly the group is still in existence. On the other hand, groups with less rigid objectives, such as those concerned with purely leisure activities like the devotees of a pop singer, may not persist together as a group for very long because their group goals are not long-lived: whilst they do exist their insistence on accepting the norms of behaviour (devotion to the idols) may be very rigid. Here again the reader will have no difficulty in finding example of many different manifestations of this kind of activity from his own experience. In general, however, we may agree that in formal organisations, particularly those concerned with business, the achievement of the group goals and the maintenance of the group tend to be joined together; those who assist in increasing business get promotion, those who hinder business are moved out. In less formal organisations this does not always apply and the holding together of the groups and the achievement of its objectives may be quite separate activities, bearing in mind that the very informality of the group may derive from the imprecision or diffuse nature of its objectives.

Lastly, groups exist so that the *members may have reference groups* which affect and influence the values and the behaviour of their members. For many groups one of the goals of the members is to set up codes of behaviour and standards of value which are esteemed by the members. These then become standards by which the members may judge other activities, whatever these activities may be. As we have already mentioned, these groups may also be reference groups for non-members.

Reference groups are thus defined as those groups of which an individual is or has been a member, or to which he aspires to be a member, or groups of which he does not wish to be considered a member, according to the circumstances. A boy who wishes to be a Boy Scout may often try to emulate the conduct and perhaps even the dress of scouts; he may also do his utmost not to be considered a member of a local "gang" of the "Hell's Angels" type. It is in this area of reference groups that we find what is probably the best known practical application of sociology in marketing activities. Codes of behaviour and the aspiration to, or aversion from, social groups with particular codes of behaviour provide a great deal of the motivation underlying customer behaviour, particularly buying behaviour. Further elaboration seems unnecessary as the phenomenon is so common.

Roles and status

As we have seen, the achievement of a group's goals requires the performance of a number of very different tasks and, according to the task he does, so an individual is appointed to, or assumes, a *role*. The roles to which individuals are assigned are decided by the differences in their abilities. The ability of an individual is partly, at least, a matter of experience and training, but it also includes his whole personality. As Adam Smith perceived two hundred years ago, it was the differences in the abilities of different individuals which gradually led to specialisation and the division of labour, in industry and commerce, as individuals learned that it was in their own advantage to concentrate on those skills with which they were best endowed.

Each individual, however, lives a whole life in which all his activities, economic, social and personal, are combined. As he is usually a member of many groups in all, he has a number of different roles to perform. These roles often have different statuses and having different roles and statuses is a problem in itself, because of the tensions it creates. In addition to this the individual may quite frequently find himself in a position where different roles which he fills require different actions so that real conflict arises between two or more roles. A simple instance of this may be the case of a senior business executive who, in the course of his business, may have to recommend an increase in prices. In so far as he may be a member of a political party trying hard to prevent a general increase in prices, he has a conflict between these two roles. In a further role, as father of a family, he endures additional conflict because in his home life he has to make his salary go round and this has been made even more difficult by his business decision.

An individual's roles may vary according to his activities at different times. A woman may be, at different times in one day, mother to her children going out to school, a buyer in the shops as she lays in provisions, a cook as she prepares the family meal and a wife as she welcomes her husband home. Each role makes a different demand on her and causes her to think and act in accordance with her current role, her perception of this role, its significance to her and her understanding of how she should carry it out. It is clearly important in our business activities that we should appreciate the extent to which an individual in any particular situation sees the roles played by himself and others and, furthermore, sees how others view *his* role. A man may be husband, father, salesman or customer; his understanding of the first two of these roles will influence his personal life and of the last two his business life; but as a salesman his appreciation of all four roles can assist him considerably in understanding and selling to another man whom he views as a customer but who nevertheless is also a husband and a father.

Status is a measure of difference. It has dimensions which are usually visible although they may not always be measurable. An individual's style of life frequently reflects both his occupation and his role in society. The kind of house in which he lives, where it is situated, how it is furnished, all usually give observers an indication of his probable occupation and status. His occupation itself reflects the amount of training needed to carry out his work. It may also indicate how many other people's activities he controls (an important measure of status).

The degree of efficiency with which an individual performs his job is another indication of status for this, too, reflects his personal ability. The level at which he operates makes little difference here, for the good craftsman may be selected for a test job because of *his* special skill and obtain credit for this among his associates much as a good managing director may be asked to serve on a public body because of his business acumen and be similarly esteemed by *his* associates.

A further indication of status is the company which the individual keeps. In Cambridge a certain University Club is largely run by the current undergraduates. It is very exclusive. Membership is by invitation and election only, and is limited to those who have represented the University against Oxford (Blues) or have come very near to this standard. The Hawks have a very distinctive tie and seldom appear at any great sporting occasion without wearing it. "Birds of a feather" may sometimes be a contemptuous phrase, but in sporting circles at least, a Hawks tie is a sign of distinction. Yet whilst a person's associates may give clear indications of his status so, also, may his beliefs which of course cannot be seen. A person's position in the world, be it high or low, be it in a technical or a purely lay sphere, does tend to influence his beliefs. A member of a successful family business tends to believe in free enterprise; a member of an out-of-work family tends to feel that the under-privileged are never considered by the people in authority. On the other hand, a man to whom the hurly-burly of business is unattractive, may seek and enjoy a successful career in the civil service or armed forces, thus showing that his position in life can be itself very much affected by his beliefs.

In most countries there is some form of social class, however it may be described. The extent to which a man is identified by others (rather than by himself) as a member of a particular social class is a measure of the status which he enjoys in their estimation. In this connection, too, it is of some interest that social class is objected to mostly by those below when they feel that social mobility (that is, their own opportunity to rise) is limited. It is a reflection on individual and social psychology that those in the higher echelons seldom consider social class a bad thing.

What then determines the status set of an individual? In the long run there are two determinants. Firstly the rareness of the ability he possesses; this is not just his technical expertise but his complete personality; his character, intellect and physical prowess. Secondly comes the degree to which he assists in the survival of the group itself. He may be a leading member of the board of directors in a company, or a newly joined junior; he may have founded the organisation or be a principal means of holding it together, as often happens in musical or other cultural groups, or he may be an occasional and not too co-operative attender. His status in the group is awarded by other members according to his performance therein.

Roles and communication

Communications, which clearly have marketing significance, as analysed by most students, consist of four elements; sender, message, medium (means of transmission) and receiver. Roles have great importance in the communication process.

Whilst individuals have many roles, the sender of a message, wishing it to be well received, must make it consistent with the role of the receiver at the time the receiver is exposed to the message. This makes good sense to most people who attempt to understand the motivations influencing their fellows. It is particularly important in view of the significance in marketing activities of certain roles. The husband or wife is at the centre of family group life and as such is very much concerned with the behaviour (including the economic or buying behaviour) of the whole group. Since people act in accordance with their perception of themselves, say as parent or housewife, this visualisation of the individual's role and its requirements very much influences his actions. Elsewhere we show an example of this (page 92) when housewives did not buy instant coffee because this would have been inconsistent with their views of what a housewife was required to do, i.e. their perception of the behaviour which this role demanded. Membership of a business organisation confers upon the individual particular roles such as buyer, decision-maker, customer and so on and similarly each of these in its own sphere influences the behaviour of the individual. Finally, whatever additional roles he may have, each individual still has the basic one of being a consumer in his own right: this in turn influences, or is influenced by, the requirement of his other roles. Nothing in the field of behaviour ever seems really simple and uncomplicated.

A study of the working of social processes

Most of us have ample personal experience of the influence of "other people" and reference groups generally. There are numerous examples of work carried out by sociologists especially those in the American Forces during the Second World War. The following is a brief account of a very comprehensive civilian study which is one of the most enlightening and fully controlled experiments in this field dealing with the influence of social reference groups.

This most interesting study was carried out in four cities in the U.S.A. to investigate the spread of the use of a new drug. This drug was used by almost all doctors 15 months after its introduction but the speed with which it was adopted by different doctors varied considerably. The specific objective of the study was to uncover the social processes leading from the initial use of the drug by a few innovators to its final use by almost all medicos.

A sample of doctors was interviewed and each doctor was asked:

(*i*) to whom he most often turned for advice and information,

(*ii*) with whom he normally discussed cases,

(*iii*) which doctor friends he contacted most, socially.

The date when each doctor first used the drug was obtained, from prescription records. Doctors were classified, from indirect questioning, as to whether they were profession-orientated or patient-orientated and the more profession-orientated doctors were found generally to use the drug earlier than the less profession-orientated doctors.

The social influences were shown very clearly when doctors were classified according to whether they appeared in the questionnaires as named, under any of the three groups above, i.e. advice, discussion or social contact, by other doctors. The degree to which a doctor was thus considered integrated with his colleagues was positively and strongly related to his adoption of the new drug, which also indicated the importance of social contacts in the speed of introduction of the new drug. There was evidence that, whilst there were individual differences in receptivity between patient-orientated and profession-orientated doctors in the way they adopted the new drug, both the "integrated" and "isolated" doctors behaved in a very similar way in the very early months of the new drug's existence. There was, however, an acceleration in its use by the integrated doctors, a kind of snowball effect indicating that whilst they were not different in receptivity they tended to adopt the use of the drug as their fellows began to use it. There was strong evidence that the integrated doctors learned from one another whilst the isolated doctors each learned individually from the journals, salesmen and publicity for the drug.

A more detailed analysis showed that at first the influence of the social networks operated only among doctors integrated into the community of their colleagues through ties of a professional nature, i.e. as advisers or discussion partners. Later the social influence spread through those tied on a friendship basis, by which time also this influence had become operative among the relatively isolated doctors. Finally the remainder did come to use the drug, but for reasons other than the influences or the social networks. A possible reason for the "integrated" doctors being more influenced by the social networks earlier may be that in the earlier stages the effects of the drug were held to be more uncertain. The researchers report that this reasoning is supported by other evidence that it is in situations which are objectively unclear that social validation of judgment is particularly important.

The paper describing this study (*The Diffusion of an Innovation Among Physicians,* by Coleman, Katz and Menzel) is reprinted in Day (Ed.), *Marketing Models,* International Textbook Co. Ltd., 1964.

CHAPTER 6

Marketing Communications and Customer Behaviour

The problem of marketing communications

Much attention has been devoted in recent years to the study of communication and this too can help us in our consideration of the customer. Whilst we shall discuss the functions of selling and advertising in later chapters it seems more appropriate to examine communications theory here as part of our examination of behavioural science approaches.

We have already seen that marketing is a process of uncovering needs in a market, devising a product to satisfy those needs, and selling this product to the customers who form the market. In a free society no customer can be compelled to buy a product however much the manufacturer believes he should do so. The manufacturer, therefore, must so inform the customer of the benefits he will enjoy by using the product that he (the customer) will be persuaded to buy it. The principal tools which the manufacturer can use in this process of informing and persuading are advertising and personal salesmanship. Both of these are essentially means of communication.

In communications, as with most other activities, there is likely to be much waste unless the goals to be achieved are clear. In communications these goals have two special purposes, one to guide the receiver in making his choice among the alternatives at his disposal (i.e. deciding which product to buy) and the second to show that the goal has been achieved and that the sender should thus cease communicating. This requires that the goals should be quite specific. Whose behaviour is to be influenced? In what direction, to what degree and over what time is this behaviour to be influenced? This may seem pedantic at first, but let us consider a possible marketing goal to be "to increase sales". This can have several meanings. Sales can be increased by £X. They can be increased by X per cent. They can be increased by X tons or X units. They can also be increased by getting X new buyers or X per cent new buyers. Clearly the goal "to increase sales" must be more clearly defined.

Even having specified the goals accurately we still have the problem of how to achieve them. The means themselves are sub-goals and are complicated with (i) a time element (is the goal *being* achieved?); (ii) a source element requiring co-ordinated effort (such as advertising aiming at increasing knowledge of the product and selling aiming at increasing the number of shops stocking it); and (iii) a receiver element in that different receivers are in different stages of preparedness or persuasion. All this directs us to the conclusion that no single goal can be set for guiding the whole strategy of marketing communications.

When we examine marketing strategy we find that there are in fact four different levels of marketing decisions to be taken and that each decision sets the goal for the next lower level. The decision on the basic marketing mix with its definition of product, price, time and place, lays down the requirements of the overall promotional strategy, that is how sales of this product are to be achieved. The share of the overall task which is given to sales promotion must then be divided between selling and advertising. The advertising function must then be divided between that part which is straightforward advertising and that which is sales promotion. Finally the advertising element has to be divided between the advertising message (theme) and the advertising media which will carry the message. At each level a goal, or objective, is set for the next lower level.

When it comes to devising the message content of the advertising actual sales do not themselves appear to be suitable as the goal of the exercise. One of the functions of a communications goal is we have said to indicate its achievement so that the activity may cease. Here this goal (sales) would not serve this function as sales occur too late in the whole scheme of things: if they are not made it is then too late for a change.

Looked at from the side of the receiver of the message (the prospect) the goal of sales again seems unsuitable. Some prospective buyers are already regular buyers, others are on the point of buying, others buy that type of product but another brand, others have no interest in either the product type or the specific brand. Actual sales give no indication of these original differences and the different effort needed to obtain sales from the different sectors.

At best actual sales can only measure the effectiveness of the whole combination of the marketing mix. Yet, perversely enough, sales are often made the goals of advertising effort and, despite this formal if doubtful goal, market research practitioners still use research studies to measure the exposure of prospective customers to advertising media, their coverage by those media, their remembrance of the advertising messages and so on. If such aspects are fair yardsticks, should they not be used as parts of the goals of the advertising in the first instance? In marketing communications the relationship between cause and effect is seldom more than a mere probability. Results are usually achieved by the use of a combination of factors such as the product itself, its presentation, its price and the selling and advertising effort. The more certain we want to be of the relationship between the results obtained and the causes of them the less certain can we be of the part played by any individual factor, for all the factors are used in combination as a "package-operation". Any attempt to identify more closely the effect of any individual factor, would be enormously expensive in time and money in relation to what could be learned in a practical world of rapidly changing conditions, and the results obtained would still relate to a situation which no longer existed. Even closely investigating the results of using a particular marketing mix has only limited practical value because the individual elements such as price, advertising or product variation are not all equally flexible and manipulable. Adjusting the marketing mix to *ensure* the achievement of goals, when the latter are judged only in terms of sales, is thus a highly speculative activity.

If, on the contrary, we approach the problem from the side of the targets for the marketing communications a great deal can be done to improve goal setting. We can divide the prospective customers for the product into those who use and those who do not use a product of that type. We can divide the users of the type into those who have used the brand and those who have not. We can divide those who have used the type but not the brand into those who know of the product and those who do not, those who are hostile to the product and those who are not hostile. Such classifications will enable us to set different goals for each group; for example to increase usage by those who already buy the brand, to get users of competitive products to switch to our brand, to improve the attitudes of non-users of the product towards the brand, to develop awareness of the brand among those who have not heard of it, and so on.

The really important thing is that to have efficient marketing communications requires the use of different goals for different sections of the market. This is certainly also a pre-requisite if we are to make any serious attempt to measure the effectiveness of the measures we adopt.

Changing attitudes

It is generally accepted that a principal goal of marketing communications is to change attitudes, or create favourable attitudes, towards a brand or product. Three common methods of achieving this are:

(*i*) To give existing categories of products new labels or names. This changes both what people consider to be the content of the category and also their evaluation of the category. "Male toiletries" has been a generic term commonly used in recent years. This may not be universally acceptable but it seems more likely to be widely acceptable than a label such as "male cosmetics" with the feminine association of "cosmetics".

(*ii*) To change the category of the product itself, either by changing the attributes previously used in connection with it or by creating new attributes for that category. The popularising of fashions in male clothing seems to have been assisted in this way. Urging prospective buyers to generalise (include a smaller category in a larger, more acceptable one) or discriminate (separate a smaller category from a larger less acceptable one) may both, in appropriate cases, be effective. For example, we may think of air travel as just "travel", and not ask for "Scotch" but the more precise "Haig".

(*iii*) To change the way in which the category itself is evaluated, either directly or by influencing the value of related categories. For example, to popularise holidays overseas as being "in the sun" or "available to everyone not just the fortunate few".

Categories, we have seen, are used to simplify life by gathering large numbers of stimuli into a relatively small number of groups. We generally form categories on the basis of prospective use. For instance we describe a stone used as a paperweight as a paperweight and there are many examples of objects which can fulfil many uses and can thus be placed in many categories. The attributes used in forming categories are usually either physical or functional. All motor cars are in a certain range of size, weight and shape and all cars to some degree can be used for the same services, personal transport, carrying luggage and so on.

All of us can, and do, create categories without realising what we are doing and without realising what attributes we have used in the process. This is another behavioural factor especially useful in marketing as the advertiser (sender) can also do this without the customer (receiver) realising it or being able to do anything about it. For example, we could advertise "a modern shave" to those to whom being "with it" is important as being synonymous with using an electric razor.

Putting a name on a category is a means of saving time and, sometimes, of being more precise. This usage can, however, create confusion when, as Crane quotes (in *Marketing Communications*), a simple word like *leaves* may mean colour or shape to an artist, or food for insects to an entomologist, whilst to a lumberjack they may not be seen at all. However, this possible confusion can be overcome by starting with a more general category and then suggesting a specific item: "I want a paperweight, a stone will do"; or beginning with a specific item and suggesting a wider use: "I want a stone to use as a paperweight"; or giving the category in its context, "a few drops of rain" (millions) "a few shillings" (ten or twelve).

Once a difference or attribute has been named it becomes easier to perceive when it occurs again. Farmers or geologists notice differences in soil which ordinary people do not. When his attention is drawn to them the layman also notices these different types on future occasions. Names can nevertheless also mislead since the name given to a category may often imply something of the attitude of the person who gives the name. The same behaviour may be described as "firm", "stubborn" or even "pigheaded" by different observers, indeed the everyday labels for categories do tend to be connotative.

Connotative words are those which include a valuation on the part of the user, such as "handsome", "Goliath", "strode". Words which merely describe without giving indications of value or attitude are called *denotative*, such as "marked", "woman", "walked". Whilst this is generally true, it is also true that words normally denotative can be chosen and used together to influence the receiver to accept a predetermined value judgment about the category to which they refer such as the now famous Procter and Gamble slogans "$99\frac{44}{100}\%$ pure" or "gets out every last possible speck of dirt".

An individual's values may be positive, neutral or negative. When a person has no category into which to place an object, or when he attaches small value to it, he is said to be in the "neutrality of indifference". One way of overcoming this indifference is to show cause why the category should be considered important. An illustration of this is that the 18th-century aristocrat did not consider body odour of any great significance whilst today millions of men and women, old and young, consider the avoidance of this natural phenomenon as essential if they are to be acceptable in the group (or to the mate) they aspire to. Has not this change of attitude been created by communicators?

Neutrality of value can be ambivalent, that is the pros and cons can be equally balanced. Although inherently unstable, when this situation does arise the individual may just put it out of mind (especially if the category is an important one to him) and try to ignore the whole matter. This may be the situation regarding annual holidays, when an individual may find it difficult to choose between the Mediterranean and, say, the South of France. The shrewd travel agent may here introduce a new category, where conflict is less obvious, such as recommending a Scandinavian cruise. The lesson we learn here is that when competition is weak, and we have the stage to ourselves, we should emphasise the importance of our product and its group; when competition is strong, we should suggest that our product serves a different purpose and is not competing at all with its powerful rivals.

Acceptability of ideas

A useful concept is that we all have in our attitudes a neutral point and that around that point we have a range of acceptance of ideas. This is not the same as the neutrality of indifference. An individual who is in this state of attitudinal neutrality can accept new ideas because he has no very strong views on the matter. If the neutral point is crossed, however, the process of perceptual defence (page 36) may be aroused and also, perhaps, that of selective exposure. These are the tendencies of the individual to avoid that which is disagreeable, because it does not fit in with his present attitudes and to seek out that which is agreeable, because it supports his present attitudes. Crossing the neutral point is crossing the line between acceptable and unacceptable positions and is a critical and important matter. The range of acceptance, however, is a form of tolerance and it helps the advertiser (or any communicator) to decide whether to advocate a larger or smaller change of attitude or behaviour. This range naturally varies with different individuals. Generally, people with extreme views tend to have a narrow range of acceptance and a broad range of rejection and the opposite applies to people with less extreme views. This same phenomenon (which has been tested experimentally) helps to explain why dyed-in-the-wool brand supporters are less easy to persuade to buy other brands than those who are only casual or chance users. The concept indicates that a small change of attitude is on the whole more likely to be acceptable than a large one and that "softly softly" may have a very sound basis in behavioural science.

The stage of persuasion of the prospective buyer is always a practical problem for there is the clearest theoretical and logical argument for treating different segments, from this aspect, differently. But in practice what *can* be done? Retail traders have been aware of this problem for years and many of them send special direct mail communications to everyone in their account lists in the belief that they are already "sold" on the shop and therefore are among those most ready to buy from it. It is more difficult with manufacturers' operations. In the area of promotion it is sometimes possible to bring together people with a particular performance but this just touches the fringe of the problem of how to locate the different people concerned and how to approach them economically with what should be a multi-stage story. Most manufacturers seem to prefer to concentrate their resources on current buyers and good immediate prospects and take little note of the remainder, and the constraints of the profit and loss account make this very understandable. Against this we may put the many cases where consumers base their product loyalties on advertising seen and remembered with the clarity and disingenuousness of childhood memories.

The study of human behaviour is full of difficulties and complexities. Nevertheless progress is being made with both academic analysis and the application to practical cases of the lessons learned from this analysis. The measurement of the efficiency of advertising has of course long been one of the chief worries of the advertiser. Eventually this may be overcome and, in the process, if it becomes possible to measure accurately the effect of one message then surely it will be possible to predict the effect of another message. Certainly at that stage the chances of reaching a desired goal are likely to be greatly improved and the relevant costs reduced.

The whole study of human behaviour in our context is not aimed merely at improving advertising but at improving the whole marketing operation starting with a definition of the customer's needs and ending with selling him a product which fulfils those needs.

We must still guard against two dangers: firstly, the perennial truth of "a little learning"; secondly, the belief that an understanding of the behavioural sciences will open the gates to Elysium. Marketing still requires judgment and a decision on which of the available courses of action to take.

Suggested Reading

ALDERSON, WROE. *Marketing Behaviour and Executive Action*, Irwin, 1957.

(One of the very earliest attempts to bring out the importance of the behavioural sciences to the study of marketing as a discipline.)

BRITT, S. H. *Consumer Behavior and the Behavioral Sciences*, Wiley, 1966.

CRANE, E. *Marketing Communications*, Wiley, 1965. (The theory behind selling and advertising.)

DAY, G. S., *Buyer Attitudes and Brand Choice Behaviour*, Free Press, 1970.

ENGEL, J. E., KOLLAT, D. J., & BLACKWELL, R. D., *Consumer Behaviour*, Holt, Rinehart & Winston Ltd., 1968.

FESTINGER, L., "Cognitive Dissonance"—see Barksdale (Ed.), *Marketing in Progress,* Holt, Rinehart & Winston Ltd., 1964.

HOVLAND, C. I., JANIS, I. L. & KELLEY, H. H. *Communication and Persuasion,* Yale, 1953.

HOWARD, J. A. *Marketing Theory*, Columbia, 1965. (A behavioural study of marketing fundamentals.)

KRECH, D., CRUTCHFIELD, R. S. & BALLACHEY, E. L. *Individual in Society*, McGraw-Hill, 1962. (A sociological classic which contributes much to the understanding of customer behaviour.)

PART THREE

The Tools of Marketing

In the first two parts we have considered the objectives of the marketing function and some of the factors which influence the behaviour of the customer. In the next chapters we shall review the tools which the marketing manager may use to help him obtain his objectives.

CHAPTER 7

The Marketing Mix

What is "the marketing mix"?

The phrase "marketing mix" is now part of the jargon of marketing. Essentially it means the marketing methods adopted in order to carry out marketing policy. The idea of a number of ingredients which are the same for all cakes but from which, according to the quantities of each item used in the particular recipe, very different types of cakes can be made is a useful metaphor as this is just what does happen in business. A heavy machinery manufacturer has a quite different marketing organisation and operation from that of a company selling packets of tea. But each of them does to a greater or lesser degree all the things done by the other.

The following comprise the ingredients of this mix:

1. The products made.
2. The promotional policy and the company's philosophy of business.
3. The presentation, packaging and branding of the product.
4. The pricing policy and its implementation.
5. The selling operation, the sales policy and the organisation of the sales function.
6. The advertising policy and campaigns.
7. The channels of distribution of the product.
8. The stock of finished goods and its location.
9. Sales, or after-sales, service.
10. Market research.

Each of these factors plays its own separate part in any business but the importance of this part varies from business to business.

1. The products made

Here quite clearly the company must decide on the type, size, variety of product required to satisfy the needs of those making up the market it has decided to operate in. The selection of the market is a basic marketing decision. The devising of the product follows from marketing's definition of the market's needs as modified by the policy considerations discussed in Chapter 2.

2. *The promotional policy and the company's philosophy of business*

What is the company's general approach to business? Is it expansionist and aggressive, or is it easy-going? Does it wish to thrust and push and grow as fast as ever it can, or does it wish to cultivate its customers and friends and grow "by invitation" as it were? This philosophy will be a major influence in all the other aspects of marketing; it underlies every aspect of the company's activities and can usually be altered radically only by a conscious desire to do so emanating from top management and planned to take effect at all levels.

3. *Presentation, packaging and branding of the product*

This includes the basic selling platform on which the product is offered to the user. The benefits it offers to the user, its name, the pack design, the product's reputation in the market, all these are bound together to achieve a concerted impression on the potential user. Branding (i.e. the adoption of a name and product character) can equally apply to any product or service, whether it be in the industrial or in the consumer field.

4. *Pricing policy and its implementation*

The importance of the company's approach to the central factor of price needs little emphasis. The level of price in the market brings together the buyer and the seller. Along with this goes also the structure of trade margins, special discounts for quantity or immediate purchase, and the integrity of the pricing policy. Does every similar company get a similar price or is it a question of individuals bargaining and the best poker player winning? The company's pricing policy is one of the most important of its marketing tools.

5. *The selling operation, sales policy and organisation*

The kind of selling operation used depends largely on the potential customer and the kind of product. Selling bridges across the Zambesi or complete electrical installations in Kuwait is a different matter from selling tea to Mrs. Brown in Edgware. Yet each of these operations is affected by the company's basic philosophy towards development and both these examples are affected by whether a middle man (distribution agent) is employed and whether the traditional channel of distribution is used or not. The organisation of the selling operation is determined by the selling tasks to be performed and the overall policies to be followed.

6. *Advertising policy and campaigns*

Advertising is a method of promoting sales by informing potential customers of the existence of the product and giving them reasons why they should buy it. Sometimes people tacitly assume that advertising is only what appears in newspapers and magazines or what is heard or seen on radio, television or hoardings. This is only part of the whole. Display material at the point of purchase, catalogues, material sent direct to the user (direct mail), exhibitions, demonstrations, all are part of advertising, the "media" of advertising. Special offers, coupons, send-away offers and so on are usually termed "sales promotion" but in the widest sense all advertising is the promotion of sales to potential customers.

The story in the advertising campaign is usually called "the theme". Combining a suitable theme with an effective media programme so that the potential sales prospect is prepared for purchasing the product is the basic skill in advertising. Clearly the advertising campaigns used in support by the hopeful bridge builder will be different from those used by the tea packer.

7. *Channels of distribution*

The channel of distribution is the method and organisation used to get the product from the factory to the final user. The channels used are varied but are usually not dissimilar within any one industry. Capital goods manufacturers usually sell direct to their customers and make delivery directly from factory to site. Consumer goods makers usually distribute their products through retail shops but may either sell direct to those shops or through the intermediary of a wholesaler or factor; some consumer goods manufacturers, however, sell directly to the consumer at the house door.

8. *The stock and location of products*

This element of the marketing mix depends on the importance to the company of having a stock of manufactured product available and so situated that speedy delivery can be made to its customers. Service is the criterion. For some companies, making custom-built products, there can, by definition, be no finished goods stock except those awaiting delivery to the customers who ordered them. For those companies, the equivalent factor to having pre-manufactured stock is the time taken to turn an order into a delivery of the product or service. This is called the "lead time". This element of the mix is one which may considerably influence the manufacturer's ability to get business from his customers.

9. *Sales or after-sales service*

In the case of consumer goods pre-sales service is help given to a buyer to make up his mind what to buy. It takes the form either of advertising or the expertise of the retailer or distributor.

After-sales service is the action taken to ensure that the performance of the product is up to a certain standard of quality. Whatever may be the law on the matter, the consumer expects the manufacturer to make good deficiencies in his product by virtue of the brand or maker's name upon it. This commonly takes the form of replacing items of small unit price or the repair or adjustment of bigger items such as domestic equipment. The degree to which the manufacturer supplies these services himself or through his distributor may have much influence on the business he obtains.

There are counterparts in industrial operations where such services may be even more important. In many industrial operations the manufacturer works with his customers to solve the latter's own production problems. He designs or modifies machinery for particular purposes and generally acts as helper, consultant or adviser.

After supplying a product (often a machine) the manufacturer frequently sets it up, makes sure that teething problems are overcome, trains operatives and gives agreed service and maintenance over a period.

Buyers in industrial operations generally expect high service standards. They do not expect them to be free but understand that the cost of them must be included in the overall price. The amount of service and the willingness of the manufacturer to give it is undoubtedly one of the most powerful incentives which he can offer to his buyer to induce him to do business.

10. *Market research*

Market research can be a valuable and potent factor in a company's marketing operation and here the company's attitude towards the basic market, information it needs and the steps it takes to get the information, is paramount. This attitude determines how much of its resources a company devotes to finding out the needs of the market, to testing out product changes or new developments, to investigating competitive action and to checking on changes in the market.

A vigorous, aggressive company uses market research as a means of keeping to the forefront in its sphere of operations, of initiating moves to increase the rate of change and not merely defensively matching the doings of others and trying not to be left too far in the rear.

Different marketing mixes

Let us look at a few examples of how different operations require different interpretations of the marketing mix.

Branded grocery products

Major grocery products such as branded foods, detergents and soaps illustrate some of the most competitive, and at times controversial, marketing situations in the country. By and large these markets are large in sterling value and relatively stable even in times of industrial slackness. The products are bought, consumed and bought again at very frequent intervals, often weekly. A very high proportion of housewives buy them and a very large number of shops sell them to the actual consumers. The stability and size of these fields makes them very attractive to larger companies whose resources can best be applied where the business is considerable. Frequently such markets are dominated by two or three large manufacturers although there usually is a large number of small (often local) competitors making up a minor portion of the whole.

Usually the product is made for stock and held in a number of places for very quick delivery to as many as 30,000–50,000 shops and wholesalers' warehouses. The larger manufacturers usually have a heavy investment in plant which gives a very low unit cost when production is maintained at a high proportion of total capacity. If this plant is operated at a low level, however, unit cost increases markedly. Such manufacturers clearly have a particular interest in maintaining (and selling of course) a high level of output.

The leading manufacturers therefore generally employ very sophisticated marketing methods. Market research is widely and intensively used to obtain as much information on which to base decisions as is practicable.

Their products are branded and packaging and presentation appeal is highly developed. They employ large well-organised sales forces, numbering up to 150 or more salesmen, selling direct to the major outlets, and through wholesalers to the remainder. They support these efforts with consistent and heavy advertising to the consumer and follow this through with considerable display and sales promotional effort in the shops (at the point of purchase) to ensure that the consumer, already prepared by the advertising campaign, will actually buy their brand when she is in the shop with her money in her hand.

By contrast, these major manufacturers try to keep their prices stable (in so far as they can, for they can no longer fix retail prices). They prefer to alter the weight or size of package rather than use the more clumsy price tool, for meaningful price changes have to go in steps often too large to allow delicate small percentage adjustments. They compete with advertising and with product improvements rather than price lists. Lord Heyworth, former Chairman of Unilever, is on record a few years ago as saying that one of the Unilever toilet soaps had had eleven product improvements in a five-year period in order to meet or surpass its competition.

The shop owners and wholesale traders are well aware of the value of heavily advertised quick-selling products. They themselves, therefore, do not accept high margins when they believe they can improve their own individual profits by keen price fixing and adopting a policy of "small profits, quick returns". As a result the percentage margins to the trade, whether retail or wholesale, are usually very small. Wholesale grocers habitually work on about $7\frac{1}{2}$ per cent gross margin on turnover; counter-service grocery shops on 20–22 per cent; large self-service shops about 14–19 per cent. The actual figures vary but with a stock turnover varying from 12 to 30 times per year these figures can obviously still give a good level of profit.

Whilst it is especially dangerous to generalise in this area, it may give the reader who is not familiar with these markets some inkling of the situation to suggest that a manufacturer may spend as much as 20 per cent of the consumer sterling value on advertising and promotion. Of this, promotion could be one-third to a half, i.e. 5–10 per cent of consumer value. His selling costs also may be around 5–10 per cent of consumer value. These figures vary very considerably and it is really not possible to generalise intelligently on packaging, market research, product development and other marketing mix ingredient costs. We can, however, bear in mind that in such operations as these we find very elaborate marketing organisations, with the emphasis always on the consumer and a co-ordinated effort to find what he (she) wants and get it to him.

Motor cars

Here we have a quite different picture. Buyers do not normally buy a car on impulse nor do they usually buy one frequently. Usually the decision to buy at all is second only in importance to buying a house (because of the large unit cost) so the decision-making process is often long and devious. Furthermore, having bought a new car, the buyer has come to accept that certain immediate adjustments have to be made soon after purchase because of the nature of this complicated piece of machinery. He knows that sometimes he will need help and advice when things go wrong (although he hopes this will not happen frequently) and that he will need periodic expert attention. As a result a highly specialised system of distributors and local dealers has been created, marrying technical service and advice to the normal retail functions of stocking and selling the product near to where the buyer lives.

This organisation consists of "distributors" buying from the manufacturers and "dealers" buying from the distributors. In either case, each company usually has a franchise giving it the sole selling rights over a certain territory. The manufacturer helps train both the salesmen and the servicing staff of both distributors and dealers, and arranges with them the responsibilities of all parties in so far as free servicing and warranty operations are concerned.

The motor car industry is already an oligopoly, with only a handful of large manufacturers and a few specialist manufacturers on the fringe. The specialist knowledge and capital investment required of a new entrant is so large that it is now almost impossible for newcomers to be a serious possibility. Outputs are large and sales high, yet there is a good deal of fluctuation in sales from year to year due largely to the relative ease with which the market can be affected by outside factors, such as taxation or control of finance available to the buyer.

The pattern of the marketing mix thus revolves in this case around a complex distribution and servicing organisation. Behind this, the manufacturer's own field sales force is small and concerned primarily with negotiating with the main distributors. Advertising expenditures are low in relation to turnover and generally amount to only a few shillings per car sold, although this still mounts up to considerable sums. Advertising is usually aimed at influencing the make of car a buyer will buy and creating a brand image to fit particular segments of the market. Competition manifests itself mostly in design/performance characteristics; pricing is keen but it is not easy to relate price and value. Distributors/dealers do not get very wide margins on a percentage basis (perhaps 17 per cent between manufacturer's receipts and the retail price, to cover all rungs on the distributional ladder) but the sums per sales unit are comparatively large.

Heavy engineering products

This is quite a different type of business. Whatever type of basic engineering is involved, the marketing problems are radically different from those outlined above. Probably there are only a few potential buyers. Almost certainly there are comparatively few potential suppliers. Most of those concerned are likely to know most of the others quite intimately. So far as the volume of business is concerned the total may fluctuate wildly with the general state of the economy and business activity. Another difference is that the time between the buyer deciding he has a requirement and the signing of a contract for plant may be many months, even into years. The reputation of the supplier for reliability and the service which he offers to the buyer are often more important than the price quoted.

Characteristically, companies in the heavy capital goods fields have only a few salesmen and these men are traditionally more technical representatives and consultants than salesmen. The company's own men are often supported (especially overseas) by agents who largely act as "scouts" and pass the word to a head office contact when new business may be in the offing. Advertising is a minor activity and often seems employed more to remind the competitors of the company's existence than to sell to their own potential customers, although this can hardly be seriously intended! Sales literature is generally used only where stock items are made or held ready. Because of the design, service and contract-financing problems serious contact is almost always direct between supplier and buyer, and often at several different levels of responsibility or of technical expertise.

Factors affecting the marketing mix

Let us conclude this brief review with a glance at some of the more important influences on the make-up of a company's marketing mix.

(1) Size of capital investment and degree of expert knowledge required to gain an entry into the industry. Little comment is required. The greater the magnitude of these the less likely will be the entrance of new competitors so that the present manufacturer may the more safely concentrate on his current competition.

(2) The total size of the market. If the "universe" is great the com-

pany may also aspire to being large. Small markets will not support large sophisticated operations—nor are the latter likely to be necessary.

(3) The stability of the market over the years. The measures and organisations required to deal with a volume of business fluctuating considerably, as trading activity waxes and wanes, are usually quite different from those which can be applied when the total market is relatively stable.

(4) The degree to which the market is constantly changing in its character. This is the question of market "dynamism". Is the market always in a state of change and flux? Are product life cycles short? Are consumer wants or the channels of distribution constantly changing? When all of these conditions apply in a large and stable market (e.g. soap or cigarettes) the most sophisticated marketing procedures are likely to be needed.

(5) The actual number of potential customers. This factor is connected with the channels of distribution but raises in itself problems of organisation and method between the extremes, for example, of the bakery industry, making the almost universal and immediately consumed loaf of bread, and the shipbuilding industry, making ships for a very limited number of shipping companies who only replace their fleets over a long time span.

(6) The geographical distribution of potential buyers. This is a refinement of the previous factor but in itself causes considerable modification to operating methods, as can be seen by comparing any small local company with a national company (in the U.K.) or by examining a company with a large export trade in several countries.

(7) The complexity or simplicity of the process of reaching a decision to purchase. This cuts right across industrial and consumer operations. Deciding whether to buy a tin of peas is different from deciding to buy a new car. The decision to buy some lubricating oil for use in an engineering company is different from deciding to buy a new piece of equipment costing £100,000. There are two very different types of consumer here but each is supplied by two quite different marketing operations.

(8) The type of channel of distribution which is appropriate and available. This again tends to be the result of other factors but, whilst there are exceptions to following tradition, this factor must not be ignored lest the manufacturer literally fails to get his product to his customers because of the power of the existing channel of distribution.

(9) The degree to which the market is seasonal. This can have many

repercussions, particularly in the consumer goods field. It is exceptionally important where there is the need to process seasonal crops for later consumption or to manufacture products (e.g. toys) for a market with a pronounced seasonal peak.

Our review has been brief for such a wide subject but this is not indeed a subject with a finite generalised conclusion. The marketing mix is a *real* thing. It varies almost from firm to firm, let alone industry to industry, and it must be for the reader himself to consider the whys and wherefores of particular cases.

Suggested Reading

KOTLER, P. *Marketing Management: Analysis, Planning and Control,* 2nd edn., Prentice-Hall, 1971. (Chapter 12 gives a useful concise analysis of how to optimise the marketing mix.)

MCCARTHY, E. J. *Basic Marketing, a Managerial Approach,* 4th edn., Irwin, 1971.

SHAPIRO, A. "Marketing Experimentation", *Medical, Marketing and Media,* Vol. 6, Stamford, U.S.A., 1971.

CHAPTER 8

Marketing Research

Market research as a tool of marketing

From the concept of marketing discussed in Chapter 1 we have the thought that a business depends fundamentally on its customers rather than on its production facilities, and that it is the function of marketing to define the customers' needs and how to satisfy them (at a profit). Fortunately we also have a list of questions which, when answered, will put the marketing man well on his way to working out a sound basic policy. We have not, however, considered how he is to get the answers which will help him in forming his policy.

One of the principal tools available is market, or marketing, research. Market research is research into the market, its past, present and future. Marketing research includes this but also goes on to encompass research into the effectiveness of different elements in the marketing operation such as sales, advertising and distribution.

It is convenient in discussing this function to speak of a market research department as the one and only place in the company where *all* market research activity is carried on. In practice, however, a good deal of this takes place in the sales office, the advertising office or the marketing manager's office. Most self-respecting market research departments would not expect to have to supply information on competitor's prices or advertising space costs to their respective sales or advertising departments, but they might very probably be the repository of a great deal of environmental data such as income levels, industrial activity, industrial or consumer characteristics in different regions, consumer habits and so on within a reasonable range around the company's field of operations. It is still worth bearing in mind, however, that much that is called "market research" in textbooks is, in practice, carried out every day under different names, such as keeping sales data of the company and its competitive companies or obtaining regular reports on advertising activity and expenditures.

Unfortunately it is true that many, many business men make no systematic assessment of the market. "I've been doing this all my life, I *know* what the customer wants" is an all too typical attitude. Sometimes he does. In this case systematic investigation is quite unnecessary. The problem is when does he "know" he is right—and is; when does he "know" he is right—and is not?

Market research is the marketing manager's principal tool for seeking the answers to his basic questions (see page 10). It is, however, a tool and does not, must not, take over his function of making a decision. Market research can find many (not all) of the answers, but these still have to be assessed and translated into recommendations and actions. The marketing man who will not invite his market research man to give him a view, an interpretation, an opinion, is clearly selling himself short, as the responsible market research man will have much to offer from his own experience and ability. All the same, the researcher will not conclude his report by saying "this means we should drop line X in favour of line XY", or whatever. His job is to get the facts as accurately as possible and explain them in their context. No more. We hope no less.

Main categories of market research

Market research can be considered under three main headings:

(*i*) Collection of facts.

(*ii*) Assembly of people's opinions, attitudes and views about products, events or companies.

(*iii*) Testing marketing operations.

Collection of facts

The relevant facts required by any one company may be quite different from those required by any other but the questions to be answered will usually include the following:

(*a*) Who buys the product? Are they men, women, old, young? Are they characterised by social class, income group, attitude to the product field or some other factor?

(*b*) Where do they live? Are there more of them in some places than others?

(*c*) How much do they buy? Are these differences, in quantities bought or frequency of buying, related to some particular characteristic (e.g. size of family, addiction to an activity such as motoring, etc.)?

(*d*) How big (in both physical terms and sterling value) is the total market?

(*e*) What influence has the external economic situation on the market?

(*f*) What are the characteristics of the principal competitors, their products and their methods of trading?

(*g*) What are the characteristics of the distributive system?

(*h*) What advertising facilities are available to us? What are their characteristics?

Assembly of attitudes

This is the field of motivational research where the primary objective is to find *why* people act as they do. We have already discussed in Part Two a number of ways *of approaching* the idiosyncrasies of human behaviour and their connection with the customer's actions. To understand, predict and even anticipate the consumer's behaviour will help us to answer his needs more accurately and thus sell more and make more profit. Attitudinal market research covers the consumer's satisfactions and dissatisfactions, his views about the product, its uses, and its reputation, i.e. what the consumer thinks about it and why he does so.

Testing marketing operations

This category is wide and includes the whole range of product screening and test marketing as well as research into sales methods and tactics, and advertising operations.

A test marketing operation is one designed to try out a new product in a small section of the market only. The location could be a town but will more probably be an area and must be as near similar in characteristics to the eventual market as possible. The package, name, advertising theme and price of the product will be that to be used later, if successful, and the advertising campaign size as well as the sales effort must be as nearly in proportion to the area used as can be arranged. It is essential that these proportions should be the same as those planned for the broad-scale operation it is hoped to mount later. The objects are to limit the manufacturer's commitment and costs until he has more knowledge of the probable future of the new product, as well as to indicate any weakness in his plans and give him data to help in assessing the probable success of the product on a full-scale market.

In practice it is not always possible to slot a particular activity neatly into any one category of market research because, as with so much in marketing, the boundaries are often blurred and imprecise. For example, products under development may be taken in plain covers to consumers who are asked to use them so that they may, in a later interview, answer questions about their relative performance as seen by ordinary consumers. This is a testing procedure, not test marketing, as no purchase is involved; it is nevertheless very much keyed to finding out attitudes and opinions. If one of the products happens to be a re-packed sample of a product already on the market and questions are asked concerning quantities of similar products used and the frequency of purchase of them by the respondent, into what category can this work be put? Obviously it fits into no one category but spreads into all three.

Market research methods

Let us now look briefly at how the market research operation is carried out. Almost all types of market research are based on the use of a sampling technique. The whole of any situation is called the "universe". Statistical methodology tells us that, if a random sample of the universe is taken, the probability of the characteristics of the sample corresponding to those of the universe within specified limits of error can be calculated. Mathematically, the accuracy of a random sample is inversely proportional to the square root of the size of the sample. If a particular sample can give an accurate result to, say, plus or minus 6 per cent, then to make it accurate to within plus or minus 3 per cent, i.e. to halve the error, means that the size of the sample has to be increased *four times*.

When accurate information about the composition of the population is already known, say by sex, age, size of family, there is a method of obtaining a closely representative sample by relating sections of the sample to sections of the population. For many purposes this technique, known as "stratified sampling", enables market research organisations to work on a sample of only a few hundred people and still obtain a good representation of the whole U.K. population. We might be tempted to think, therefore, that once an accurate sample of the population has been devised the researcher, seeking information about what people do, is home and dry. Not so. There is still the problem of how to get accurate information from the people in the sample.

Cost of marketing research

Before continuing we must consider the cost of market research operations. In absolute terms, a great deal of market research is costly because of the amount of time it takes up, the difficulty in searching out information and the need to employ people skilled in specialist activities. This is particularly true of both specially commissioned surveys and the setting up of continuing studies of particular activities. For example, a quite simple study involving interviews of housewives in their homes may cost around 30s. to £2 per interview. Seeking out and interviewing specific business people may cost more, perhaps as much as £5 to £10 per interview. If 400 to 500 interviews are required in their homes may cost around £2 to £3 per interview. Seeking out and interviewing specific business people may cost more, perhaps as much as £7.50 to £15 per interview. If 400 to 500 interviews are required in the former or maybe 100 in the latter, the cost is already quite

In considering the cost of market research the following three issues must be faced:

(*i*) It is necessary to estimate the value of the information which is sought. There is no formula for doing this but it must be attempted. Clearly the cost of the work to be done must be less than the estimated value of the answers for the project to be worth considering.

(*ii*) It is vital to define quite precisely what information is required. On the precision of this definition largely depends the accuracy of the answers obtained and, if the market research department is given an unclear request, then its answers, however skilful the work, will necessarily also be lacking precision. If the results do not give the information required then the value of the research is correspondingly lessened.

(*iii*) Prudence demands that the researcher should begin by first examining the cheapest ways of obtaining information and then continuing in ascending order of cost. Simply doing this may often show that the information to be sought by the more expensive methods can be far more precisely defined because of what is learned earlier. The author had a chastening experience in this direction some years ago when he undertook to reconnoitre the U.K. domestic pet food market. At first it was considered that the canned goods side was certainly the most important and that the problem was to find suitable products for dog owners to feed to their dogs. At a very early stage information, which was not difficult (nor very expensive) to obtain, indicated that at that time far more canned foods were bought for cats than for dogs. A subsequent national investigation was therefore directed quite differently from the form it might have taken without this knowledge.

[The problem of evaluating market research in advance may not be easy, in which case deciding whether the cost involved is worth incurring is correspondingly difficult. Here some help may be found by using the Bayesian statistics approved. This relies on an analysis of the position based on subjective estimates of the probability of the various possible outcomes occurring. There is an interesting paper by F. M. Bass, "Marketing Research Expenditures: A Decision model", originally published in the *Journal of Business*, January 1963, and reprinted in *Marketing Models: Quantitative and Behavioral*, by R. L. Day (International Textbook Co., 1964).]

Sources of information

Most textbooks draw a fairly clear distinction between *desk research*, or *library research*, and other types of research. Certainly the former should be used first. Briefly this consists of making every effort to obtain information which is already available somewhere or other before doing original field work.

Often the first place to look is in the company's *own files*. Much information may be found there which, when analysed and considered, throws a great deal of light on the problem. Such matters as seasonal variations in sales, geographical distribution of sales, characteristics of competitors' marketing methods, all may bear on an investigation, say, of the usefulness of a projected new product.

There are many *published statistics* (see appendix to this Chapter) which are easy and cheap to find including the Census of Production, Monthly Digest of Statistics, Census of Distribution, National Income and Expenditure Blue Book. Then there are regular issues of trade association figures, publication of market data by advertising media owners, such as T.V. programme contractors and magazine publishers, and numerous others.

Some research organisations regularly issue broadsheets containing general information (usually to whet the appetite of potential clients) and indicating the possibility of more detailed figures being available. A. C. Nielsen, Attwood, A.G.B., National Opinion Surveys and similar professional research organisations all from time to time publicise the kinds of information they have to offer and this published material is usually quite cheap—often free.

Most professional research agencies sell generalised information which they obtain in the course of their basic routine operations for a fee. These include the work of Nielsen in a number of retail trade fields where, by means of a bi-monthly stock audit of a sample of shops, detailed information is produced on purchases and sales by the shops and levels of stock in them for specified products or groups of products. Complementary operations are carried out by the Attwood Panel and others who arrange for a diary of all household purchases each week to be maintained by a sample of housewives so that the purchasing situation can be seen from the consumer side. For those unfamiliar with this kind of operation it is not difficult to appreciate why, in large active markets, such expensive services should exist.

Let us consider one manufacturer producing a range of foods in two different factories and selling via wholesalers, as well as direct to the retail trade, from ten depots spread around the country. He cannot immediately match his ex-factory shipments with his sales force figures of orders taken because of the time lag in dealing with the paper work. He has no means of knowing how much stock his wholesale customers currently have. He has no means of knowing what stocks his own retail customers have, and he may not even know of the existence of some of the retail shops serviced by the wholesalers. So his current level of information of the present situation is low and may well mask what is actually happening. All this is true for his own products where at least he has accurate information on the orders taken and delivery and production made. He has, of course, even less information about what his competitors may be doing and whether he is gaining from or losing to them.

The use of both shop and household information is a refinement but a useful one. Some of what is sold to shops goes out to various types of institution, such as hospitals or schools, which may mask the movements in the household sector. Similarly, not all types of shop (e.g. Woolworths) are covered by the shop audits so a knowledge of what the housewife herself is doing is of great value.

Such panels are naturally expensive to form and maintain. The detailed information obtained is therefore sold to the subscribing clients of the research companies at a fairly high fee but at a much cheaper rate than that which an individual company could achieve with its own sample panel of shops or homes. Outside companies (i.e. non-subscribers) can usually buy information on such aspects as total market size or geographic breakdown, but the interests of the subscribers are protected by the research company not allowing outsiders to have information about individual brands or companies. No one has yet been able to devise a satisfactory equivalent scheme for industrial products because so few of these are sufficiently similar and sufficiently frequently bought.

Finally (and most expensive) there are the ad hoc surveys. These are mounted by the market research department itself, in the case of companies having their own interviewers, or more usually by subcontract to a research group. They cover both industrial and consumer goods operations and all aspects of marketing research—fact finding, motivation, testing operations. Some, not too detailed, examination of how such surveys may be carried out is necessary to an understanding of the value of market research—and its limitations.

Market research techniques

We now return to the problem mentioned on page 84, that arriving at a sound sample of the universe is only part of the battle. Let us assume, therefore, that our market researcher has gone through all the areas where desk research can help him. He has examined all published information and purchased what he could from the research groups. Now he has decided that specific surveys are required to uncover factual matter about a specific area in the consumer field and also to find out why people buy the products they do buy and what their opinions of these products are.

If he belongs to one of the handful of companies in this country doing enough market research to warrant the cost of maintaining a market research department with experts in devising appropriate sampling and interviewing techniques and his own staff of investigators, then he might handle the whole matter internally. In the majority of cases, however, he would use an outside specialist research organisation. This has advantages in that (*a*) the agency's experts may well be more numerous and specialised than his own could possibly be; (*b*) they will almost certainly have a wider experience of research, with clients in many industries, than he can possibly have; (*c*) they will have specialised facilities for either mechanical or electronic data processing relative to the kind of information to be analysed and organised, so that they may be able to work much quicker than he could.

Research agencies usually have their own supervisors in the field but employ freelance investigators (usually part-time married women in consumer work) who are often very well trained.

The research requirements, as indicated, may entail two different types of survey. The first may be termed a fact-finding operation and the second a motivational operation.

Fact-finding surveys

These may appear to be relatively straightforward matters. We have already indicated that a skilfully arranged sample of housewives will give accurate information because the sample will represent the whole. It would seem, therefore, that our researcher only needs to ask them what they do, count up how many do this as against that, and all that remains is the presentation of the figures.

Why should this not be so? To begin with we said "he only needs to ask them". Yet, even in the simplest of cases, if the question asked is incorrectly phrased the whole basis of the exercise is falsified.

For example, let us suppose two groups of motorists A and B all live in the same village and each individually own the same kind of car and travel about the same mileage. Let us also suppose there are three garages, one selling petrol X, one Y and one Z. We then ask each motorist "Which brand of petrol do you usually buy?" Group A answer "X", Group B answer "Y" and it would thus appear that Z has no business.

In fact brand Z has 40 per cent of the business and brands X and Y 30 per cent each!

If the researcher had asked:

(*a*) "Which brand of petrol do you usually buy?" then

(*b*) "Which other brand(s) do you occasionally buy?" and

(*c*) "How much of each brand do you buy each month?"

it would have come out that Group A buy 60 gallons of brand X and 40 gallons of brand Z each month; group B buy 60 gallons of brand Y and 40 gallons of brand Z each month!

These may not be the precise words which a professional researcher would use, but the danger of using poor techniques must be obvious. There are other, more complicated, reasons for even "head counting" methods being troublesome to carry out.

Without attempting here an analysis of the psychological processes, there is always difficulty in finding out what people think about a subject or what is in their memory about a past action. They have, first of all, to recognise what is being asked, they then have to relate this to what has happened in the past, then try and remember what did happen, then try and put into words their own assessment of what it is all about. This of course is understandable and reasonable. But the subject matter may be vastly more complex. So far we have postulated that the respondent will be willing, even anxious, to help. This, in itself, may cause a change in the answer inspired only by the wish to be helpful. That can be guarded against—but what if the respondent wishes to be *unhelpful* for one reason or another? Again there is a technique of cross checking, carefully phrased questions, carefully ordered questions, which can overcome this difficulty.

Frequently, however, a much more complex difficulty than understanding, clarity of expression, memory and degree of co-operation arises. Often the area of the information touches on matters where vanity, social competitiveness, fear and similar factors cause the respondent consciously or unconsciously to twist the facts in a way which cannot be foretold (and thus be forestalled) by the interviewer. "Did you have a hot bath last night?" sounds innocent enough. What if the respondent has a weekly bath but feels he is "expected" in that neighbourhood to bath daily? What if he has run out of fuel so that he could not have his usual tub? What if his house has only a shower? Clearly even such a simple question may raise problems.

That this is so was indicated when some of the author's course members were doing a project on the marketing of French wines in this country, during which they carried out a small, pilot-scale, housewife survey to find if some of their hunches were worth pursuing on a larger scale. They started off "Good evening, we are doing a research study into people's drinking habits" and before they could get out another word the door was slammed shut. This happened three times. The two men concerned, who had never done any work of this kind before, then conferred. They continued "Good evening, we are doing a research study into various beverages, do you and your family ever drink tea?" It may not have been the perfect introduction but it worked and they then progressed via tea, coffee, soft drinks, beer and spirits to wines on the table—and had just one refusal out of fifty-odd calls.

For straightforward fact-finding, i.e. "what did happen" type surveys the questionnaire or interview framework must be skilfully constructed to avoid the kind of pitfall we have indicated. Without further detail it is clear that the whole success of interviewing lies in putting questions to the respondent which he can understand and answer, and putting them in an order which will enable him to do so honestly and without bias, deliberate or otherwise.

The market research investigator must be a skilled person. She (or he) must be adept at not "leading" the respondent, at being persistent in following a line through, in being sympathetic whilst not actually helping the respondent, above all in maintaining the routine and interviewing only the appropriate respondent so that all respondents fit into the projected sample and all answer the same questions. If this routine is not followed, interviewer bias can ruin any survey by producing plainly untrue information.

In all cases, market research organisers who know their job work out their questionnaire and method most carefully beforehand. They then pilot-test it with a few calls made by a very experienced investigator so that any snags can be ironed out before the survey is made. Nevertheless all investigators should be *personally* briefed before they go out making calls. The survey should be discussed with them in detail and any difficulties which are anticipated by the interviewer answered. As a final safeguard, when the interviewers are carrying out the investigation, good research organisations arrange for a supervisor to make calls with each investigator, to ensure that all are working in the same way and also to make a proportion of "call backs" on interviews already made, to check for interviewer bias. This kind of work is expensive but it would be fatal, as we have already said, to have conclusions based on false or misleading information.

Motivation surveys

Many techniques are used in motivational research to uncover the "why" information but we need only indicate here the kind of work being done.

Many market research people themselves have been very suspicious of work done in motivational areas on the grounds that people are so very different from each other and that there are additional difficulties in getting representative samples in psychological areas, as well as the difficulty of actually finding out why people act or think as they do. Nevertheless, considerable improvements in technique have been made in recent years and most research (and marketing) practitioners believe that a good deal of progress has been made. The basic problems are firstly to find out why a person thinks or acts as he or she does; secondly to evaluate and measure the influences in this area; and finally to try and do the same thing for all the people concerned in the particular activity under consideration. Whilst there is much experience showing that a good deal can, in fact, be learned about an individual's reactions, there is still much doubt as to whether motivations for a large group of people can be classified, evaluated, and then added together.

The following approaches are among those employed:

Depth interviews. Individual respondents are interviewed by a trained psychologist over a protracted period—often up to three hours or more—usually in a consulting room. In the course of these interviews the psychologist believes he can usually uncover the important motivations, reactions, associations and opinions relevant to a particular field. He believes that even a few such interviews enable him to present a description of the position to the initiating research group. Perforce there is no quantitative backing to the report but the qualitative material in itself can be of great value. It is a subjective technique based on the psychologist's own assessment.

Group discussions. A number of people are brought together and asked to discuss the relevant subject area. The organiser is usually a person skilled in keeping a discussion going, or keeping it to the point, without participating himself and is not always a fully-qualified psychologist. A tape-recording is made and the material is later analysed so that a summary of the important factors can be produced.

Both these methods are clearly much dependent on the judgment, skill and experience of the investigator.

Individual interviews. A great deal of work has been done on the use of various indirect questionning techniques, where individuals are interviewed with the objective of validating hypotheses formed after conducting group discussions or depth interviews. Here all the problems of normal head counting procedures are recognised, but it is also taken into account that people cannot answer some questions as they do not realise what the answers are. They are, as we have seen, reluctant to answer questions which involve their own personality, and even their preferences for products, and especially branded goods, depend on impressions conveyed by colours, shape, package, name and so on rather than their physical performances. Interviewing along lines apparently not concerned with the respondent's own situation does however allow inferences to be made about the respondent; his attitudes and opinions can usually be deduced by indirect methods.

Role playing is one such method. Here the respondent is asked to put herself in the position of another (defined) person and then give her own reactions to the situation. Her interpretation of the situation is examined by the researcher to enable him to deduce the respondent's own reactions. A good example of the use of this technique is seen in research by Mason Haire into the comparatively slow early development of instant coffee when it was first introduced to the American market (described in *Motivation Research* by Harry Henry). Two matched groups of women were each shown one of these two shopping lists and asked to describe the kind of person who would use such a list:

A

1½ lbs. hamburger	1 Nescafé instant coffee
2 loaves Wonderbread	1 can Del Monte peaches
1 bunch carrots	5 lbs. potatoes
1 can Rumfords baking powder	

B

1½ lbs. hamburger	½ lb. fresh ground coffee
2 loaves Wonderbread	2 cans Del Monte peaches
1 bunch carrots	5 lbs. potatoes
1 can Rumfords baking powder	

Of those who saw list A 50 per cent said that the woman was lazy or failed to plan well. Of those who saw list B only 12 per cent said the woman failed to plan well and none saw her as a lazy person. There being only one difference in the lists the clear inference is the association in women's minds, at that time, between Nescafé and laziness or bad planning.

There were similar problems with new cake mixes when they were introduced. It was found that women could not believe a cake could be good when they had no work to do in producing it. When the makers recommended the housewife to add an egg and mix the cake themselves (hence be involved) sales increased.

Other methods involve sentence completion, word association and similar tests of the general type used in the now familiar psychological tests used in personnel selection and similar procedures. There is also a method based on a scaling technique—for example a respondent might be asked, concerning a hair dressing,

"Did it leave your hair

(1) Not dry at all?

(2) Not very dry?

(3) Not dry?

(4) Only slightly dry?

(5) Dry?

(6) Very dry?

(7) Very dry indeed?"

Such a "battery" of questions can be allocated a rating where, in the example given, each question is awarded 1–7 points, say, in the order shown so that an overall assessment for each battery can be made. Similarly it is often possible to add together ratings for a number of such batteries to get an overall rating in a particular area.

The use of carefully devised batteries covering many aspects of the same problem area does seem to offer some hope of quantifying, or at least verifying, hitherto purely qualitative concepts. (See also notes on the measurement of attitudes on page 49.)

Industrial market research

The concept of investigating a market through the medium of a sample has been widely accepted in the field of consumer goods and an increasingly large number of companies have adopted this practice. The acceptance of the general principle in the marketing of industrial goods has been much slower. More and more companies in this field are beginning to realise that industrial market research is practicable and valuable, however, and we may expect that in the near future a much higher proportion of the total market research effort in the U.K. will be devoted to industrial market research.

There are a number of practical difficulties which have prevented industrial market research from developing so quickly as the consumer counterpart. It is difficult to tie down the concept of "markets" into meaningful categories. In the first place there is an enormous variety of products and a very wide area where products are custom-built to suit the buyer's needs. Secondly a wide range of products, particularly when they can be modified or adapted for different uses, can be bought and used by industrial companies not only in the same basic industry but also in quite unrelated industries. Further, whilst there is a growing body of basic information about industrial activity and output from official sources, there is not available anything approaching the detailed figures which are a feature of some consumer goods fields. There is not, for example, any equivalent of the Nielsen shop audits or the various consumer panels, largely because of the absence of large areas where the same kind of product is being frequently and consistently purchased.

Another snag is the frequency with which a "market" consists of a relatively small number of companies of which two or three companies, out of perhaps two hundred users or potential users, dominate the market. These may be difficult to interview or may pose problems of breaking security. This problem of security in the development of new products or ideas is far more difficult for the industrial manufacturer than for his consumer goods counterpart. The latter can develop a product and arrange for it to be tested anonymously by a sample of, say, housewives without his competitors being likely to hear about it. If the industrial goods manufacturer wishes to sound out the market on a new idea it is much more probable that the potential customer (who may indeed be his competitor in some fields) will allow an indication of what is projected to reach competing companies. This is also the more likely, if, as we have seen, the "market" is dominated by a very small number of larger companies some of whom *must* be approached to obtain a fair representation of the whole.

Industrial market research, therefore, has very special problems in the obtaining of a representative sample. Even when this can be obtained there are further problems in the actual fieldwork. The companies to be approached may be widely scattered throughout the country. This alone makes it more costly, in both time and money, to reach the respondents required. Depending on the information needed, there is still the difficulty that, although the buyer in the company may often be able to give the required information on other occasions, the only useful informant may be the production director or even (especially where future developments are concerned) the managing director. In any of these cases it may well be necessary to arrange for an interview on a specified date, again slowing down the fieldwork and increasing expenses.

In industrial market research three methods of obtaining information in the field are generally used. The most popular one is the use of a mailed questionnaire. This has the advantages of being comparatively cheap and allowing a large number of firms to be contacted. The method is weak in that the number of completed returns is usually quite low (not more than 20 per cent is a normal experience). Additionally there is no safeguard as to who fills in the information and how reliable it is; furthermore the questionnaire has perforce to be quite simple and not very long or the number which is returned suffers considerably.

Occasionally field work can be carried out by telephone. This method is not very common in the U.K. but can be used for very simple needs which can be asked and answered very briefly. Telephone interviews can, however, be restricted to those individuals who are able, if they are willing, to give the requisite information.

The third and most satisfactory method is by personal interview, and the practical difficulties of reaching the right people have already been indicated. In many areas, such as those of looking into the future and estimating future needs, or those concerned with the development of new products, this may nevertheless be the only method of real value to the researcher.

Finally we should emphasise that, except in the motivational area where qualified specialists may be needed, in consumer market research the interviewer, so long as he or she is trained in interviewing techniques, seldom needs any special technical knowledge of the subject being investigated. The position with industrial market research is exactly the opposite. Here the interviewer must not only be trained as an interviewer, and moreover one capable of interviewing senior business men, but he must generally have a sound background knowledge of the subject under review. Such a combination of talents is rare and the shortage of skilled researchers is one of the reasons why industrial market research has been comparatively slow in development. A comprehensive account of industrial marketing research is given in *Industrial Marketing Research* by N. A. H. Stacey and A. Wilson.

It is not really essential that the marketing man should himself be an expert in these technical research matters. What he does need is an understanding of what it is practical to consider.

Over wide areas he can hope to get quite accurate information on what has happened in the recent past, who does what, how much is spent, what the size of a "market" now is, what products make up what proportions of the whole. Over the other areas of why this happens he can obtain guidance and insight but mostly on a qualitative rather than quantitative basis.

The marketing man with this background must still realise that he has to lean very heavily on his market research experts. He should consult them and discuss with them what specific information he wishes to have and the reasons why he wants it. In turn he must listen to them when they advise him as to what he can expect to obtain. Above all, in the actual work of devising methods to obtain the information he should rely on his judgment of their abilities and his knowledge of their past achievements, and let the experts go their own ways. In market research as elsewhere "a little learning is a dangerous thing".

Suggested Reading

HENRY, H. *Motivation Research*, Crosby Lockwood, 1958.
DELENS, A. H. R. *Principles of Market Research*, Crosby Lockwood, 1950.
 (This is a very useful account of how to use and organise market research.)
HOLMES, P. M. *Marketing Research: Principles and Readings*, Edward Arnold, 1966.
WILSON, A., *The Assessment of Industrial Markets*, Hutchinson, 1968.
WILSON, A., *The Art and Practice of Marketing*, Hutchinson, 1971.

APPENDIX TO CHAPTER EIGHT

Some sources of information

H.M.S.O.:

Annual Abstract of Statistics	Basic figures on population, housing, labour, production, industrial raw materials, fuel and power, building, manufactured goods (10 categories), agriculture and food, retail distribution, transport and communications. External trade (some countries, some commodities). National income and expenditure (includes domestic and public spending). Prices. Index of sources.

Monthly Digest of Statistics	A continuation of the *Annual Abstract* but less comprehensive, more up-to-date.
Economic Trends	Monthly assessment of national economic situation, plus much other statistical information largely presented graphically.
Census of Distribution, 1966	Published 1970. Statistics of retail and distributive trades; data on other services.
Census of Production, 1963	Published 1968. 135 volumes including summary tables; enterprises, output, employment; area breakdown.
Census of Production Reports, Guides to Official Sources, No. 6	General introduction also giving bibliography of publications by various associations.
Department of Employment Gazette	Monthly; articles, news, statistics.
Government Statistics for Industry, 1972	A guide to departmental responsibilities for statistics and the main published sources.
The Business Monitor	Production and sales figures in 36 prescribed industrial categories.
Profit from Facts	Includes a list of government publications in a valuable section "finding your way around Whitehall statistics".
Trade and Industry	Weekly issue of business features and statistics including much on export.

Basic Economic Planning Data (Institute of Marketing, 1965)	Population, employment, retail sterling turnover, average income—on regional basis.
Commercial Information (D. E. Davinson, 1965)	Useful reference book.
The Economist	Weekly current commentary. (Various research and consultancy services available from publishers.)
Fortune Directory, 1971	200 largest industrial firms outside U.S.A.
Retail Business Marketing in Europe	Monthly reports by Economist Intelligence Unit on U.K. and European Marketing; special features regularly appear on individual markets, review of current situation.

Geographia Marketing and Media Survey	Marketing maps with hinterlands of main centres; population, local business (retail and distributive), advertising media.
Industrial Marketing Research (Nicholas and Stacey, 1963)	An informative survey of problems and methods in carrying out market research.
"*JICNARS*" *Reader-ship Studies	Six-monthly studies of audience of main national press media, commissioned by IPA on behalf of all interested parties.
"*JICPARS*" †*Research Studies*	*Ad hoc* poster audience studies.
"*JICTARS*" ‡*Research Studies*	Weekly T.V. audience studies.
Kompass (U.K.)	Annual index/directory of companies and products broken down by county and by town.
Literature of the Social Sciences (P. R. Lewis, 1960)	Historical, but lists many sources in U.K. and overseas, including United Nations and private sources, e.g. Royal Statistical Society.
Market Research (Library Association, 1964)	Bibliography including many papers published in journals.
Marketing and Market Assessment (J. L. Sewell, 1966)	Lists government offices and professional organisations.
National Institute Economic Review	Quarterly assessment of the economic situation, forecasts, statistical tables.
Sources of Statistics (J. M. Harvey, 1969)	Principal sources of statistics in U.K. and U.S.A.
Sources of Marketing Information (G. Wills, 1969)	A useful starting point for many searches, includes product fields.
The Sunday Times Business News	Useful business articles.
The Times Business News	Includes quarterly forecasts from London and Cambridge Economic Service.

* Joint Industrial Committee for National Advertising Readership Surveys.

† Joint Industrial Committee for Poster Advertising Research Studies.

‡ Joint Industrial Committee for Television Audience Research Studies.

Who Owns Whom   Annual directory of parent, associate and subsidiary companies.

Board of Trade Statistics and Market Intelligence Library, 35 Old Bailey, London E.C.4.   Contains a vast amount of data on overseas markets.

C.B.D. Research Ltd., 154 High St., Beckenham, Kent BR3 IEA   Specialist publishers of reference books and guides to research information.

CHAPTER 9

Pricing

Pricing is often misunderstood

The function of price as the critical final factor in the whole process of bringing together buyer and supplier in a mutual bargain is generally understood. The buyer should feel that the price is a fair one for the satisfaction he gets from his purchase and the supplier should feel that he has made a reasonable profit from the sale. Most readers will probably agree that the pricing of the product is one of the vital elements in the marketing mix, yet there is daily evidence that this is a much misunderstood area.

In 1964 the Purchasing Officers' Association formally complained that the prices of certain engineering products were being increased without any corresponding rises in costs "to justify them". Did they honestly believe that price increases without preceding cost increases were always unjustified? Did they truly believe that they could always rely on some suppliers surviving and being able to supply their needs and that there never was a danger of their suppliers being forced to cease production because they were making losses at the prices ruling? Might mistakes not have been made in fixing the previous prices? Is the concept of both buyer and supplier being satisfied (i.e. making a profit) of no validity? Do the marketing executives of the same buyers' companies themselves apply the same philosophy?

Let us then examine the important marketing question: "At what price shall we sell our product?" For simplicity we will assume that there is only one product and examine the basic factors involved in the pricing decision:

(*i*) The characteristics of the product and its consumers.

(*ii*) The competitive characteristics of the industry.

(*iii*) The company's policy.
(*iv*) The cost situation.

The characteristics of the product and its consumers

What kind of a product are we considering and why is it bought by the consumer? Are we considering a product quickly consumed, such as matches, food, newspapers, or are we considering a durable or semi-durable (i.e. a product with a longer life) such as domestic equipment, cars, fountain pens or even men's clothing? Are the goods concerned sold in shops—if so are factors or wholesalers involved? Or are they sold direct to the consumer by the maker's own salesmen as happens with most milk, some bread, Avon Cosmetics and Kleeneze and Better-wear Brushes? The questions of course can be endless when considering the whole field of both industrial and consumer products but naturally when *in* business we know whether we are selling to a private consumer or an industrial buyer; we know if it is a low price frequent purchase item, like razor blades, or a high price occasionally bought item of furniture. We also know, or ought to know, the conditions operating "in the market" such as the normal behaviour of the consumer, the extent to which "shopping around" occurs and how much the consumer knows about competing products.

Competitive characteristics of the industry

Here again the practitioners usually know what we here have to outline. Is the product an industrial one or in a consumer market? How price conscious are the competitors? Do they operate on narrow profit margins and change price frequently, or do they try to maintain stable margins and show their competitiveness by heavy advertising, perhaps allied to minor product variations which provide good "selling points", or extra sales service? Is advertising a major weapon? Are there traditional margins for middlemen which can be ignored only at great risk? Are the mechanics of price change relatively easy or are there physical and mechanical difficulties, such as large stocks in the pipeline from factory to consumer which have already been sold at the current price?

Company policy

An important factor in deciding pricing policy must always be the over-riding philosophy of the firm itself. Is it defensive or is it aggressive? Does it, can it, lay down the law from strength or must it be persuasive because it is relatively weak? Again this is an area which must be considered—but necessarily can only be explicit in terms of the company concerned.

Cost situation

Despite the opening paragraph of this chapter, cost does play a part in almost any pricing situation. It may not always be specifically considered, but it is there at the end of the day and if a company's costs are not finally covered we all know the consequences. As a general factor, however, the cost situation must also be considered to see whether the proposed price leaves any room for manœuvre. A company which is shackled to an inflexible price structure because of very small profit margins can be in difficulties if its competitors have more room for manœuvre. These are marketing considerations and the marketing manager must give them full weight when he is exposed to the inevitable pressures brought to bear by his own financial management, who may well be more influenced by his company's internal situation and less mindful of what is the marketing manager's first preoccupation, the market situation. As we have seen, the marketing function's responsibility includes profitability and, although other functions inevitably claim a share in this responsibility, no other function can claim to be in an equal position when it comes to the determination of the price which customers should be asked to pay.

Economic argument

In conditions of perfect competition price is fixed by the interplay of supply and demand. Perfect competition requires buyers and sellers with complete knowledge of everybody else's actions, a product which can be bought in either large or very small quantities and, lastly, that no one buyer or seller is big enough to affect the market as a whole materially.

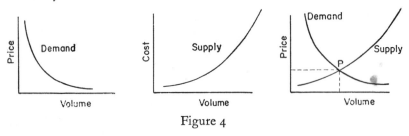

Figure 4

Under these conditions supply and demand equally interact to bring about a market price (P in Figure 4) and a stable supply and demand situation. If we read again the conditions for perfect competition—

perfect knowledge for both buyers and sellers, an easily divisible product and no buyer or seller big enough to affect the market as a whole by his own actions—then it is quite clear that the business man cannot himself decide the price of his product in a market where competition is perfect. Conversely it is also true that, where competition is less than perfect, he can influence the situation and can operate an active pricing policy. This is the situation over the vast majority of business, but we must realise the implications and remember that perfect (or very nearly perfect) markets do exist in some products. Mineral and basic raw materials markets provide good examples where price at any particular time depends entirely on the interplay of buyers and sellers of one particular product (assuming that one "grade" is one product).

Another economic concept which helps in discussing the pricing situation is that of elasticity of demand. Demand is said to have an elasticity of 1 (unity) when a small change in price results in the total revenue remaining constant. If a small decrease in price causes the total revenue to increase, demand is said to be elastic (to have an elasticity greater than unity); if a small decrease in price causes the total revenue to decrease, demand is said to be inelastic (to have an elasticity less than unity). This can be readily seen from the following numerical illustration:

Price	Quantity sold	Total revenue
£11	60	£660
(a) £10	70	£700
(b) £10	65	£650

(a) The reduction in price from £11 to £10 causes sales to rise to 70 and total revenue increases to £700. Demand is therefore elastic.

(b) The reduction in price from £11 to £10 causes sales to rise to only 65 and total revenue decreases to £650. Demand is therefore inelastic.

One of the major factors distinguishing normal business from the state of perfect competition we have just described is that products are not normally completely interchangeable. Within the same grade, a sack of wheat or a bale of cotton is exactly the same whoever offers it for sale, but one model of motor car is not quite like another, nor is one brand of cigarettes quite the same as another. Whatever the reasons, when customers consider that there are differences between products so that they value them differently, we term those products differentiated. Only with a differentiated product, then, can there be any pricing policy in the sense of the company having any choice or influence in deciding what the price shall be. The reader may also reflect that with well-differentiated products (i.e. where the buyer will not readily accept a substitute) demand is relatively inelastic.

It is somewhat unreal to try and treat price in isolation, for differentiation is closely bound up with quality, reputation and advertising and these all have their own interrelated elasticities. The practical outcome, however, is still that a well-differentiated product—one with *distinct* differences between itself and its competitors—has a different demand schedule from that of any other product. It is this which allows

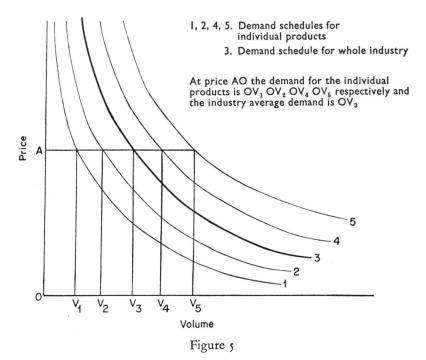

1, 2, 4, 5. Demand schedules for individual products

3. Demand schedule for whole industry

At price AO the demand for the individual products is OV_1 OV_2 OV_4 OV_5 respectively and the industry average demand is OV_3

Figure 5

the existence of independent prices and pricing policies. At a particular price competing products will be bought in different quantities and a common change in price will have different effects on these different products. The "demand" for any industry is made up from the individual "demands" for individual firms or products, some must be above the average, some below. Some must also have a greater elasticity of demand than others, so that if the level of prices in the industry falls then some products will be able to hold at least some of their customers without cutting price or by cutting their price less than their competitors cut, and vice versa if prices increase (see Figure 5).

Company pricing objectives

In its pricing as well as in other directions a company can have many objectives. These are more involved and complex than it was once considered fashionable to think, so let us now examine some possible objectives of pricing policy.

(*i*) *To maximise profit.* This clearly is a valid and important objective but few companies now accept it without some modifications. Such elements as the time span have to be taken into account, and some consideration must be given to problems which maximising profits may cause in other directions, such as fluctuating levels of employment (especially if it is difficult to regain employees once they are allowed to leave).

(*ii*) *To achieve or maintain a target return on investment.* This is a basic marketing objective which we have already discussed (Chapter 2). The pricing factor clearly carries much influence on whether it is reached or not.

(*iii*) *To stabilise prices.* This is a legitimate objective but is a means to an end rather than an end in itself. Price stability can have great advantages in the development of goodwill among both consumers and traders (where applicable). It also helps very considerably in matters of administration, and in generally smoothing operations. As we shall see, if the company is a leader in its field this may be a major objective.

(*iv*) *To make entry into the market by a competitor difficult.* By limiting the probable profitability, and hence the attractiveness, of the market to a competitor a company may hope to achieve some advantage for itself. How far it can succeed without harming its own long-term position must depend entirely on the individual circumstances.

(*v*) *To meet, follow or anticipate competitive price changes.* In practice companies often adopt this policy because they are not strong enough to be independent. Not all companies can be leaders, however, and the whole system of free competition demands that companies must match the competitive actions of their rivals or risk the loss of some, at least, of their business.

(*vi*) *To expand the market.* Here too is a policy which is eminently legitimate. But expansion of the market is also not so much an end as a means—to more profit. Without that there is little justification for the expansion and all the additional use of resources this must entail.

(*vii*) *To maintain or improve the company's share of the market.* Market share is a useful yardstick in seeing how a company is faring in relation to its competitors. In itself it is of minor importance. Once more this is a means, not an end.

Restrictions on pricing freedom

Whatever may be a company's views and basic policies, however strongly its product may be differentiated, a company is seldom completely free to do just as it will in its pricing decisions. There are a number of restraints apart altogether from the possible reaction of its customers.

(*i*) *There may be governmental restrictions.* How long we shall have the Prices and Incomes Board in the U.K. seems uncertain but these matters have a habit of continuing (Gladstone's revived income tax was only a temporary measure). What is more, the procedures of this particular governmental action seem to be based on historical data. Where margins or return on capital have been poor in the past little hope seems to exist for their improvement in the future once the P.I.B. becomes involved. Apart from this, governmental policy has in the past required that manufacturers and traders should cushion their customers against at least part of increased costs which have been incurred. No doubt this will happen again; when such action is required those concerned must conform voluntarily or be prepared for the possibility of legislative action and enforcement to secure what government requires. In such cases the manufacturer can only try to reduce costs elsewhere or face a smaller profit margin.

(*ii*) *Resale price maintenance and the pattern of retail trading.* As a growing proportion of consumer trading is affected by the abolition of R.P.M. the consumer goods manufacturer has correspondingly less freedom of action. The actual price to the consumer is determined partly by the manufacturer's prices to the trade, partly by the trade's decision to take a greater or lesser margin for itself. When a manufacturer sells through the retail trade, his price weapon is automatically blunted for he has no direct control over prices to the consumer and the margins on price taken by the intermediaries. At the same time the growing competitiveness of most retail trades and the emergence of many large companies as customers with considerable bargaining power also restricts the manufacturer's freedom of pricing action. Whether this same growth of strong retail companies will also lead to even more retailers selling products with their own house names on them is not clear at present, but this, too, could be a basic long-term influence on pricing freedom.

(*iii*) *The presence of substitutes.* This is a very real factor. How great a degree of differentiation has the product in question? Is it a leader in Drucker's sense, i.e. that customers will pay more for it either in cash or in time (by waiting for it)? In the final analysis it is the customer's decision that carries the day, it is his favour that is sought. He is going to choose between this product and some other and his decision is swayed by many factors, only *one* of which is price.

(*iv*) *Price leadership*. In the practical world around us there are many instances where one manufacturer leads the way in the market. In such diverse fields as canned vegetables, cable making, manufacture of industrial gases, companies such as Heinz, Enfield-Standard, British Oxygen have at various times set the pace in the matter of pricing. The industry has expected them to do so; mostly they have complied. Perhaps the decision to increase price is easier in modern times, when we are accustomed to frequent increases in prices, than when a decrease is required. Smaller companies are often, in practice, dependent on the price leader for their very existence and business does not always demand that the smaller companies should be squeezed out. Some, maybe, but not all . . . and it is the way in which the leader reacts which may determine the existence of the small company. This acceptance of the leadership of the market is an additional responsibility, and possible restraint, when a company is deciding its price policy.

(*v*) *There may be a strong tradition of particular prices.* In the past there have been traditional convenient prices such as twopenny newspapers, threepenny phone calls and so on, but in recent years these have become much less powerful influences as the declining value of money has led to more and more price increases. More important, now, is the problem of changing prices in the growing vending machine area where, despite much more versatile machines, adjustments have to be made when prices are altered. Another "barrier" was the presumed psychological value of 9s. 11d. instead of 10s. as "sounding so much cheaper". Here, too, the growth of the affluent society and the constantly expanding horizons of the mass of the people seem to be denying the validity of the older pricing assumptions.

(*vi*) *Market pricing.* As we have seen, if a firm is in the commodity or raw materials markets it will almost certainly have to accept market pricing because it is in an almost perfect market. That this is so may be confirmed by the occasional action of some traders in order to free themselves from the market pricing mechanism. An example of this is the growing move towards pre-packing and branding potatoes and fresh vegetables. The consumer gains from the convenience (and usually the cleanliness) of the package and the assurance of quality which attaches to the use of a named product. The producer gains because his now differentiated product enables him to have a policy towards price and some independence from the normal action of the market. Generally he gives more service—and is rewarded with more profit.

Pricing new products

When the price decision has to be taken the marketing manager must first of all find out what is the range of choice available. This he will do by closely examining his position against his competitors (and potential competitors), the trade customs and margins and the relative merits of his own product and that of his competitors. He must then decide on a strategy. There are three principal approaches:

(*i*) High profit, low sales.
(*ii*) Wide coverage of the market.
(*iii*) Exclusion of competition.

High profit, low sales is sometimes called "skimming the cream". The objective is to fix a high initial price so that high profits will be obtained from a modest output. This policy may well work with a novel product where demand is relatively inelastic and buyers may not be able to compare prices readily with other products. It is also useful if the company intends to divide the market into segments according to the price the market will be prepared to pay. As a policy it allows quick recovery of investment, to be followed by a later exploitation of the mass market, as often happens in the pharmaceutical market where prices two to three years after the introduction of a product frequently fall to about 75–80 per cent of the original level.

"Skimming the cream" is a policy frequently adopted where there are great uncertainties about the reaction of the customer, or when both demand and costs are very doubtful. Caution, lack of information, the knowledge that it is easier to put prices down than to put them up, all tend to make this a compromise solution which also allows the company to avoid committing itself to a very high capital outlay for large-scale production plant in the very early stages of a new product venture.

The policy has one particularly awkward disadvantage in that it not only permits but actually stimulates competitive entry into the market. The high profit margin cannot be disguised; somehow someone will find a product to compete.

Immediate wide coverage of the market commends itself where there is considerable information about the market and especially if the company can afford the time for a deliberate wide-scale entry. It is the course preferred by companies aiming at a medium- or long-term profit. It is very effective where the elasticity of demand (and therefore better response to modest pricing) is high in the short term, i.e. that the product is readily acceptable.

The transition from aiming at a wide initial coverage to aiming at *preventing or at least discouraging competitors from entering* is only a short step. Henry Ford originally aimed at creating and preempting the market with his aggressively low pricing policy and Rael Brook shirts in this country aimed similarly at seizing the lion's share of the new drip-dry shirt market. The difference between such operations and a wide initial coverage is one of degree. Whether to go all the way may well be decided by the assessment of whether it seems likely that competitors will attempt to enter the same field or not.

In all cases, however, the product life-cycle must be considered before the decision is made. In the early days of developing the product a skimming policy may be justified during the novelty stage. Later in the product's growth stage, a market penetration policy may be appropriate. Finally, in its full maturity, exposed to competition on all sides, the product may be in a market-price situation. This in fact is what happened with nylon and it must surely happen with many other new man-made materials. Not all products, however, go through this pricing cycle and the estimated life of the product, together with the investment needed to produce it, may well be the decisive factor.

Influence of cost on price

We have almost avoided discussion of this topic though, as we have seen, cost must play *some* part in the fixing of price. Certainly cost is especially important in the case of a product already on the market. But the question to be answered is not "Does cost fix price?" but "Should cost fix price?"

In many companies price *is* fixed by rule of thumb—or the hunch of the poker player—"price equals cost plus X per cent", X varying according to estimates of what other companies will do and what the state of the market is. This policy has two very clear weaknesses. In the first place "cost" is not at all easy to define or calculate. invariably the argument turns on overhead cost, what this will be, and how it shall be apportioned over products *not yet made* and therefore of an unknown number. The second weakness is that it ignores the customer and the value of the product to him. An example can be given of a company making filling machinery. A new machine was developed which saved customer companies about £2,500 per year in operating costs. A basic price (subject to a charge for modification) was fixed at about £4,000. Customers were very willing to buy this machine, which saved its own cost in well under two years and then continued to save them £2,500 per year. Yet the basic manufacturing cost was estimated at well under £2,000. "Cost plus 10 per cent" would surely have been a wrong pricing concept here. What reward do we pay ourselves for inventiveness? What is the product worth to the buyer?

In the last analysis the cost of manufacture fixes the lowest limit to which a manufacturer could go in dire circumstances. In the short run, of course, one product or even more may be retained simply to keep the loading factor in the factory high and thus carry a proportion of the total overheads which the remaining products could not cover if the "unprofitable" line were cut out. We have already mentioned this under the simplification of the range in Chapter 2. In pricing, it is well to bear in mind that the vital cost in any competitive industry is that of the lowest cost producer. Those who cannot match him must persuade their customers to pay more, accept a lower return on their investment or leave that business!

Suggested Reading

TAYLOR, R., & WILLS, G. *Pricing Strategy* (readings), Staples Press, 1970.

CHAPTER 10

Channels of Distribution

Marketing operations take the form of another eternal triangle consisting of the product, the customer or user, and the channel of distribution which conveys the former to the latter. The channel of distribution, as we have already seen, is an ingredient in the marketing mix and it can be an active and positive force in the service of the thoughtful marketing man. It can also be a barrier and real hindrance to those who do not appreciate its true characteristics. Let us therefore review the principal channels of distribution, for convenience considering consumer goods and industrial goods separately.

Consumer goods operations

There are a number of distinct channels for the distribution of consumer goods from the manufacturer to the ultimate purchaser, ranging from direct contact between manufacturer's representative and customer to the use of inanimate vending machines.

Direct contact between manufacturer and consumer

In this type of selling operation representatives call at the house of the prospective customer and there is direct delivery from the manufacturer to the home. This is a commonplace for local services and utilities such as property repairs and the supply of milk or bread on a local or a national scale. Few national manufacturing companies reach their market this way though there are exceptions, such as Avon Cosmetics, Tupperware, two brush manufacturers and some industrial assurance institutions. The manufacturer who sells direct to his customer has a number of advantages over his counterpart who sells through the retail trade. *Firstly*, by using his own staff he has more control over the selection of potential customers and the selling techniques used. There is always some argument as to whether people paid on a commission basis only, as often occurs in direct-to-house selling, are "employees". The advent of Selective Employment Tax has apparently made this clear since such people can be classified as "self-employed". Nevertheless companies do have more influence over men in this category than over true freelance agents who may have several different "lines" to sell, all from different companies.

Secondly, his staff is more involved, has greater interest and will usually be trained to have more knowledge of both his product and his customer than is usually the case with those outside his own operation (i.e. the salespeople in shops). *Thirdly,* a selling interview at the house takes place with a semi-captive audience; that is, the prospective customer cannot very easily close the interview and walk away. *Fourthly,* when a sales interview takes place at the house there are no competing (and tempting) products, no other sales talk being made. These are all strong arguments in favour of selling directly to the consumer in his home.

The disadvantages to the manufacturer of selling direct to the house stem mainly from the costs and the calibre of the people involved. The number of calls which have to be made if individual consumers are to be contacted directly, the time taken merely moving from one to another, the high proportion of people who are out at any one time during the day, the problems of administering large numbers of salesmen, or women, all make this form of direct contact cumbersome and relatively costly. Furthermore, the corollary of individual calling is individual delivery and again the sheer cost of delivering small quantities of product to large numbers of houses becomes a huge deterrent unless arrangements can be made for the salesman to deliver on a later call (selling and delivering at the same time may raise questions of hawkers' licences).

Finally there is the question of the calibre of person employed. Generally speaking (there are obvious exceptions) knocking on doors to sell something is not a highly rated occupation. Some people like it, many do not. Some women will welcome a part-time, evening job but many will not. Recruiting staff for work of this kind is not easy and those prepared to work at the house door are usually not quite such good salesmen as those employed in the more traditional "commercial" sphere so that the actual ability of those thus employed may be less than in other "more desirable" fields.

From the consumer's point of view there are also advantages and disadvantages. Clearly the saving in time and trouble of buying a product delivered to the house is considerable. So is the value of a more expert knowledge, when this is applicable, and the opportunity of considering a purchase without the distractions of other merchandise or other customers.

Against this there are the disadvantages of the over-forceful salesman, who may not be easily dismissed when he is once in the home, and the lack of an opportunity to compare merchandise. For many consumers, women in particular, there may well be another disadvantage, the feeling of being deprived of what is a pleasurable and ritualistic experience—"going shopping".

Nevertheless, if a company has the right kind of product, can overcome the administrative and organisational problems posed by vast numbers of potential direct customers and large numbers of its own staff (Avon Cosmetics is believed to have some 40,000 sales representatives), it should gain on balance from the intimacy of a direct to consumer operation. In the past there has been a tendency to accept the view that the traditional channels of trade via wholesaler and retailer must be the most efficient as they have "stood the test of time". This whole argument is already being challenged within the retail trade itself and we cannot necessarily assume these days that the old traditional method is the best.

Traditional retail trade operations

Here the manufacturer sends his salesmen to the retail trader or perhaps to the wholesaler or factor who then goes to the trade. Very often both retailer and wholesaler are visited, the former when he is big enough to warrant the cost of a direct call, the latter to deal with the large numbers of smaller shops which exist in most trades. The trading organisations involved are well-established and cover the entire country in proportion to the level of business existing, for they have been developed purely by individuals and firms pursuing the profit motive and providing service where they see it is needed.

By specialising in particular fields such as food or furniture the retail trade makes shopping easier for the consumer. This specialisation also enables the retailer himself to acquire greater knowledge of a particular range of merchandise so that he can offer better advice and help to his customer, as well as holding a wider variety of items in that group for the customer to examine and compare.

The various sections of the retail trade are, as a general rule, very knowledgeable of consumer taste from their accumulated experience of what has sold and what has not sold and their knowledge of customer enquiries for goods or services. Much retail trade has tended in the past to be very conservative and by no means venturesome but it has provided an organisation, an institution indeed, whereby the manufacturer can make his products conveniently available to his ultimate consumers near their homes. Furthermore the specialisation of retail trade has other advantages for the manufacturer which are often overlooked. Because of retail specialisation the business for his products is concentrated in a comparatively small number of specialist shops which are aware of his kind of merchandise and have already developed trade in that field. This saves him selling time by defining his outlets, and by concentrating his sales in a smaller number of shops reduces his delivery costs. On the other hand his competitors are equally aware of this, so his product is directly alongside its competition—and who is to know whether the shopkeeper, with his presumed authority and knowledge of the field, will push the one or the other? Modern thought tends to consider that reasonable proximity of shops, whether competitive or complementary, attracts more customers and creates more business for everyone.

In recent years there has been a great change of heart in retail trading. Once there was little attempt by the majority of shopkeepers to take trade from one another, little attempt to build up bigger and more efficient units which might give better service or cheaper prices to the public. Broadly, there was an atmosphere of live and let live which was fostered by the acceptance, by most manufacturers, of a fixed traditional retail margin according to the type of trade. Now the position is very different. A wave of more intense competition is spreading over much of the retail trade. It began in the grocery field and since the abolition of resale price maintenance has spread very fast into many other sectors.

Larger trading units have developed as multiple stores applied the weight of their greater resources and knowledge to enlarge their business. Individual shops have become larger in the main shopping centres. In this process some of the smaller shops have been very roughly treated, but surprisingly few have closed. Even in the grocery trade it has been estimated that the total number of shops has only fallen from about 146,000 to 110,000 in the last ten years—and this mostly because of slum clearance and demolition of premises. In some sections of the market, such as in food, clothing, footwear and department stores, there has emerged a number of large strong companies each operating many—sometimes hundreds of—shops or stores and each in itself capable of standing up to and negotiating with the manufacturer on equal terms. These companies are often more needed by the manufacturer than he is by them and his terms of trade tend to move accordingly.

In passing, it may not be inappropriate to consider another by-product of the more thorough, scientific approach of the modern retailer, especially in the grocery trade. Here close records are kept of all facets of the business and one measure of efficiency is reckoned in terms of profit per foot of shelf or floor space. Traders tend to limit their stocks to two or three leaders in each field, because of the need to retain only the most profitable lines as well as the physical impossibility of stocking everything (many supermarkets stock up to 20,000 lines). What then of the new, unproven product? If it is not available in the big supermarkets it will never make real headway, but these same outlets wish to have only the proven winners. The weight and prestige of the larger manufacturers usually enable them to strike a bargain and the new product is accepted on trial, but the smaller company trying to build itself up from small beginnings has a very stiff hurdle to jump.

In some retail trading areas there have been examples of manufacturers using their own shops as means of distributing their products. This has been the case for many years in chocolate and sugar confectionery and even more notably in footwear and clothing. The manufacturers' objectives were partly the ensuring of an outlet for their goods, and partly a diversification operation looking for additional profits via vertical integration. Usually in trades such as confectionery and tobacco these shops did not noticeably flourish, perhaps because the manufacturers' own products alone did not always give the choice which consumers wished. Because of this the shops had to be run strictly as normal profit-making shops stocking a wide range of products and the manufacturer was left with but little advantage for his own brands. Footwear and clothing shops still continue, however, under manufacturers' auspices and this may be due to their providing not only an acceptable range of their own merchandise but also one which is fully advertised and with a favourable reputation or brand image in its own right.

Mail order selling

This began in this country as an extension of retail trade operations and many department stores have used it for more than forty years. An advertisement is placed in the press; customers send an order by post, with cash; the store sends the goods direct to the home.

More recently this has been extended in two directions. In the one the manufacturer himself places advertisements in the press and carries through the whole transaction. Here he risks offending the retail trade whose function he is abrogating but, if he is successful, he may take for himself the margin of the intermediary as well as his own manufacturer's profit. (He may of course still use the retail trade for part of his business if they are willing to trade.) That this sector of retail trading has not turned the others out of business is partly because so many consumers prefer to trade in the shops and see the merchandise and partly because of the peculiarities of, and special skills involved in, mail order trading.

Mail order is founded on the existence of a section of the public which is prepared to buy on description or illustration, without ever seeing the goods, in the belief that a saving is made in money or trouble. From this has developed a second mail order variation based on a number of specialist *Mail Order Houses* who have large central warehouses and carefully organised departments to buy, assemble orders, pack and deliver. They are retailers in the sense of being between manufacturer and consumer, but they are not shops in that their customers cannot normally visit them and see their merchandise.

Furthermore these companies now rely more and more not only on ordinary press advertising but on the additional influence of an elaborate and colourful catalogue attractively printed and running to several hundred pages—usually twice a year. These catalogues are too expensive to be given to each customer or potential customer so agents are recruited to visit a number of customers each, solicit orders and strengthen the appeal of the catalogue by their personal approach. Most mail order houses also offer instalment buying terms or some form of extended credit as an additional and nowadays crucial inducement. This is now a well-established channel which is dominated by a few large companies. In 1972 "mail order" trading is estimated at almost 4 per cent of *all* U.K. retail trade. In the sixties it was developing almost twice as fast, in sterling terms, as the total retail business. Whilst there was some hesitation at the end of the decade, this sector now seems to be buoyant again and many good judges believe it will again grow more rapidly than retail trade as a whole.

Those who built up the tradition of mail order trading did so on the basis of two kinds of service to their customers. The first was a factual one of good merchandise, quick service and readiness to replace faulty material without question. The second was the psychological satisfaction of receiving and opening a parcel which many ordinary people seldom experienced. Today, in addition to this, they offer more credit and easier terms than do most retail traders. There is often pressure to prevent consumers having easy access to credit purchasing, and mail order is often the only means whereby many consumers can obtain credit, for they have no bank facilities and shops seldom grant long-term credit. Mail order houses must have, from the outset, a considerable knowledge of the market and their customers. Immediately after a new catalogue is issued there is a surge of orders which have to be dealt with very quickly or extra costs of writing letters and arranging later deliveries are incurred. To deal with the orders at once means having stock, which often has to be ordered even before the catalogue is printed, certainly before there is evidence of how a line is selling. Perhaps this unusual and highly specialised operation has not been taken up successfully by more competitors because of these problems. Many knowledgeable people believe that the additional weight of credit facilities added to quality and fair price is what has made this such a successful area. This is certainly valid reasoning, but two other aspects must have played some part, though they may in turn be part cause, part result of the expansion in this sector. These are the increasing use of mail order facilities by department stores suffering from more intensive competition from specialist shops (food, clothing, etc.) and the general swing from the onetime smaller, low-cost items to the present merchandise lists which include even such items as refrigerators and washing machines.

Trading franchises

A fourth and more recent development in distribution is the use of trading franchises. These are not new, but they have developed very rapidly during the 1960's.

The manufacturer (franchisor) contracts with the retail trader or distributor (franchisee) to work with him over a period (often ten to twenty years). The franchisor supplies a product or service (usually branded and well advertised) exclusively to the franchisee in a certain area. He also agrees to help, advise, train and generally provide "know-how" to the franchisee.

The franchisee provides the capital and, with the guidance of the franchisor, establishes a business such as a café, launderette, petrol station or even an employment agency. He owns and manages this but sells the franchised product exclusively in that field. The franchisee may pay an initial franchise fee but more usually pays a royalty on his turnover in the franchised product; terms, including arrangements to break away in certain circumstances, vary from contract to contract.

The manufacturer employing a franchising operation gains by having closely tied to him an active enthusiastic distributing organisation without having to put up the capital himself. The franchisee (often an experienced and able manager displaced in the great changes caused by mergers and takeovers) gains from having the backing, knowledge and advertising of his franchisor.

Franchises often exist without the knowledge of the general public and apart from those mentioned above they are found in the operation of snack bars, motels, dog parlours, ice-cream vending and no doubt many others. It seems probable that many similar types of business will also use franchises. But abuses and sharp practice may well lead to legal regulation in the near future.

Vending machines

Lastly we should mention the use of vending machines. For many years these have been used for the sale of cigarettes and chocolate after shops were closed. More recently vending machines have been used to extend sales well beyond shop premises by offering a much more sophisticated product. Machines can now supply a variety of hot or cold drinks or even a complete meal, and are widely used in factories and offices where they are convenient for the purchaser and help the manager in organising facilities which can be widely used in short refreshment breaks.

Fully automatic retailing may well develop much further with the elaboration of machines. Already there are specialists who arrange for the siting and servicing of machines and who have no other retail interest nor ever meet their customers face to face. It will be the latter who will decide if this is to continue as a fringe activity or become something much more important.

Industrial goods operations

The channels of distribution for industrial goods are rather different, as may be expected. We must remember, too, that there is always a doubtful boundary between industrial and consumer goods and that when necessary the manufacturer will use channels appropriate to both; for instance, the typewriter manufacturer will certainly want to make his product available in the appropriate shops but he will also find it necessary to deal with big users, such as large companies, direct.

Probably the most important channel in industrial operations is the direct contact between the manufacturer's own salesmen and the customer company, with corresponding delivery. The variations on this method are many. At one extreme there may be several technical design people involved on either side over many months before the product is agreed, made and delivered, or erected, on site. At the other end the manufacturer may have fifty or a hundred men making regular frequent calls on companies and delivering from a series of strategically sited warehouses where stock is kept ready for immediate despatch exactly as happens in many consumer goods operations.

The important features here again are the control, knowledge and interest made available to the manufacturer when his own man contacts the customer. The main problem is whether or not customers buy in sufficient quantities and are so situated that they can all be visited economically. This particular problem is precisely the same as that in retail trading and the answer is similar. Where business for standard products does not warrant a call from the manufacturer's man he usually uses a factor who serves all the same functions as in retail trading. Factors carry stocks of industrial goods in common use, nuts, bolts, standard tools and suchlike items but, as in retail trading, they have many products to handle and they cannot have the same approach and specific interest as the manufacturer's own man concentrating on his own range of products.

One other channel is available in industrial operations which is much less common in consumer goods fields. This is the agent or commission agent. This man (or company) is really a freelance salesman. He knows a particular industry or territory and "carries" agencies for a number of non-competing lines or products. He takes orders and transmits them back to his principal who usually arranges direct delivery and invoicing and remits the commission to the agent on settlement of the account.

Agents can be a great asset to a company starting up in business, or not knowing a new territory and the potential customers in it. They can be very useful when the business available, or the distances involved, do not warrant the company employing its own salesmen because of the cost in money and time in relation to the volume of trade. On the other hand agents, like factors, tend to be weaker in knowledge of the particular product than the company's own men and they cannot be so easily controlled and directed. An agent paid on commission will naturally spend his time getting the easiest, quickest sales. This may not always be in the true interest of his principal who might perhaps be trying to introduce a new product with all the inevitable need of extra time and trouble compared with selling a current "runner". On the whole the use of agents seems to be slowly but surely declining in this country although they are widely used in the export trade.

Organisations used in channels of distribution

Having described the more important channels of distribution we must also look at the various organisations involved in operating them.

The reader seeking statistics on this area will find much information in the Census of Distribution and the many marketing data publications (see Appendix, page 97, for a list of some sources of marketing data).

The manufacturer's own sales department comes first in any list of organisations. This is the focal point in the company for all dealings with the company's customers. It may be a large group in the case of a national food-manufacturing company or it may be one man in the case of a small company subcontracting in the engineering industry.

The sales force in the field may be the company's own man or it may be agents or factors or a combination of all of these. These are the people who actually sell to the company's customers.

The depot organisation is a system of depots or warehouses, as required, spread around the country for the holding of stocks of products ready for immediate delivery to customers. This is generally essential when operating on a national basis with standard products in common use or for consumer consumption. The depot organisation may be owned and operated by the larger manufacturers or it may be hired on a pro rata basis, using specialist companies who operate depots in various parts of the country.

Retail distribution is the system of shops and stores covering particular trades and products which is used by manufacturers as a means of making it easy for the ultimate consumer to buy them.

Transport is becoming more and more important as companies try to save money by reducing stock held but requiring at the same time quicker delivery of orders to make up for this. Whilst some companies can carry out their own deliveries with their own transport many find it cheaper to use specialist transport companies which are usually available either on a national or a local basis.

Commodity markets. These are still the great market places for many raw materials, much produce and some services. Metals, grain, cotton wool, shipping, insurance, money are all dealt with in their appropriate exchanges.

Finance and insurance groups. The operation of business needs finance, banking and insurance. Here we need only mention their existence but few businesses operate without the services of these organisations somewhere along the line.

Selection of the appropriate channels

Many marketing managers may rightly feel that this decision need only be taken at rare intervals. This is true, and even for a new product the best channel may be the most obvious, but that is no reason for not taking the opportunity of examining the position and either confirming the obvious or making a change.

The decision depends partly on the characteristics of the channels in relation to the objectives aimed at, partly on the kind of operation involved, partly on the company's philosophy.

To take the last point first, the company approach will be one of the key determinants for if it is an aggressive company, determined to thrust forward and upward at speed, it will need a channel (if one is available) which will make it possible to use these characteristics to the full. A slower-moving company, or one with close relations with an existing channel(s), will probably prefer to use the more traditional channels.

The basic approach cleared, what are the requirements of the market? Where are the prospective buyers? Who are they? This may indicate using a local, a national or an international channel. Then, what size of order is likely to be taken each time? How often will this occur? Will it be a seasonal trade only? Where will the orders be taken? The answers to these questions will indicate the cost of obtaining an order and help further to define the mode of operation. Finally, though perhaps of greatest importance, how big is the market both in physical and financial terms? Will it require or even support an elaborate organisation, for the organisation must be appropriate to the size of the operation?

These questions and the answers to them will go a long way towards deciding the most suitable channels of distribution, but the marketing manager still has to evaluate the importance of his own representation against the use of agents and possibly factors too. He must also decide whether he can or should for other reasons (maybe cost, maybe the effect on his present trade customers if he changed) stick to the channels he already has established. Whatever answer he comes to, the problems of maintaining stocks in depots and overcoming the difficulties of geography and climate are always there—and always have to be dealt with. What he must always do is to examine the whole situation and *consciously* decide to continue with the channels already in use or to change them if the reasons for doing so are valid.

Need for constant review

One of the characteristics of the successful marketing manager is that he insists on continuously reviewing his operations. The marketing environment is never stationary, never quiescent. Consumers change or move about, the products they need must therefore move correspondingly, so the channels of distribution are never static. Further, as we have seen, the channels themselves, the shops, the organisations, the men, are constantly changing and seeking for better ways, more profitable ways, of carrying out their functions as the pressure of competition becomes even stronger. Review, evaluate, improve must be the key words of the progressive marketing manager. The trade itself may be revolutionised in its methods (as happened in the grocery field from the mid-fifties to mid-sixties), or a product field may move en bloc (as happened with kitchen paperware, cakecups, paper towels, etc., as the business changed until most of it became centred on grocery shops instead of the traditional stationers). In the motor car market both Ford and British Leyland have completely reorganised their dealer network (1967–72). This has not been done simply because of internal reorganisation but because the market for motor cars has changed considerably and many of the old dealers were badly sited or otherwise not in tune with the needs of the new car-owning public.

In the end, however, we must still remember that the channel of distribution and the closely allied selling operation are both parts only of the marketing mix. The overall marketing plan must itself be integrated and balanced. Distribution is important. So is selling. Both must work together—and with all the other functions involved.

Suggested Reading

MENDELSOHN, M., *The Guide to Franchising*, Pergamon, 1970. Most marketing textbooks have sections devoted to channels of distribution.

CHAPTER 11

Selling

> "*The price may be right, the quality acceptable and the channel chosen for distribution the appropriate one, but it still takes another force or two to get the product into the consumer's hands. These forces are advertising and personal selling effort.*"
>
> M. Zober: *Marketing Management*, Wiley, 1964.

The sales function is a wide subject, but most literate people in this country have some idea of what it is about. In our approach we may start by asking four questions:

(*i*) Why do we have salesmen at all?
(*ii*) What tasks must they carry out?
(*iii*) What kind of organisation do we need to enable them to do this?
(*iv*) What special problems do we face in the selling function?

Why are salesmen needed?

Basically people suffer from inertia. They will not exert themselves more than they can avoid. This applies both to individuals in their daily life and to buyers in their official capacity. For anything other than a staple need, therefore, the individual has to be encouraged to buy even when buying is in his own interest. Until such time that buying becomes part of his nature, a habit even, the process of encouragement and persuasion must go on—and the essence of competition is that another manufacturer or another shop has an alternative to offer which has *some* advantage(s) to the buyer against all other alternatives. So no one in competitive business can really relax. Further, the personal interview, with the opportunities it offers for statement, counter, rebuttal in all their ramifications, is commonly agreed to carry more persuasive power than any other selling technique. This, then, is the reason for having sales people, whether they be in a shop or out "on the road" selling, on behalf of the manufacturer, to the retail trade or a customer company.

For the manufacturer, a salesman has other functions, too. Being the man on the spot he can locate new outlets, new customers of which the manufacturer is unaware, for no amount of experience, or record books, or reference books will show all potential customers. In addition, when the salesman visits a new outlet he can decide whether it is *suitable* for the company's operations. The manufacturer can make enquiries and obtain information about most known potential customers but, without actually seeing them, it is often impossible to be sure that they are the right kind of customer for him—this is especially true of trade outlets where the image of the trader may be an important factor and where the trader concerned may either be moving up or declining.

Another reason for personal representation is the need to have a man on the spot to negotiate terms of business or to work out specific requirements, specifications or designs. This needs personal contact, not just correspondence or telephone conversations. In the same connection the availability of a man to *represent* the manufacturing company as a whole, including all its products, to explain its policies, aims and methods, is a source of strength to the manufacturer and is seen as a welcome service, sometimes an essential one, by the customer.

In these considerations we must also include the advantage to the manufacturer of having his own representative, rather than an agent or factor, in contact with the customers. The company's own salesman is more involved and more interested in his own company's products. He knows more about them. He can iron out problems as a member of the organisation rather than as a part-timer or third party with a more tenuous link. Furthermore, the company can, when necessary, use a full-time employee to further its long-term marketing aim even if this should be at the expense of current sales (as may happen when a salesman is required to spend a high proportion of his time introducing a new product). This may mean lower immediate sales (for a new product may take time to gain momentum) in the hope of really large sales in the future. Factors or agents on the other hand are often more interested in present sales, on which their immediate income depends, regardless of what may come at a later date (their goals are not in fact congruent with those of the manufacturer).

Lastly, by having his own sales representative in direct contact with the customer, the manufacturer creates an immediate means of obtaining information about his products, the buyer's reactions, the market generally. This business intelligence or *information feedback* can be more than just a useful by-product for, according to the type of sales operation and the skill and experience of the salesman, it can be an important source of market information.

What tasks should salesmen perform?

These naturally depend on the kind of operation in which he is participating, particularly whether he is in a consumer goods field or an industrial goods field and whether he is selling standard products of low or modest price or custom-built plant and machinery of high price. Some tasks follow naturally from the considerations in the previous section, such as the negotiation of prices or contracts or the dealing with enquiries or complaints. These are tasks common to most types of sales operation.

Specifically in the consumer field, the salesman's tasks may include keeping up stock levels in shops, arranging trader special offers, collecting cash, introducing new products and finding new trade outlets. In industrial operations he may be especially required to maintain a certain standard of contact frequency, to develop good relations with potential customers, and generally to ensure that present customers are retained and not lost to competitors, even when orders are only placed at long intervals.

The tasks are varied and sometimes perhaps apparently contradictory, but what is really important is that the company and the salesman should both know what specific tasks he is to perform and their relative importance; and the company, if not the man, must know the cost in time and money of carrying them out. It goes almost without saying that the specific tasks in any particular case must be reviewed from time to time to make sure that they are still appropriate in view of the ever-changing market conditions.

What sales organisation is needed?

The first step in answering the question is to determine how many men are required on the ground. As always in marketing matters, let us begin with the customer to be called upon, that is the shop or firm to whom the manufacturer sells, not necessarily the final consumer. The total of such customers (including any provision for calling more than once in the appropriate period) gives the total number of calls which have to be made in that period. Then the average time taken to make a sales interview, including waiting to see the customer and the travelling time from one customer to the next, must be calculated. Dividing this time into the period (or journey-cycle as it is called) will now give the number of calls a salesman can make in the period. Dividing the total calls to be made by this number of calls per man/journey gives the number of salesmen required. Allowance has to be made for variations in territory (calls near each other or far apart for example), illness, unpredicted call needs and holidays, but the calculation can still be made.

The numbers of salesmen required varies enormously, perhaps from half a dozen in quite typical engineering firms to some hundreds or even thousands in the case of large companies calling on many shops or direct at the house door. In every case some form of organisation must be developed. Most companies begin with the formation of a team of seven to ten men. If that is the total number they may all report direct to a sales manager at head office. If there are many teams, three or four teams may be grouped under a local manager. If many managers are involved, two or three may be grouped in a region and perhaps two or three regional managers finally report to the general sales manager at head office.

In a large operation of this kind, ancillary services require the formation of subdepartments as the sheer volume of work to be done is beyond the capacity of one manager and in an elaborate organisation quite sophisticated services will be essential. These usually fall naturally under:

> Operations
> Training and recruitment
> Personnel, promotion and development
> Sales planning
> Technical service
> Administration
> Sales accounts

According to needs, these may be joined together in whole or in part or other sub-divisions may be added. As the size of the operation increases, so problems of control and communication become more complex, organisational activity itself becomes considerable and more and more "staff" are needed to keep the salesmen at "the sharp end" serviced.

The administration of a large sales organisation is quite complicated, but the function and its problems—other than those due entirely to communication because of the many strata of control and responsibility

—are similar in most sales situations. Information has to be collected, sorted and passed on, upwards towards the general sales manager, downwards towards the salesman in the field. Records have to be maintained both for current control purposes and to help make plans for

Industrial Sales Department

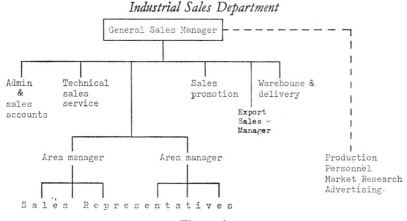

Figure 6

Consumer Sales Department

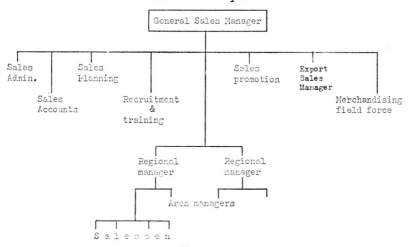

Figure 7

the future. Orders must be processed and delivery arranged; invoices have to be issued and accounts maintained. Liaison with the production departments regarding manufacture or delivery has to be maintained. Instructions regarding the deployment of sales effort and the co-ordination of this with promotional effort, advertising or technical sales help have to be decided and transmitted. Finally, the recruiting of men, their training, payment and promotion must all be properly arranged. When the total force is numbered on the fingers this may not be an onerous task and might well be conducted by one man, but in a large-scale operation the sales department may run to several hundred people including those in the accounting office.

The organisational skeletons (Figs. 6 and 7) show typical sales organisations for consumer goods and industrial goods situations. The foregoing implicitly assumes the division of sales territories on a discrete geographical basis. Many companies on practical grounds have specialist salesmen, dealing with special customers or "house" accounts, cutting across sales areas. They accept complications in comparing sales results with geographical market data on the grounds of greater efficiency in selling. Another common variant is for a company with many, or very complex, products to divide its sales force into product or customer/industry divisions and to subdivide its divisions geographically when the size of the operation demands this. Such an organisation enables the salesman to be more expert in a narrower field, albeit at the expense of having more than one man covering a particular piece of ground or even one particular customer.

Problems peculiar to the sales operation

All business consists of problems and the overcoming of them, but there are a number of factors affecting the sales force which do not apply elsewhere in the company. Salesmen tend to be extrovert characters, ebullient by nature and subject to cycles of elation and depression according to how their work is progressing, whilst generally those in the more technical departments tend to be characteristically more stolid and detached. Yet salesmen are also different in their traditional adoption of a group character as people different from others. Is their claim to be an esoteric group apart well-founded or is it a piece of mumbo-jumbo fostered over some generations of this different activity? Is selling an art that you are born with, or can it be taught to anyone? Is the cult of the customer and the view that "you can't organise a salesman, he has to work according to the customer's needs" entirely justified?

Let us realise that a salesman has a *responsibility* for communicating with the customer so that, in behavioural terms, the customer learns to buy from the company. Whilst they have this responsibility (and are given assistance by other elements in the marketing mix) salesmen are in a position where they may not succeed in their task for reasons quite beyond their control. The customer may not buy for one of a dozen reasons despite all the salesman's efforts. The customer is not predictable, he has to be influenced; sometimes this cannot be done. The position is by no means the equivalent of making a product in a factory when the operative can carry out his task (assuming the materials, tools, etc.) provided he applies himself. Yet the salesman still has to get his figures, meet his responsibility.

A salesman spends most of his time in isolation among the enemy; not for him the comfort of feeling, in an office or factory, that he is a member of a group or corporate body, all allies, all working towards a common end! Despite this isolation, a salesman is constantly required to perform psychological hand-stands. To his customer he represents his company, and he therefore wants to be considered a helper not an outsider; but to his company he must represent his customer, his customer's views, his customer's needs, whilst still retaining his own identity as a member of the organisation. Perhaps it is in part because of this constant changing of ground that sales management, having usually had the same experience out in the field, tends to protect its outside staff, to be unwilling to accept that salesmen are not "different", to develop an almost pathological fear of outsiders interfering with the sales force, trying to organise them, tending to upset them.

Apart from these psychological and sociological problems there are very real physical problems of communication with the sales force. The salesman is not down the corridor or even on the next floor. He is normally not even obtainable on the telephone except by prior arrangement. In the larger organisations too there are additional hindrances to rapid communication caused by the lengthy chain of command and the need to avoid several different people contacting and instructing the salesman for different purposes. All this tends to make the actual exercising of control a difficult matter and to require management's spending much time and effort visiting salesmen, rather than reducing their time with their customers by calling them home for consultation. It also helps to explain why a failure to reach a certain performance may not necessarily be due to a shortcoming on the salesman's side, but partly at least be due to factors external to his or his company's control. A salesman obviously cannot be as closely supervised as an office or factory worker for he is not on the premises. This is why so much has to be left to his own personal motivation and it is easy to see why sales managers try to encourage and exhort their men rather than drill and order them, why some of them resist operational research into selling, why some believe special incentives are needed to get full effort from their men.

There are also other characteristics indigenous to the sales force. Very often sales people dislike forecasting future sales, however many or few customers they have. They are always conscious of the little things which bring about a sale or those which cause one to be lost—and they know a forecast tends to become a target to be reached. There are practical problems of evaluation too, not in themselves difficult in concept but certainly difficult to solve in practice. With a wide range of diverse products (as many companies have) and an understandable reluctance to allow figures of profit margins to be too freely available, there is the general problem of priorities among products and the agreeing of a satisfactory yardstick. The usual one is sterling receipts, because this is the only common factor, but this of course masks differences in profitability. How much time can a salesman give daily to filling in accounts of what he has done; what orders have been taken; answering questions from his superiors (within or beyond his own knowledge); dealing with enquiries, offers or complaints; when at the same time he has no office, no typist and is expected to use all normal office time for calling on his customers?

Finally, salespeople are faced with a different situation from that applying to some other functions of the business. They do not know all the facts pertaining to their operation and information is often not only incomplete but frequently quite inadequate. Competitors' activities, customers' policies and real needs are often unknown, or at best the information is out of date. Yet somehow the effort has to be made —and is made. Is the salesman really different? We must surely answer "yes". He is different because he has to work on his own, partially uninformed, partially isolated, yet with a heavy responsibility for achievement. He must always be prepared to accept that not every customer wants to buy from him and that a thick skin to turn away positive rudeness may occasionally be a pre-requisite for success. A factory worker or office worker can leave to get away from unpleasant superiors, but a salesman cannot ever get away from his customers. Fortunately, whilst some of them may be tough negotiators the majority are by no means really unpleasant to deal with.

Sales management

The foregoing has outlined some very complicated matters. How does the company ensure that the sales tasks are in fact carried out? The answer is the use of sales management.

The sales force consists of the men in the field who contact the customers and it should be built around the tasks it has to perform. When those tasks change, the sales force must equally be changed to meet its

new tasks. Similarly the sales department indoors must be organi?
perform the duties necessary in that particular function. The
department is the office organisation which is the link between the
of the company and the sales force.

Again the organisation should be built by defining the main objectives and then breaking these down and sub-dividing in succession to
arrive at comparatively narrow sub-goals which form the basis of the
sub-departments and their activities. A great deal of activity can of
course be "programmed". That is, certain tasks are dealt with in a laid-
down routine which automatically begins when a particular signal is
received. A simple programme, triggered off by the arrival of the company mail, is described on page 210. Routines of this kind can be set up
to enable the bulk of straightforward matters to be pushed on, using
a minimum of managerial time, so that when some more important
decision has to be made, appropriate managerial time is available. What
is vital here and throughout the organisational plan, is that everyone,
every department, should know what is the objective of his particular
exercise and how that fits in with the whole. Nothing is more wasteful
—or derisive—than to find individuals or whole groups or departments
sincerely working with all their hearts in a direction contrary to the
main objective of the company. This should not happen if the organisation is sound and communication is good between departments and
individuals. But it does happen.

Budgetary control

Once a sales operation has been organised around sub-departments,
each with a specific function and goal, it becomes possible to use
budgetary control as a means of checking expenditures and performance. In essence this means estimating beforehand what the expenditure
of each sub-department should be and what performance it should
achieve when making this expenditure. Periodically, usually monthly,
the actual achievement is checked against the forecast. Variances can
then be examined, explained, and the necessary action to correct or
amend taken. Departments with no "output" can still be periodically
examined to see whether their costs remain within the budgeted figure
because sub-departmental budgets should cover both output and expenditure as may be applicable.

Sales forecasting

We have earlier stressed the importance of a company having a
specific objective which it aims to achieve. Ultimately this results in the

marketing department having to forecast and plan specific sales achievements for the future and these lead to the setting of actual targets
which are to be met in, say, the following year. These targets must
necessarily be divided among the specific products and these in turn
must be shared out among the various sales force strata. Much has been
written about sales forecasting and what can or cannot be done but,
whilst many companies practise forecasting sales as a matter of course,
some few protest that it is not possible. The essence of planning is to
decide on an objective and then to work out a way of reaching it.
Companies should have an objective of profit but to reach this they
must achieve the necessary sales level or target. In order to make such
a target future sales must first be forecast.

There are many ways of doing this and most companies normally
have at least two independent approaches. One is largely a statistical
one, wherein past performance is examined, trends noted, and statistical extrapolation made.

This appears at first sight to be a quite simple exercise. In fact it can
be a most elaborate and difficult affair involving complex statistical
techniques. The assumptions made, and the detail into which the fore-
caster must go, vary from company to company but the following are
among the considerations usually included:

(1) the anticipated level of activity in the whole national economy
(or international if exports are a major factor);

(2) the probable situation in the industry in which the company
operates;

(3) the price levels expected to apply during the period;

(4) the competitive activity which is anticipated;

(5) the company's own intentions regarding the promotional effort
it will use and the likelihood of introducing new (or eliminating old)
products.

Another method is the purely pragmatic one of building a company
forecast upon the individual salesman's own forecast. Here the forecasts are accumulated and refined at each stage of the organisational
ladder until they reach the general sales manager. Basically, this method
is weak in that salesmen are usually too optimistic as to their future
achievements and also that they can have little or no knowledge of
what changes and new support the marketing division may be planning for the future.

There are variants on both these opposites and some compromises in
between but this book is not the place to try and discuss existing techniques in detail, particularly as much has been written around the sub-

ject already. Certainly sales forecasting can be done successfully; it *is* done by successful companies. Kotler is particularly readable in the area of sales forecasting.

Once more, however, we must emphasise the importance of not treating the sales operation in isolation. Selling is part of marketing. All the activities in the sales division must fit it with all the other activity in the advertising and promotional functions to work to a common goal. Timing, for example, must always be considered so that selling and advertising work together at the right moment to get the best return from the customer. Let us assume that the company has a product with a heavy concentration of consumer purchasing in the autumn. In this case the advertising department will wish to advertise a little earlier because it takes time for the advertising effect to be felt by the consumer. The sales department in turn must ensure that the product is available in the shops before the advertising starts, or early buyers will be unable to purchase and may possibly buy a competitive product—which would be a waste of the advertising effort due to bad timing by the sales department.

Remuneration of salesmen

We have already discussed some aspects of the salesman's approach to his job. Traditionally it had become accepted that a salesman was, and had to be, paid largely according to the results he achieved. The reasoning behind this was that because of the peculiarities of the job and the type of man, it was not really possible to control the work by instruction and order, and that the inducement approach was the only one possible. This general belief has been breaking down for some years, and whilst it is usual to have some form of a sales incentive in the form of a payment related to results as well as a basic salary, there are now many instances of salesmen who are paid a straight salary (and actual expenses) like any other member of the company's staff and who have no direct incentive element in their earnings.

What normally governs the way in which salesmen are remunerated? As might be expected, this depends largely on the functions the man is expected to perform and the type of organisation in which he works. If the work requires the considerable exercise of discretion, high intelligence and much negotiation, with perhaps a considerable lapse of time and many visits between initial contact and final order, the salesman's remuneration will be correspondingly high. If, on the other hand, the work required is closely supervised, offers little opportunity for the exercise of discretion and initiative, requires many fairly straightforward and routine calls each day, then remuneration will be correspondingly lower.

This does not answer the question whether the total remuneration should include a carrot incentive or whether control should be exercised finally by the big stick and the ultimate sanction of dismissal. There is no hard and fast rule. Speciality salesmen, selling expensive items direct to consumers such as domestic equipment, double window glazing or hearing aids are often paid entirely by commission. Grocery salesmen selling to retail shops are often paid entirely by straight salary. There are many exceptions and the particular method used seems to depend very much on the upbringing of the members of the management themselves.

If a man is paid by commission only (i.e. a percentage of his sales turnover) his self-interest will be in maximising turnover and this as we have already seen may not always be in line with the company's marketing goals. Remuneration by a straight commission payment may produce very high total sales turnover but it has other weaknesses. If a company paying its salesmen by straight commission develops very fast it will have difficulty in being fair both to the men and to itself. A high commission may be needed to persuade its first salesmen to take the risk of joining the enterprise. If sales increase very quickly these men may have such high commissions that there is no real incentive for them to work hard and they may prefer to play golf two or three days a week. Should the company then wish to expand its sales force it will probably have difficulty in taking away territory from men "who have borne the heat and burden of the day". Furthermore, any attempt to decrease the rate of commission will also lead to resistance and ill-will from the men on the former rate. Payment by straight commission on the other hand clearly offers little security of earnings to the salesman and in these days of the welfare state and security consciousness it is becoming less attractive to the majority of them.

At the opposite end of the scale, a man may be paid by salary and expenses (car, travelling, etc.) only. Here he has maximum security and certainty of earnings. The company, too, has an advantage in being able to direct the man to do any work it may require, since his self-interest lies in obeying the company. As we have seen, the question here is whether this form of remuneration creates an adequate motivation in the man and this method is therefore usually associated with very close supervision by sales management.

In between is the salary and bonus method of payment. Here the bonus can be fixed over any length of time and can be attached to physical sales (as against sterling turnover) or other variables as appears desirable. It contains within itself some answers to problems existing in other methods for a bonus tied to physical sales does not suffer from the unfairness to one party or the other of a method of payment directly tied to sterling sales when prices fluctuate for reasons outside the control of those out in the field.

Salesmen, themselves, usually like some form of incentive payment and usually prefer schemes where payment follows soon after performance, i.e. a monthly payment is preferred to a quarterly one, and a quarterly one to an annual one. Clearly, there should be a fair relationship between salary and bonus (if used) to give the salesman some security but also the incentive to try harder. A ratio of about 80/20 salary/bonus seems to be effective and acceptable in many relevant sales situations.

Incentives should primarily be related to the *effort* put in by the salesmen themselves not to the "raw data", that is the actual invoiced sales figures. For example a man in territory A may have a turnover of £2,000 per week and a colleague in territory B may have a turnover of £3,000 per week because of differences in customers, local needs and so on, yet each works equally hard. This is another aspect of problems arising after setting up a new company and paying salesmen high commission for immediate business. As the company develops its own corporate effort, quality of product, advertising, promotion and general company strength play an ever greater part in the procuring of business, so that if the salesman is still on his introductory commission rate he may obtain a much inflated income for less effort on his part. Conversely, if a salesman moves to a less well-developed territory no amount of skill on his part may be enough to enable him to match his previous figures elsewhere.

Where salary is the main element in earnings, or bonus is paid at long intervals, a company may mount appropriate sales "drives" and, as a means of encouraging the salesmen and overcoming staleness, sales contests or prize schemes run among the sales force may be used. These can be extremely effective, particularly in getting away from the humdrum sameness of the work. In this connection, however, it is worth throwing in a word of caution for if too many such schemes are used, the man may get into the habit of working for the current prize and lose sight of the fact that he is also paid a salary for doing a fair day's work. At the other extreme, some men resent too many prize schemes as turning their work into a circus performance. The sales manager has to be a psychologist in dealing with his own men as well as his customers and he is left with the decision of how to balance control by management and direction against encouragement by incentive.

The sales interview

This subject is one of the most fully documented areas in business, although somewhat surprisingly there seems to be little treatment of the subject from the behavioural sciences approach apart from the title mentioned for further reading at the end of this chapter. Modern practitioners regard selling as being a skill which can be taught and learned; sales techniques play an increasingly large part in all sales training. Let us therefore briefly consider the outline of the sales interview itself.

The sales interview can be divided into sections. There is usually an introduction or opening where the intention is to arouse the interest of the customer. Next comes the creating of a desire for the product, which as we saw earlier should centre round telling the customer the advantages *to him* of buying. In most sales interviews the even flow of an irresistible sales talk is then broken by objections from the potential customer and reasons why he does not wish to buy. These are overcome (if the salesman is successful) by a restatement of particular benefits conferred by the product. Finally, the salesman comes to the most difficult part which is the "close" of the sale, i.e. obtaining the agreement of the customer to buy.

When his interview is finished—successfully or otherwise—the good salesman will include some gesture or action helping to prepare for a subsequent sale. This must not be a dreary renewed selling (or he may find he loses the order altogether) but more probably a mere confirmation of friendly anticipation or some assistance to the shopkeeper (for example) to sell current stocks.

The most difficult sales interview of all is that where no actual close or sale can be made. The salesman or representative can only discuss, negotiate, give service, for the decision is taken elsewhere and often at another time. Not all the training in the world can get him to the "decision factor" (the man who decides) and the decision is taken in private. Here the real value of a concerted marketing effort is seen to full advantage for if the company has put forward more and better reasons for buying than its competitors have done, it will usually find the order come along in due course.

Sales manuals

"What is the use of a 'sales manual'?" This question is asked mostly by those who do not fully accept modern selling approaches and the emphasis put on selling technique and sales training generally. A sales manual should be a comprehensive up-to-date compendium of what the company's salesman needs to know to carry out his job to the fullest extent of his ability. It should give background of the company's history and philosophy of business. It should give adequate information about the company's products, prices, performance, delivery, terms of trade. Finally, it should contain detailed administrative instructions so that the salesman knows what is expected of him and can refer to the book in most cases and need not call on the office, or his immediate superior, except when really necessary. Both administrative instructions and the use of set-piece training methods, i.e. giving the salesman the points he should make about a product in the order most likely to be effective, can be regarded as means of further reducing areas of activity into programmes. Intelligently used, this does not in any way detract from the use of the salesman's initiative and intelligence, in fact selecting the right programme is intended to enable him to achieve better results with less difficulty.

The manual should build the salesman's morale by giving him on paper, complete (and reassuring) information about his company's products. Especially to the newcomer, the complexity of the range of products can seem very formidable to the man who is facing, and being questioned by, a customer (who often seems to know more than the salesman).

Finally the sales manual should aim at the general improvement of selling techniques in the field by encouraging a degree of uniformity of basic approach to the selling situation based on the successful experience of sales managers and leading salesmen. And the very fact of having a sales manual and having to keep it up-to-date in turn requires that the sales management itself must keep on reviewing its own operations. The "bible" is useful—but it must be very practical and completely up-to-date.

Suggested Reading

THOMPSON, J. W. *Selling: A Behavioral Science Approach*, McGraw-Hill, 1966.

KOTLER, P. *Marketing Management: Analysis, Planning and Control*, 2nd edn., Prentice-Hall, 1967. (Chapter 5 gives a comprehensive but concise account of current thinking and practice in sales forecasting.)

BLAKE, R. R., & MOUTON, J. S. *The Guide for Sales Excellence: Benchmarks for Effective Salesmanship*, McGraw-Hill, 1970.

"Direct Selling in the U.K.", Retail Business, No. 154, *The Economist*, 1970.

CHAPTER 12

Advertising

The pervasiveness of advertising

Advertising, the last of the elements in the marketing mix, is one of the most powerful weapons in the marketing manager's armoury. The total expenditure on advertising in the U.K. was, in 1971, of the order of £650 million and annual expenditure has been consistently between $1\frac{1}{2}$ and $2\frac{1}{4}$ per cent of the gross national product over the past twenty years. This figure is between $\frac{1}{4}$ per cent and $\frac{1}{2}$ per cent less than the equivalent figure for the U.S.A. The total expenditure is in itself considerable, although the proportion of the G.N.P. is small; but the proportion of the final price of the product which it represents varies very considerably indeed.

Some companies spend very little on advertising (few spend nothing, although they may not consciously regard what they do as "advertising" as we shall see later). Others may spend on individual products, especially in such highly subjective and emotional areas as cosmetics or pharmaceutical products, as much as 30 per cent of the ultimate consumer price. The mergers in the brewing industry have reduced the number of brewing concerns from about 450 in the early 1960's to about 78 in 1972, but of the dozens of brands still left about five or six between them carry most of the several millions of pounds spent on advertising beer and allied products each year. So that a straightforward allocation of funds to brands advertised would show these few with appreciable expenditures in relation to turnover and the rest with negligible expenditure.

Since we are all surrounded by the manifestations of advertising in our ordinary everyday lives, we tend to consider advertising as a subject on which we are entitled to air our views as authoritative, whether we have experience of working in the advertising field or not. Against this "lay" background there has been a considerable change in recent years in the business background where emphasis has been moving rapidly from the importance of production as a function to the importance of distribution (including selling and advertising) as a function. This is clearly shown by the relative increase in the proportion of total employment provided by distributive and service activities compared with that of the employment in productive industry in the more advanced national economies. Despite the best efforts of those who are conscious of this, the spirit of the cloth cap economy is still active and advertising in particular is still seen by many to be wasteful and not nearly so "productive" as mining or making iron and steel, or indeed any other specific production activity.

Those in advertising scarcely support this viewpoint; nor do the shrewd heads of businesses who sign or authorise the cheques for large advertising expenditures in the certainty that over the years their money is well spent.

The literature on advertising is prolific, ranging from highly academic treatises on communications theory through to detailed examinations of the techniques employed in devising advertising campaigns. Our approach will again begin with the posing of four questions:

Why do we advertise?
To whom should we advertise?
What should we say in our advertising?
What means are there for conveying our advertising messages to their audiences?

Our narrative will mostly turn on consumer advertising for reasons which will be clear as we proceed, but the underlying principles apply, *mutatis mutandis*, to industrial advertising too.

Why advertise?

Basically, advertising is concerned with conveying information about a product or a service, and the company producing that product or service, to potential buyers. Competition implies that our competitors will always be trying to sell their products to our own previous buyers, therefore we must include in our potential buyers those who have bought before as well as those who have not. As we have already said (page 122) personal contact is the most persuasive form of selling, but it is clearly very difficult and costly to try to locate, and get someone to visit, each of our potential buyers; certainly to do this frequently would be prohibitively expensive. Advertising, therefore, is used as a substitute for personal selling. It is not a perfect substitute, for any one sales talk by advertising is generally less effective than one by personal contact, but far greater numbers of prospects can be reached, far more often and far more cheaply, by advertising.

In the case of advertising which is printed, whether in the press or in a catalogue, it has another advantage. Seeing is believing and people often attribute to the printed message an authority which they withhold from the spoken word or personal salesmanship. Selling is inducing people to learn to buy (page 127) and buying is generally the culmination of a long process of developing a favourable attitude towards the item concerned. The function of advertising is to provide an economical means of directing a series of selling messages to the prospect to assist in this process.

There is growing support, from those who have studied the psychological and sociological aspects of human behaviour, for the theory that human beings are very much influenced by group behaviour. This we have already discussed, but if individuals *are* influenced by group leaders, as is suggested, and buy products because the leaders do so and the others follow their example, then advertising for new products, at least, should be primarily aimed at starting the process of personal recommendation (i.e. personal selling) by these leaders or innovators. Whichever theory we accept, advertising is an economical substitute for direct selling and is dependent for its existence on the saving in cost it affords to the manufacturer. It is the natural mass-selling counterpart of modern mass-production.

To whom should we advertise?

The product, as we have seen, has been devised to fill a consumer need. The advertising should, therefore, be directed to those same consumers whose need has been uncovered. First of all, then, we must define the market and then project the advertising messages to that same area.

This is reasonable though still rather imprecise, but it is not difficult to see the general procedure. If we are selling a Rolls-Royce it is of little practical value to place an advertising message before impoverished pensioners or lowly paid wage earners. If, on the other hand, we are selling processed peas, a traditional staple food of workers in the heavy industrial areas, our message would not be very well received in the rarified atmosphere of Belgravia.

Yet both of these examples have at least one thing in common. The actual buyer may not be the only person involved in making the decision to buy. The housewife buys for her family and if they don't

like the peas she won't buy them. The buyer of the Rolls-Royce may
a rich private individual or a business tycoon, but neither is likely
buy unless the purchase is approved by his wife and family, or h
associates, respectively. The decision-making unit is the group whic..
is involved in, and helps to form, the decision to buy. Here then are
refinements to the definition of the market. We should advertise to the
decision-making units who make up the market and, particularly important when a new product is concerned, the leaders who set the trends for
others to follow.

When selling to consumers through trade channels we also have to
consider the position of the trader. He buys our product by way of
business, to sell it and make a profit. He will be influenced by knowing
of and seeing the advertising for the product, for this will indicate a
probable demand for it. He is also, "ex officio" as it were, a target for
a second specifically "trader" campaign aimed directly at his business
involvement, the dealing in our product for the profit he makes in
servicing his customers.

What should advertising say?

Our product is made because it fills a consumer need. So we should
present it to the consumer as fulfilling that need. We sell the *benefits* of
the product to the consumer. This is what he is interested in, no more;
so we show how our product helps him by filling a need of which he
may or may not be conscious but which he will recognise when it is
pointed out. Whether we do this by a "logical" approach or an "emotional" one depends on consumer attitudes; whether we show an argument giving both sides or merely stress our own advantages depends on
the complexity and importance of the product to the buyer and the
competitive situation. One thing we have to avoid, however, is running down or "knocking" the competitive product. This has a bad
long-term effect. The consumer knows that the competitive products
have their own positive advantages; to decry them discredits us ourselves and indeed tends to bring all business into some disrepute.

ᵢ If there are market segments with quite different characteristics, then
these should be treated as separate markets. Sometimes it is possible to
have an overall theme to cover the whole, but the greater the area and
the more diverse the segments to be covered the less closely will one
theme fit the individual elements concerned. An instance of the practical working of this is seen in the cosmetic field. The approach, need
and attitude of the young woman to personal adornment is quite different from that of the more mature woman. As a result, manufac-

turers tend to have different names, presentations and advertising campaigns for the two requirements, though in fact some of the products may be quite identical.

Devising the actual message content of advertising is beyond the scope of this book, but the reader will have seen many different ways of presenting almost any particular message. Some advertisements consist of an illustration and perhaps the name of the product. Here the advertiser is relying on the impression conveyed by the illustration, and probably also on the familiarity of the consumer with the product and all it implies. Other advertisements may have a closely reasoned, wordy argument such as that used with such success by David Ogilvy for advertising Puerto Rico in the U.S.A. The method will vary because there is no one correct way and different creative advertising people can achieve the same result in quite different ways.

Advertisements can be divided into two: those aiming at immediate action, i.e. promotions, and those building up the knowledge and understanding of the product by the consumer, usually termed "theme" advertising. The objective of long-term theme advertising is to create and develop a personality or image for the product in its market, i.e. to evoke favourable attitudes in the minds of prospective buyers. What this image should be is dependent on the product, the market and the interpretation of these by the marketing manager. The right image is one that tends to get the potential customer to buy; trite—but true.

Advertising media

Let us now turn to the vehicles by which the advertiser can convey his advertising messages to his prospective buyers. One such vehicle, such as a newspaper or a television station, is called an advertising *medium*; when more than one medium is concerned we speak of *media*.

Communications theory holds that the effectiveness of any communication depends substantially on the authority of the communicator as seen by the receiver. In the case of advertising communications this also applies in some degree to the authority of the medium. Many women consider that *Good Housekeeping* speaks with authority on household matters; many business men consider that *The Financial Times* similarly speaks with authority in the business world. Advertisements appearing in media which have particular characteristics in the eyes of their audience are also considered by that audience to have some of that authority merely because they appear there. So, financial advertisements are placed in *The Financial Times* and household advertisements in *Good Housekeeping*. This is an important factor when choosing specific advertising media because the particular audience will consist of people who buy or look at the medium because of their interest in its contents and at the same time they will tend to regard what they see there as being invested with the same authority as the medium itself possesses. The owners of media are, of course, conscious of this and use it as a strong argument when selling their advertisement space to advertisers.

Making a media plan, that is selecting appropriate media and the size and dates of appearances of the advertisements in them, is a highly technical operation which takes into account the authority of the medium, the extent to which an advertisement in that medium can reach all the potential buyers of the product and the extent to which the message is made available to an audience which consists only of potential buyers. The extent to which all potential buyers are reached is termed *coverage* and the extent to which the audience is limited to potential buyers is called *selectivity*.

To get the best value for his money, the advertiser tries to reach all his potential buyers but not waste money on people who are outside the scope of his market. If he fails to reach them all he misses business; if he spends money on "non-prospects" he is wasting his resources. To see the considerations involved let us consider a national newspaper like *News of the World*. It has a circulation of over six million copies but a total readership (audience) of about 16·5 million adults because on average nearly three people read each copy printed. Its advertising space costs are fixed on the basis that all this huge readership is available to any advertiser; this certainly is a bargain to him if he is advertising a product (let us call it "Allbuy") which appeals to all of them. But supposing he is advertising a product "Whatsit" which could only appeal to 1 per cent of that audience? Then the cost of reaching each potential buyer of "Whatsit" is in fact 100 times as great as the equivalent cost to the advertiser of "Allbuy".

On the other hand if there were a smallish periodical called the *"Whatsit User"* which was bought by perhaps 75 per cent of "Whatsit" buyers then even if the cost in relation to circulation were high compared with the *News of the World*, it would still be an economical medium for "Whatsit". The scheduling difficulty arises over reaching the other 25 per cent of buyers who do not read *The Whatsit User*.

One other broad consideration is the factor of *impact*. This is the depth of impression which an advertisement makes on the audience. Impact is partly a function of the sheer size of the advertisement, for example a full page against an eighth page. It is, also, partly a function of black and white print against colour. Here the selection of media is involved because some publications can only print in black and white or rather poor colour, whilst others offer much more sophisticated reproduction. Compare a newspaper advertisement in colour with one in, say, *Good Housekeeping*.

Another factor creating additional impact is the use of movement (as in films or T.V.) against the static illustration in printed advertising, for the ability to show an action incident, either in real life or in cartoon form, adds greatly to the impact. Finally, there is the use of sound and speech (as in radio, films or T.V.) either alone or in conjunction with sight and/or colour. Additional impact, however, costs more money as the media owner quite naturally bases his prices on the estimated value to the advertiser. The advertiser again has to choose between fewer, high impact, advertisements or more advertisements each with lower impact. So, given a sum of money for advertising, impact and frequency have to be balanced more or less in inverse ratio.

Advertisers are closely concerned with the cost of using various media and their relative value. Media owners sell advertising space on the basis of what they consider the space is worth to the advertiser, allowing for all the special characteristics such as a specialised audience or the use of colour. Before valid intercomparisons can be made, a good deal must be known about the characteristics of the audiences of the media concerned and a great deal of information is therefore obtained by market research and published by both the media owners and independent bodies such as the Institute of Practitioners in Advertising (the association of advertising agencies).

Cost concepts

Whilst special terms, bulk discounts and special offers abound, there are some basic cost concepts in general use.

For newspapers mil/inch cost. This is the cost of the space reduced to a common level of 1,000 circulation and a size of one inch in one column, e.g. an advertiser pays £375 for a space 10 inches deep by 3 columns wide in a newspaper with a circulation of one million copies so that the mil/inch rate is therefore 1·25p.

For magazines page rate per 1,000 circulation. This is the cost of the space reckoned in terms of a full page per 1,000 circulation, e.g. an advertiser pays £1,000 for a half page of space in a magazine with a circulation of one million copies. The page rate per 1,000 is £2.

For posters   *cost per week*. There is no audience figure in common agreement. The rent for a site is determined by its size, the estimated passage of people by it and whether it is "solus" or one of a number of positions forming a composite site.

For radio and television   *cost per 1,000 audience*. This is the cost of the space brought down to a common level of 1,000 audience. Sometimes this is also compared on a standard 30 secs. of time, e.g. cost of 30 secs. time is £1,000 for an audience of one million. Cost per 1,000/30 secs. is £1.

It should be noted that media owners sell the space as such, i.e. "half page" or "20 seconds" and are under no obligation to guarantee an audience though in practice they do vary their rates according to the audience and usually allow rebates if the audience is not "delivered". In the older media of press and magazines *circulation* figures not *readership* are used and the leading media have circulation figures audited by an independent organisation, the Audit Bureau of Circulations. In the newer radio and T.V. media total *audience* figures are used and are based on audience estimates from an independent research organisation (Audits of Great Britain Ltd.) which carries out a full T.V. monitoring service on behalf of all those interested in the business of T.V.

Media available

Let us now look briefly at the media available and their principal characteristics.

National newspapers such as *Daily Express, Sunday Times*. These may be weekly (Sunday), or daily publications. Usually their circulations are large and fairly evenly spread according to the population over the whole country. There are some distinct differences in their coverage of social class and occasionally of age groups. Mostly they offer black and white printing of moderate quality and the dailies, though not the Sundays, are often read in haste and thrown away. The printing of colour in newspaper advertisements, formerly postponed because of disputes in the industry, is now becoming commonplace.

Local newspapers. There are a comparatively few, quite large, local newspapers (mostly evening papers in the larger cities), but none of them is quite so large as the national newspapers. There are also several hundred local weekly newspapers. Local newspapers offer facilities for advertising in restricted geographical areas and are thus of especial interest to local traders. Mostly the print is in black and white, though a few are adopting a limited amount of colour printing. The local weekly newspapers are often read from cover to cover and the other local newspapers may perhaps be read slightly more carefully than the national daily newspapers—but generalisations in this respect are hardly meaningful.

Magazines and periodicals. These may be weekly, monthly or quarterly publications. They include general interest and high coverage magazines (e.g. *Radio Times*), mass circulation women's magazines (e.g. *Woman*), special interest periodicals (e.g. *Amateur Gardening*) and trade and technical press (e.g. *Chemical Age*). Many offer good colour printing on high quality paper. They are not controllable geographically except for rare "county" magazines. Publications in this group are often read at leisure and retained to be referred to later.

Television is split into a number of regional stations which are available individually or can be employed in groups for advertising purposes. With live action or cartoon action, personality sponsoring, a semi-captive audience in their own homes, this is a powerful medium. Costs are related to a mass audience which is biased away from the higher socio-economic groups. Almost 85 per cent of families in the U.K. can view advertising on T.V. The T.V. picture is, however, transient and cannot be referred to later, which is a real disadvantage for some advertisers. The rapidly growing use of colour transmission is of course a further strengthening of T.V. as a medium.

Cinema and films. Whilst the cinema audience has greatly declined in recent years and has a pronounced composition bias (a high proportion consists of younger people), films can have considerable impact with colour, movement and sound. The audience is captive (i.e. it has to see the advertisement) and geographical control is good, for most people attend cinemas somewhere near their own homes. All newspaper and magazine media have the advantage that they can be laid aside and referred to later. T.V. and films are essentially ephemeral and not available for reference later.

Outdoor advertising. This essentially consists of various types of hoarding on which posters are exhibited. The audience consists of the passers-by and may be difficult to measure or identify. Hoardings, with large size and full colour, can have considerable impact. They are completely under geographical control. Their message usually has to be exceptionally simple because of the short time viewers have to read the message while passing.

Direct mail is theoretically the most efficient and most controllable form of advertising, provided there is available a complete list of names and addresses of prospective buyers. In colour or black and white, the advertisement should go to a real prospect, whether at home or at work, but the medium still suffers from an attitude of irritation on the part of many recipients towards unsolicited mail.

Exhibitions and demonstrations have very great impact and are usually sited in an exhibition hall or in a shop. The demonstrator can show complex products in use and answer questions with real authority. A weakness is the high cost and low coverage; a great deal of work is required in organising demonstrations, booking sites and obtaining staff.

Catalogues and leaflets are often not considered as "advertising". They can be strictly tailored to the market and product but they tend to be rather expensive and of limited coverage (depending on the mode of distribution). They often form an important part of the armoury of the salesman.

The package. The dressing of the product so that it appeals to a potential buyer is a potent advertisement before and after the act of purchase and should be an important means of evoking the correct image. The cost of producing the package varies but it is seldom accounted for as advertising (see page 171). This is merely treating the pack as an important advertising medium. For packaging as an element of the marketing mix, see page 72.

Summarising: what we say in our advertising is the theme; where and how we say it is determined by those to whom the advertising is directed and the media available; how much we spend is determined by considerations of impact, frequency and coverage as related to the tasks allocated to advertising in the overall marketing plan and the money available.

The advertising agency

Let us again approach our subject by posing questions:

What is an advertising agency?
How is it organised?
What does it do?
Why should a manufacturer use it?

What an advertising agency is. An advertising agency is a specialist organisation which helps manufacturers to handle their advertising. Originally advertising "agents" came into existence to sell advertising space on commission for the early newspaper and magazine publishers. Gradually they built up a connection with manufacturers and traders, by offering advice on what media to use and by designing advertisements to fill the spaces their clients bought through them. This history still shows in the fact that an advertising agency is the legal principal in arranging a contract with a media owner for advertising space. By the rules of their own business association, an advertising agency may not have a financial holding in a client and vice versa.

How is an advertising agency organised? The very small agencies—some hundreds of them—are partnerships or one-man-bands. A small agency may handle "billings" (total receipts from clients for space, services and so on) up to about £½ million per year and the partners carry out all the essential work on an *ad hoc* basis. The very largest agencies on the other hand handle well over eight figures sterling in billings each year and mostly follow the same trend in organisation.

Looking from the client side inwards there are usually five main divisions:

Account executive
Creative
Media
Marketing and market research
Administration/accounting

The account executive division is the link between the client and the agency as a whole. Usually each "account" (an advertising area which may cover the whole operation of a client or just one of his products or brands) has an account executive, who is responsible to an account director, but whose main function is to receive and interpret the client's brief to his colleagues and in turn to advise the client of the agency's views and its advertising recommendations for the client's approval. In many agencies a "client group" is formed (usually different for each client) with specialist representatives from each section and this group, presided over by the account executive, becomes in fact his particular "agency" formed of those particular specialists who are best qualified to deal with the client's special needs.

The creative division may be sub-divided in several ways. Fundamentally this is where the advertising itself is conceived and developed. Some agencies still divide the work between visualisers and copy writers—i.e. those who sketch out the form of an advertisement and those who write the words for it and carry on the division of work on this basis. Others begin with specialist newspaper, magazine, television, radio, exhibition and so on sections and co-ordinate their work with "creative managers". Whatever the particular method there is a great deal of further work to be done in filming, photography, painting, drawing, lettering, etc., much of which is often subcontracted out to specialist suppliers by even the biggest agencies.

Media division is concerned with evaluating and buying space in advertising media. This was once considered the poor relation of creative or account work, but is clearly of no less importance in the final success of an advertising campaign. The media division usually has specialists in the main media areas such as newspapers, magazines and television and also maintains a close connection with all sources of market research intelligence regarding media audiences.

Marketing division is still quite a newcomer in many advertising agencies. It has come into existence because agencies found that so many of their clients did not have departments to organise their marketing thinking or did not really understand marketing. Fundamentally, of course, the agencies also realised that advertising was but a tool for achieving marketing objectives and therefore if they could get nearer to the policy-making area by helping their clients with their marketing problems, the agency's own standing would also be improved.

Market research in an advertising agency serves two basic needs, (*a*) it enables the agency to learn more about media and the advertising it produces (i.e. improves its own expertise), (*b*) it is also a further service which it can sell to its clients by carrying out market research for them.

Administration and accounting division is obviously important to an advertising agency. The paper work and contact which has to be made to create, maintain and obtain payment for a sizeable advertising campaign is enormous and the machine has to be set up and kept in efficient order.

What does an advertising agency do? The agency in principle should turn itself into an appendage of the client company. Depending naturally on the manufacturer's own resources and organisation it should help him analyse his marketing and advertising objectives and recommend the best way of achieving them. Many agencies do just that. At the other end of the scale some agencies are merely shown a product, given a list of its physical characteristics and told that a certain sum is to be spent on advertising—sometimes even specifying the media.

The essence of the advertising agency operation, however, is the provision of a highly specialised expertise. Because an agency has many clients—none of whom are competing directly in the same markets—it has to deal with a wider variety of advertising problems than any of its client manufacturers and may for example produce advertising for a soup, a cigarette, a petrol, a cosmetic product, a motor car, a men's tailor, an airline and a nationalised industry all at once. It can therefore find enough work to justify the employment of a highly competent and specialised body of people, who can all be used wholly in their own specialisms, and then deploy their higher skills "part-time" on the problems of its clients so that each client obtains the use of talent he could not possibly afford to buy "full time".

To say therefore that an advertising agency produces advertising is not just an over-simplification, it is distinctly misleading. This is but the first service it renders to the client. The other services are to help its client with specialist advice on a wide range of marketing topics including advertising, market research, selling and even product policy and to carry out the client's instructions in any or all of these fields as mutually agreed. The modern advertising agency is prepared to take over, if need be, any or all of the marketing functions for a manufacturer and in many instances it has done so very effectively for new or developing companies which are not fully staffed on the marketing side.

Why should a manufacturer use an advertising agency? An advertising agency should be considered an extension to the client company's marketing department for its contribution is complementary to, not in competition with, the client's operation. Unfortunately, in the past there has been much distrust between the client and his advertising agency. The latter has been seen by the manufacturer as a necessary evil but not one to be allowed into the client's full confidence, to share his real worries, or his triumphs. This was partly because the agency was suspected of "making money out of the client" and also because, with the known high rate of migration of personnel from one agency to another, and the frequency with which clients changed agencies, it was feared that confidential information would reach competitors. In recent years the need for closer and more stable relationships in their mutual interest, together with a growing appreciation of the value of advertising agencies, has been fostered by the growth of competition, the development in stature of the advertising agency as a "real business", and the growing understanding by the manufacturer and agency of marketing and the need for an integrated marketing operation.

Much of the earlier mistrust was due to the obsequiousness of many agencies towards their clients, who were often perceived primarily as their paymasters. Some of it was the suspicion of the client, used to thinking in terms of bricks, mortar and products, towards an agency which dealt so much in intangibles, in ideas and people, not factories. The agency's real interest, like that of any other organisation selling to industry, is the client's prosperity. The client's interest lies in getting from his advertising agency a skill and expertise which can only be developed in the advertising world itself. Evidence of the increasing acceptance of mutual interest is seen in the growing number of relationships between client and agency which have lasted twenty years and more; some of them as long as forty years. The existence of long successful relationships among some of the biggest advertisers in the world such as Procter and Gamble and Unilever is not without significance.

But what does the manufacturer gain from using an agency? Firstly, he gets good advice and a second opinion on any marketing matters he raises. Secondly, he gets the use of highly specialised top calibre brains. Thirdly and consequentially, he gets better advertising than he could himself provide. Fourthly, except where extra services are provided on a fee basis he gets his advertising created for him *free*, for the system of agency remuneration means that the commission is rebated by the media owner and the advertiser who made all his own advertising would not only have to pay the cost of this but without the commission which is allowed to his agent, would also pay more for the space.

Public relations (P.R.)

The concept of public relations is that the creation of a background or reputation which is favourable to the manufacturer will also be favourable to his product, and therefore will predispose people to do business with him. P.R. may or may not be connected with the product. It is not merely concerned with creating a favourable attitude so that people will buy the product, but creating this attitude so that people and companies will know about the company, buy from it, sell to it, tell it about new developments, even work for it. P.R. begins with the way the switchboard girl answers the telephone, continues with the way in which a complaint is answered, and ends with a renewal of business. If a favourable attitude is a pre-requisite for doing business then P.R. is a means of developing that attitude, and the essence of the operation is that a P.R. campaign is *not* an advertising campaign. It does not rely on advertisements paid for by the manufacturer but attempts to influence third parties to speak or write favourably about the company and its activities. Those who see the results of this effort do not connect them with the manufacturer speaking from self-interest, but regard them as independent and unbiased comment. (This is another instance of the importance of the source's authority in communications.)

The media used by P.R. include all those means of propagating information which are used for theme advertising purposes and the method is to influence favourable comment in the editorial or commentary sections of the media concerned. Frequently the division between advertising and P.R. is shadowy. If a brewery company presents and endows a prize for a horse race called the "Newtown Cup" and it makes "Newtown Ale" do we classify the expenditure as advertising or P.R.?

As with advertising there are specialist practitioners of P.R., either as a group within the larger advertising agencies or as independent groups. They are skilled in fostering and changing public opinion and adept at turning everyday incidents in the affairs of a company into favourable news items which will create a "good feeling" towards the company. Again, however P.R. is conducted, it is very important that the aims of the operation should be clearly defined. Is it to overcome an unfavourable historical reputation? Is it to pave the way for a new product, the prosperity of which requires that prospective buyers have a new way of looking at life? At least let the objective not be "to create good P.R.", an aim the author has come across more than once.

Advertising in action

We saw on page 141 that advertising can broadly be divided into two categories. The one, *theme advertising*, is aimed at giving information about the product and building up a favourable attitude so that the potential buyer will sooner or later succumb to the blandishments of a salesman or a display. The other is that part of advertising called *promotion* which is specifically aimed at taking advantage of the theme advertising which has gone before and obtaining immediate buying action. Promotion is the creating of an advertisement aimed at immediate action by using very heavy impact and consequently usually limited coverage. It aims at persuading buyers to buy now, to obtain *now* the response to stimulus of our learning theory (page 36). Promotion can also be directed to industrial operations, for example by offering free trial quantities or special prices for buying now, but it is much more commonly seen in the full variety of its operation in the consumer field.

The most common types of promotion are:

Price offers: obvious inducements for immediate action seen in many forms—3p. off, buy one get one free, buy one get another product cheaper.

Premium offers: this is a special type of price offer, the essence of which is that upon proof of purchase of the product (usually sending a label or carton top), the customer is entitled to obtain from the manufacturer another item such as a breadknife or a flower vase at a much reduced price. If the premium is a popular item and the "bargain" a good one this form of promotion can create much interest and excitement around the advertised product both in the consumer's home and in the retail trade.

Sampling: the giving of free samples in the shop, or at the house door, or upon purchase of another product. It is an expensive but highly effective means of eliciting action. If, having tried the product free, people will still not buy, then they may not be open to economic persuasion in the foreseeable future.

Coupons: a variation of sampling designed to enable the consumer to try a product more cheaply. It is not so expensive to give a coupon as to give a completely free sample since it is easier to distribute pieces of paper than actual samples. It is not so effective, of course, although there are cases where the manufacturer believes that his prospect will think more highly of his product if he buys it at a reduced price than if he gets it free. Coupons can be distributed by post or by hand, door-to-door, on the packages of other products, or printed in newspapers and magazines. Each method has its own advantages and disadvantages.

Competitions: a form of promotion periodically in favour (there seems to be a fashion in advertising and promotion as in many other activities). Here the advertiser offers an opportunity for the buyer to enter a competition for a (large) prize upon showing proof of purchase of the product, but as we shall see the real measure of the success of such a promotion is the level of subsequent sales, not the number of entries for the contest.

Personality promotions are very similar to competitions but rely on the publicity value of well-known personalities, usually from the entertainment world, who recommend the product and thus lend it their personal authority. There is a useful and full summary of promotions in the Economist Intelligence Unit special report in *Retail Business* (June 1966).

Dealer offers. When selling to the consumer through the retail (or wholesale) trade the manufacturer has to consider his relations with the trade and how best to develop the trade's co-operation, or at least avoid its active displeasure. The growing competitiveness of business in all fields has made most retail traders now realise that it is in their own advantage to co-operate with most manufacturers but usually not to tie themselves unduly to any one.

The manufacturer, on the other hand, knows that the retailer stocks many products, including his own competitors', and thus tries to woo the trader to give him some advantage. This he usually does by special price inducements or some form of combination offer whereby the

trader gains by buying an assortment of goods. The objects of all such
offers are, firstly, to encourage the retailer to put more sales pressure on
the manufacturer's own line(s); secondly, to persuade the trader to take
so much of that product that he has neither the money nor the physical
space to buy in so much of the competitors' products; and thirdly, to
hope that the pressure of stock will make the retailer try even harder to
sell that product quickly so as to turn his stock into cash.

Point of purchase display. No account of marketing consumer goods
would be complete without some mention of this vital link in the chain
of events leading to a purchase. The prospective purchaser has seen or
heard many advertisements extolling the virtue of the product, but
mostly when she was very far from the shops and thoughts of shopping. Here she is now, money in hand, ready and anxious to buy. Then
she sees the product, the object of all the marketing effort. If it is not
bought now, it never will be. And if it is not *seen* now it has but little
chance at all.

The presence and display (i.e. prominence) of the product at the point
of purchase is what finally brings about the sale. A great many marketing men in the consumer field believe (and there is a good deal of
evidence to support their belief) that many of the ordinary everyday
requirements of men and women are bought "on impulse" when they
"happen to be seen" in a shop. Manufacturers believe this implicitly
and many of them know that the greatest value they get from competitions and similar promotions is the extra display in the shops which
produces far greater sales than merely those from people who actually
enter the contest. For many promotions a principal objective is the
raising of stock and display levels and pressure on space is so great
that a promotion is needed to achieve any display at all.

All promotions should be examined at the outset to see what it is they
are intended to achieve and whether they are likely to do this. For
instance, how far would a free sample distribution, covering all homes,
entail giving samples to people who would never buy that product
subsequently and how far would it be subsidising current buyers by
simply giving free samples to many who would buy in any case? The
subsidising of current buyers is a matter for careful consideration, and we
shall discuss this again when considering brand switching (Chapter 15).

Timing of advertising

All marketing activities must be co-ordinated in one concerted effort
and it is essential to link together the selling effort, the delivery of actual
stocks of the product to the shop and the advertising of the product

to the consumer to get the fullest value from each. This applies universally to new or old products, seasonal or stable products, wherever a drive for more sales is mounted.

Is there, nevertheless, a case for "teaser" advertising appearing before the product is available and leading people to wonder and question so that when the product does burst upon them they will rush to buy? Some manufacturers clearly believe so and at least one successful grocery producer—a liquid bleach called Lanry—achieved considerable success using similar techniques in the late 1950's. Before making a judgment we need to know if people are in fact favourably influenced by a message which may seem almost gibberish ("Look for XY"), or does their perceptual defence merely filter it out and thus cause the advertising expenditure to be largely wasted? All our behavioural studies would tend to question the teaser technique and the author's own experience has led him so far to believe that he for one would rather not spend money persuading people to think about his product unless they could buy it when they were so persuaded.

There are other, equally important, questions. Is it valid to say that people will accept and be more influenced by advertising when they are in the appropriate mood or involved in the appropriate activity? Is this merely desirable or is it really important? We all know the irritation of being asked to think of something when we are occupied with something else. Do we shut out the new message entirely or merely pay half attention? This creates something of a dilemma for the manufacturer —should he intrude into the family's evening television entertainment or put his message in the leisure interest magazines? Not everyone can have the same answer, which is one reason why marketing and advertising are such fascinating activities, but here are areas where British students of marketing might do some basic research into the behavioural field.

Advertising efficiency

We have already (page 139) described advertising as mass selling designed to accompany mass production. We have also indicated many advertising areas where opinions differ and doubts exist, especially in the actual presentation of the advertising message, the selection of media and the decision between impact and frequency of appearance. Despite this our whole business approach must be consciously directed to optimise our advertising effectiveness. In this respect what have we to help us apart from sheer guesswork and educated hunch?

There is, of course, historical data. Some of this may be mere qualitative judgment but we have, nevertheless, the results of the particular marketing mixes (we cannot separate the elements) we have used in the past and we have the effectiveness (as estimated) of campaigns and promotions. All of these lead us to an informed appraisal based on our actual experience, and our insight into their meaning.

We can also use market research (and encourage our advertising agency to do the same) to find out more about the audiences of various media and the reaction of our prospective purchasers to our advertisements. Some manufacturers and advertising agencies have gone further than this by pre-testing advertisements before they are either finalised or used; all these techniques are far more advanced (albeit more expensive) than those available a few short years ago and it is often possible to screen out an advertising theme of doubtful efficacy, even if it is not often possible to pick out the real winner of the future.

Other factors bearing on the efficiency of advertising are the life-cycle of the product and its position in that cycle, the gross margins available in the field of operation, the total size of the market, the stability of the market, the proportion of the population involved in the market and the state of our knowledge of competitors and their policies.

There are also, fortunately, a number of useful yardsticks which we can use to check and improve on the effectiveness of our advertising. The actual costs of selling personally to our prospects instead of advertising can be estimated fairly accurately. The cost and results of offers, promotions, alternative media can all be assessed and compared. The coverage of the media to be used can be estimated; research surveys can show how far our messages have been received (seen) and understood.

The real problem is that only with great difficulty can our full advertising effort be checked separately. We are always working in the environment of the complete marketing mix, in the background of our ever-restless competitors. Even if we could find two similar situations and have everything the same except for advertising, we could only check one aspect of advertising at a time, and we have four or five variables here alone. Besides all this, we cannot use the level of sales as even a direct reflection of our current marketing mix for some part of our present sales will surely be due to our advertising effort last year, or the year before. So we are left with a number of separate and often unrelated pieces of information which tell us part of the truth only—never the whole truth. This may seem a somewhat defeatist account but it is true that few facts can be set out in black and white showing what progress has been made. Nevertheless it is also true that progress *is* being made by empirical methods and it may not be out of place to hope for steady progress in the years ahead.

Advertising expenditure

Kuehn in the U.S.A. and Professor Lawrence in this country are among many who have been attempting to work out a rationale for optimising advertising expenditures. Conceptually this is by no means impossible, although some of the assumed factors may not be very clearly quantifiable. Practically, from the point of view of practising marketing management, the barriers preventing accurate quantification of the factors involved do not appear to be surmountable in the near future but what we have already achieved is a clearer view of what are the factors which have to be taken into consideration before optimum advertising appropriations can be calculated.

One consideration is particularly applicable to the launch of new products, yet still applies in a lesser degree to current runners. Advertising, as we have seen, does not usually produce immediate and final results. Expenditure this year does not have *all* its effect this year (especially that part of it which occurs late in the year). To the extent that advertising is undertaken either to start off a new product or to provide for sales at a later date, should not this advertising expenditure be considered as capital expenditure undertaken in the one case to launch the product, and in the other to provide for later sales in the same way as plant is installed to make a product for sale later?

In the case of current advertising expenditure, some of this, especially promotional expenditure, is devoted to immediate returns and some to longer-term effects. Can we separate these? It is particularly difficult to achieve this when the rate of return and the period over which the return is expected cannot be precisely identified, but any progress towards overcoming this difficulty will clearly help.

A third factor which theoretical approaches tend to "assume" is the "advertising value" of the campaign, which is clear enough in concept but so far not solved in practice. Every marketing man knows that a good advertising campaign can achieve far more than an average one —witness the famous man with the black patch for Hathaway shirts (another Ogilvie masterpiece); but no one has yet succeeded in quantifying this area, particularly the super-brilliant campaign. The best practice to date only goes some way towards avoiding the really mediocre by using a pre-testing technique. This of course helps the avoidance of the really bad advertising, but it does not give the evaluation and grading on a quantitative basis which the theory demands.

In practice, when deciding advertising appropriations many advertisers tend to use rule-of-thumb methods such as applying a percentage of anticipated profits or sales. Other, more marketing minded, companies attempt to estimate the magnitude of the task to be done and work backwards from the cost of carrying out each element in this task.

The two earlier methods can scarcely be commended from the marketing aspect. Such approaches lead to heavy advertising when times are good and light advertising when times are bad, which is exactly the reverse of what the environment requires and which in fact tends to make boom or slump even more pronounced. Such methods are understandable from the point of view of the accountant, only concerned with his budget figures, but they are not what the marketing man, attuned to his market and the need to make sales to get profit, should have in the forefront of *his* mind.

Whatever course a company follows in deciding what its advertising appropriation should be, it must take account of the estimated life-cycle of the product and its present position in that cycle. This factor usually carries considerable weight in the practical world as well as in the theoretical approach. If the product is just beginning to develop then more effort should be placed behind it; if it is past its peak and in decline then perhaps nothing should be spent on it, but it should be drained of all possible profit before withdrawal.

As we have said, no one has yet produced a practical solution to the concept of quantifying the advertising value of a campaign so that less money will be spent on the brilliant campaign than on the merely competent one. So far even the most sophisticated advertisers find it far easier to pick out and stop the weak advertising campaign than to inspire and obtain a brilliant one. When the latter does appear there is at least as much ground for believing that many companies *increase* their advertising appropriations in order to "reinforce success" as there is for believing that companies decrease their expenditure on such (brilliant) advertising because the normal level would then be wasteful and extravagant.

Suggested Reading

ADAMS, J. R. *Media Planning,* Business Books, 1971.

GRAVES, R. *More About Creating Customers,* George Allen & Unwin, 1970.

JEFKINS, F. *Advertising To-day,* Intertext, 1971. (A most useful book, largely descriptive, good for reference.)

OGILVY, DAVID. *Confessions of an Advertising Man,* Longman, 1964.

WEBSTER, E. *Advertising for the Advertiser: A Client's Guide,* Murray, 1970.

WILLIAMS, D. *Advertising and the Social Conscience: Exploiting Products not People,* Foundation for Business Responsibilities, 1972.

PART FOUR

Managing the Marketing Function

In the earlier parts we have examined the functions and objectives of marketing and the tools available for carrying out the necessary action. We have scarcely touched on marketing management however and actually directing and managing operations is very different from just knowing what to do. In the remaining chapters we examine some of the techniques of marketing management and control. A chapter on differences in and the application of marketing methods to industrial operations is also included.

CHAPTER 13

Controlling Marketing Operations

Managing the operation

In its widest sense marketing means making legitimate profits by supplying a customer need. This also means not only being "in business" but staying in business; so the marketing man who is to be successful must be a good business man. His objective is the making of continuous profit, so obviously he must understand finance and the financial situation of his company; on the other hand, he himself must understand the effect on his company's finances of his own marketing operations. All this must be included in his appraisal of the market and his formulation of policy, or strategy, for from the latter stem the objectives aimed at and the plans for achieving these objectives.

Merely creating plans is not in itself sufficient. If everyone were perfect and did the right thing every time, at the right time, the majority of the members of any company's management team would be superfluous. Things do not work out like this (we are all fallible humans) and therefore the marketing manager has to follow up and see his operation right through to a successful conclusion. This is a management function and a management requirement. In the end the marketing manager has to "manage" his operation.

Assuming that the basic objectives have already been decided upon we may consider this part of management to be a control function involving a sequence of operations:

(*i*) setting up an organisation to carry out the necessary work;
(*ii*) selecting individuals to fulfil the various functions required;
(*iii*) setting sub-goals for each sub-unit involved;

(*iv*) defining, if possible in quantitative terms, the sub-goals;

(*v*) examining performance against these sub-goals and, if necessary, taking remedial action to ensure their achievement;

(*vi*) constantly being alive to the possibility of revising both the sub-goals themselves and the methods of reaching them.

Let us now look at these operations remembering that though they have to be put down in some order, this does not necessarily mean that they must be carried out in this sequence. Nearly always in marketing several things are going on simultaneously and none can be tackled in absolute isolation.

Marketing organisation and personnel

A full-scale marketing operation is seldom conceived and developed absolutely from nothing. Most companies start in quite a small way and grow little by little, especially in the early days. As they grow a management structure is developed and additional pieces are grafted on to it as required. Occasionally a major overhaul is necessary and quite drastic changes may be made—but they seldom if ever involve cutting out everything and starting afresh.

We usually find, therefore, that the marketing manager has some kind of an organisation to work on and no matter what changes may be desirable, he should first make the best use of the material he has. Only when a particular individual is not only unsuitable for a particular job but is also unsuitable for any other job which has to be done (and which is available at the time) should he be required to leave.

This is not altruism. On the contrary it is good business sense. Using to the full the talent already available in a company avoids the cost in money, time and effort of seeking out new men, indoctrinating them into the company's way of operating and training them to do their job in the company's way of doing things. Using talent to the full goes beyond this, however, for it helps to develop loyalty and team spirit and generally raises morale. The marketing department, with its special interest in people and their motivation, should be among the first of all departments to remember that its own personnel are also people with all the usual human characteristics and that their motivations are important also.

Nevertheless, new members of the department will be needed from time to time, especially in an expanding operation. Finding them is a costly and time-consuming job for those seniors involved. Let us not take time discussing the types of men and women who have successfully filled marketing jobs; the work itself will have indicated the intellectual and personal attributes needed. We cannot, however, overlook the difficulty still being experienced in finding suitable new marketing staff. This is partly due to a considerable increase in the number of companies which are beginning to realise the importance of setting up an integrated marketing division. But it is also partly due to the relative paucity of candidates who have been trained on the job by companies using modern marketing techniques and the lack of facilities (until very recently) for the training of suitable candidates outside the company. Most of all, perhaps, it is due to the lack of perception by large numbers of companies that they should have been raising marketing men (but how could they if they did not even understand marketing?).

We have discussed the various elements involved in the marketing function as a whole and how the mix of marketing tools varies from one type of operation to another. Advertising, selling, planning, market research, distribution, technical service, invoicing, product development, product management are some of the functions which *may* be involved but it seems likely that any attempt to set down an organisational plan for a hypothetical company may be more misleading than helpful. We have discussed the considerations which should be borne in mind; the marketing manager should look first at the job he has to carry out and then see whether it is necessary to alter his organisation in order to do it.

Usually this organisation will stem from the sub-goals the marketing manager has fixed. This is not to say that every secondary objective needs a sub-department or even a separate individual to carry it out. Objectives can be grouped under departments, as most readers will appreciate, hence the use of sales departments selling a variety of products and advertising departments advertising (or arranging the advertising of) a variety of products. An interesting point, however, is the growing tendency to delegate marketing responsibility to brand or product managers who carry responsibility for planning and organising a product profitably: these functionaries tend more and more to absorb the advertising function, possibly because of the increasing ability of advertising agencies to provide marketing thought and advice as well as purely advertising services. The physical selling tends to be kept separate largely because it demands more personal time with the customer.

Nevertheless the elements decided upon in the organisation must be given clear and precise briefs on their responsibilities and their authorities in carrying out the actions necessary to perform their tasks. The precision with which these can be defined increases as the tasks fall into the lower levels of operations, as we shall see later (Chapter 16), so that eventually the means and end amount to the same thing; which is the opposite case from higher managerial responsibilities where the object-ive to be reached rather than the means of reaching it is what matters.

Value of goals and targets

We have already postulated that the company's operations must stem from an overall objective. This should need no argument yet many companies deny either their ability or their need to have such an objective. There is an old saying that "if you don't know where you want to go then any road will do", and many would agree that if you aim at a star you may not reach it but you will probably climb higher than if your eyes never leave the ground.

Although we have already discussed the fixing of communications goals and sub-goals (Chapter 6), let us again examine a goal as an object-ive, or target, to be reached. The goal may be a level of sales, a number of customers, a level of profit, but it can also be a level of output in the factory, an amount of time taken to produce an item, or a level of cost. Cost, or expenditure, targets are in themselves equally as important as any other objectives and the fixing of cost standards is as urgent and necessary as the fixing of standards of achievement in amounts of product produced or to be sold.

Whatever the goal—and each one must be considered separately— the precise definition of it is the first step towards the marketing man-ager's making sure that he achieves it. At least he knows what it is he is trying to do.

The second step is to see where he is now and how far away that is from where he wants to go. This clearly requires the use of some form of measurement and the introduction, wherever possible, of measure-ment and figures. Once he can identify his target in measurable units and similarly identify his current performance in the same units, the problem becomes much easier to handle.

There are many sets of figures which a company needs, but from the overall marketing standpoint we may consider these under three heads.

The *net cash flow* is the rate at which total receipts into the company exceed total payments outwards. It can be positive or negative. If the net cash flow is not large enough at the relevant time to meet planned capital expenditure when that is due, then the company must obtain funds from other sources, or change its whole development plan unless the cash flow can be rapidly improved.

The second category of vital figures is the detailed presentation of the company's *sales achievement*. Whilst in theory this should be continuous, in practice the figures are usually present at intervals, sometimes monthly, sometimes weekly and occasionally daily. The form of these figures depends entirely on the kind of operation the company is involved in. For example, the figures used for a large civil engineering company will be quite different from those of a company selling foodstuffs in the grocery trade. In each case, however, separate receipts should certainly be shown for sales of groups of products or activities, possibly also by different geographical areas; certainly non-sales income should be shown separately from sales income.

The third category of basic figures is the *marketing cost* of obtaining the sales achieved. Essentially this comprises selling costs, advertising costs and physical distribution costs. These we discuss separately later.

In the case of both sales achievement and the costs of making this achievement, the overall objective must be broken down into a series of sub-goals and the means of obtaining them, so that targets for both income and expenditure can be set up in a series of budget figures showing anticipated income and anticipated expenditure in the appropriate time intervals. As the marketing operation proceeds the actual sales figures and marketing expenditures will be shown against the budgeted figures; this then makes the way clear for the third step in the marketing control procedure.

Budgetary control

This third step is to examine the actual figures achieved against the planned target figures, whether of sales income or marketing expenditure. Where there are variances these must be explained and the marketing manager must then take action to correct them. This is straightforward enough in principle but is, of course, not so easy in practice. The whole procedure hangs on the initial planning of the operation, the breaking of it down into constituent parts so that total income can be estimated in terms of the sales from each part of the operation and expenses for each part can also be examined under specific heads such as advertising, selling, administration and so on in detail.

Comparing performance with budgeted aims clearly must be done frequently so that early action can be taken before any discrepancies get out of control and conversely so that advantage can be taken of any success beyond that anticipated. If this is not done at the earliest moment then later on may be too late and the plan may become unattainable because the corrective action (a standby in the initial plan) cannot be applied in time. In practice, many companies find it convenient to have marketing target and achievement figures produced monthly as a good compromise between the high cost of presenting the figures more frequently, the need to have long enough periods to obtain meaningful figures (by avoiding the distortions which tend to creep into very short periods) and the dangers of going too long without proper examination of the situation. There is of course no need to have all figures presented at the same time interval; for example, sales achieved may be looked at weekly in the case of a new product launch, and monthly in the case of general sales, whilst in the same operation salesmen's expenses may only be examined quarterly.

Revision and reappraisal

Correcting variances in performance against budget in marketing operations demands a degree of judgment more finely tuned than in many other activities. The first need is not to be precipitate in taking counter-action. The reasons for variances must be identified as accurately as possible and the manager must be sure that the variance is a real one and not just a random skew result which will be self-corrected when the operation has run, say, another month. Secondly the remedial measures, when selected and instituted, must be given enough time to work through the market (if the variance is a shortage of sales, for example) and some possible remedial measures, such as a new presentation of a product or a new approach in an advertising campaign, may not even be an appropriate answer because they need too long to become effective.

Nevertheless the prudent marketing manager, who must be presumed to have evaluated the possibilities when making his original plan, will institute necessary remedial measures at the earliest moment when he is sure that he has a problem and has identified the cause. What should he do if the variances turn out to be so great that the most rigid analysis shows that the plan cannot be achieved? Opinion here varies as does practice. In general, basic objectives should not be altered and the marketing manager should still try to keep them in view; but if for some reason completely beyond his control his targets are genuinely unattainable, then certainly the targets must be re-assessed and a new plan built around the new situation. What would seem to be misguided would be a constant and frequent changing of main objectives; this makes the whole operation unstable and formless.

The skill and judgment required is, therefore, the ability to read the situation accurately and keep the company on course. The company's overall objectives are usually long-term ones and should not be changed frequently. The principal marketing objectives fall into a similar category but are likely to have a somewhat shorter time span and to be changed accordingly. Short-term objectives and short-term plans devised to meet the needs of the overall objectives may and often do go astray and thus need more frequent adjustment. The key lies in choosing suitable objectives in the first place and when this is done later alterations will certainly be minimised—which is the most we can practically expect.

Suggested Reading

DRUCKER, P. *The Effective Executive,* 2nd edn., Pan, 1970.
KOTLER, P. *Marketing Decision Making: A Model Building Approach,* Holt, Rinehart & Winston, 1971.
MUDDICK, R. G. *Mathematical Models in Marketing,* Intertext, 1971.

CHAPTER 14

Analysing Marketing Costs

Need for quantification

We have already indicated the close connection between marketing and human behaviour and the consequent need to emphasise the contribution made to marketing thought by the behavioural sciences. From this aspect it is clear that marketing, being so closely linked with human behaviour, must be an imprecise subject and its practice an art rather than a science. Nevertheless, attempts are being made to try and introduce precision and measurement even into the realm of the traditionally unpredictable human behaviour.

At the same time marketing is a *business function*; business is concerned with profits and profits are reckoned in money, which is a very quantifiable product. It is natural, therefore, that marketing people should try to incorporate operational research and quantitative methods into as much of marketing practice as possible and that figures, statistics and scientific approaches have become a large part of modern marketing. Some indication of ways in which the marketing man can use these figures, not merely to picture what has already happened but to help him analyse his operations and to discover areas where improvements may be made, appears to be both desirable and necessary.

From a narrower point of view, having reached a decision on what product(s) to make, marketing may be considered to be a matter of distributing the product to the user and in this sense the marketing expenses which are inevitably incurred are substantially the cost of distribution in the widest sense of the word. The reader should, in fact, take care when seeing "cost of distribution" in print for, according to the context, this may be the cost of the entire marketing function, the actual cost of transporting the product from factory to shop, or anything in between. Let us, therefore, keep to "marketing costs", when this is what we really mean.

Marketing costs, including by definition expenditure on selling, advertising, promotion, transport and so on through the whole marketing mix, differ from production costs because they are capable of actually producing, or increasing, revenue for the company. For example, an advertising campaign may increase net sales revenue from a "no advertising" situation by 50 per cent, or whatever the figure may be. Alternatively, advertising may also add to the desirability of the product in such a way that the consumer would willingly pay 12½p. instead of 10p. for it so that the net revenue is greater than before. In either case net revenue is greater with the marketing cost of the advertising expenditure than without it. Nevertheless any sensible marketing man will want to know what his company is getting for this expenditure and whether the constituent elements making up the total are all pulling their proportionate weight. This means that we must introduce some form of marketing cost analysis as a prelude to the use of one of management's most fundamental tools, control of costs.

Advantages of marketing cost analysis

Almost every marketing manager tries to analyse his marketing costs because the information he gets by doing so is very valuable. Some typical items which he may separate are the cost of using his own sales force of salaried employees or (if used) the cost of agents paid by commission; the cost of distributing free samples, the cost of distributing coupons which enable buyers to make a trial purchase of a product at a reduced price; the costs of different lengths of advertising time on different T.V. stations; the costs of different sizes of advertising space in magazines or in newspapers.

Merely separating such items draws attention to the levels of expenditure different marketing activities require. Further than this, however, possessing this kind of information in itself invites the marketing manager to make comparisons between the items and to ask himself what he is getting for his expenditure and whether his money is being spent to the best advantage. When he can measure the results of different activities and can compare these with the costs of carrying out these activities he has of course the basis for a rational choice between alternative possibilities.

Unfortunately it is often difficult to measure precisely the return from any particular activity. Sometimes, when very specific promotional activities such as giving coupons to each household are concerned, fairly accurate information can be obtained. At other times—perhaps over the majority of the whole field—it is almost impossible to get a meaningful measurement of results such as the return from an individual advertisement or the return from a change of pack design. Nevertheless there are instances where it is much better to have some factual information than none at all and where a value judgment must be placed on those factors for which no measurement proves possible so that not only can past activities be analysed but conclusions of comparative values can be drawn and future plans adjusted accordingly.

How far to extend the detail of the analysis must depend on the sophistication and complexity of the operation being reviewed. In manufacturing operations it ought always to be possible to have figures which show the contribution of individual products (or at least narrow product groups) to company overhead and profit. It should generally be possible in marketing operations, to examine the direct sales costs for an individual salesman (i.e. those costs which would not occur if that salesman did not exist). In some consumer, as well as many industrial, operations it may be very reasonable to examine costs of, and contributions from, sales to individual customers. In retail trading operations multiple shop proprietors would normally expect to have figures showing the contribution to overhead and profit of individual shops. The reader may elaborate the requirements for any business but once the return for different expenditures on different activities is determined the marketing manager has then at his disposal the basis for making a calculated rational choice between alternatives because he can calculate what effect changes in his marketing mix will have on his current situation.

The analysis of costs and the results they bring in the marketing operation has a further advantage: it enables the manager to assign responsibility to a person or department on a fair and precise basis. Whereas formerly he appointed a sales or demonstration manager to fulfil a functional need he can now give him a precise measurable task to perform, thus tightening up his whole operation. Indeed it can well be argued that a detailed analysis of cost and return in the manner outlined not only exposes the facts of the situation but, as already stated, offers a very strong incentive to compare results and look for improvements.

Types of marketing cost

There are almost as many variations in costing procedures as there are company accountants; we must therefore opt for some system without perhaps going into minute details.

Direct marketing costs are essentially costs which vary directly with the volume of sales. In practice these are mostly associated with the package, its design, its production and its delivery to its destination with the user.

Indirect marketing costs are those supporting the general operation such as the administration of the marketing department or the cost of maintaining warehouses.

Whilst all costs can be considered to be direct or indirect they can also be considered *variable, semi-variable* or *fixed* in relation to sales levels and these terms are particularly sacred to accountants. For marketing purposes, however, we may be permitted to consider categories of cost which suit our own convenience in carrying on a marketing operation.

Variable marketing costs we thus define as those which vary directly with the level of sales. In practice this means items like special packaging devised for a particular operation, sales commissions paid to agents or salesmen in relation to actual sales achievement or the cost of *physically moving* the product (not keeping a warehouse or distributing organisation in being). That part of the cost of the package which is incurred for the holding, protection and safe carriage of the product purely from the point of view of physical requirements is properly a cost of production. All package costs intended to beautify, enhance or improve the presentation of the product are properly marketing costs. Sometimes, for ease of calculation, a normal printed carton is charged in its entirety to production, although initiation costs for new designs may be charged to marketing; special advertising presentations on the other hand are a marketing cost.

Semi-variable marketing costs are then defined as marketing costs which are fixed over a short time but can be altered over longer periods. These include temporary staff employed for particular operations, or periods of time, or advertising expenditures which are contracted ahead but can be cancelled with appropriate notice.

Fixed marketing costs by our definition are those basic expenses which cannot be varied over anything but a very long period and are independent of normal fluctuations in sales levels or other work to be done. They include such items as office space, executive salaries and expenses which are incurred because the marketing department is an establishment in operation.

The bulk of marketing cost analysis is concerned with variable or semi-variable costs because in most marketing operations delivery, advertising and selling expenses cover the vast majority of the costs incurred.

This is also the area where control can be most readily applied and changes made. It is nevertheless true that the fixed costs may not always be at the correct level and the manager should certainly check expenditures made under this heading and review the basis of their acceptability at reasonable intervals.

Setting cost standards

It is pointless to analyse costs without setting up acceptable standards, or targets to be aimed at, so that there is a yardstick by which to judge variances and there are many of these standards which may be useful according to the type of marketing operation.

(*i*) *Historical costs*. Recent figures can be used and projected forward as a basis for comparison. This method is most useful when external environmental conditions such as wages, or materials costs, or selling prices, have not changed markedly. If there have been environmental changes, of course, these must be allowed for in any forward projections.

(*ii*) *Potential costs*. A geographical area, a representative or a customer may be taken as a standard against which to compare others. This type of standard can be helpful (when used fairly) in default of more objective means.

(*iii*) *Work study*. This can be used to examine how a salesman makes use of his time, particularly in order to arrive at a standard for the relation of selling time to travelling time and administration. This also is an area where comparisons between men can be grossly misunderstood yet, with due allowance for known differences in conditions, they can still be very helpful.

(*iv*) *Profit/volume analysis*. This is a means of calculating the extra sales required so that the total gross margin earned by them will cover the cost of a specific activity, such as advertising, or alternatively will cover all costs before any net profit is earned. (See Figure 8.) In the former:

$$\frac{\text{cost of advertising campaign}}{\text{gross margin per unit}} = \text{sales to cover cost of advertising}$$

(*v*) *Ratio analysis*. This is the examination of any ratio which is useful to the operation, e.g. the cost of a salesman can be examined as a cost per call made by him.

(*vi*) *Averages*. These provide a popular rough and ready means of comparison. They can be useful but apart from the difficulties of comparing unlikes (e.g. two sales territories may be very different in particular respects such as past level of attention or differing types of customer), averages being what they are, some figures will always be above and some below. Sales managers may use averages as a control for their men who fall below and as a compliment for those who are above.

Profit/Volume Chart

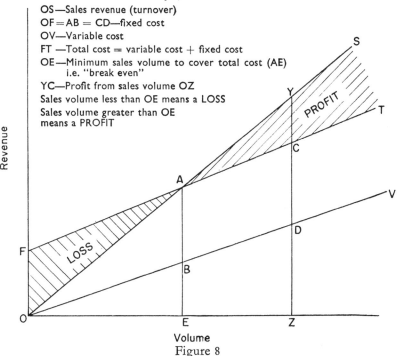

OS—Sales revenue (turnover)
OF = AB = CD—fixed cost
OV—Variable cost
FT —Total cost = variable cost + fixed cost
OE—Minimum sales volume to cover total cost (AE) i.e. "break even"
YC—Profit from sales volume OZ
Sales volume less than OE means a LOSS
Sales volume greater than OE means a PROFIT

Figure 8

Useful information for marketing cost analysis

(*i*) Product contributions, i.e. the gross margin towards overheads and profits for different products. (Gross margin is revenue minus variable costs.)

(*ii*) Costs for different channels of distribution.

(*iii*) Average cost of obtaining an order.

(*iv*) Cost of obtaining orders by size of order group (i.e. low range, medium range, upper range).

(*v*) Costs for individual areas or sales territories.

(*vi*) Profits by customer/volume group (i.e. size of annual sales to customer).

(*vii*) Sales cost per call; per order; car miles per call, per order; salesman's expenses per man; car expenses per man.

(*viii*) Advertising costs: cost of space per 1,000 circulation; cost of space per 1,000 audience; cost of space/cost of preparing advertisement (photography, blocks, etc.).

(*ix*) Promotion costs: coupon cost per 1,000 redeemed; sampling cost per 1,000 people sampled.

(*x*) Transport costs: cost of an average delivery; cost related to size of order (large, medium, small); cost as a proportion of revenue.

Sales operations study

Let us now look at an example of the practical application of marketing cost analysis. Although a good deal of work has been done to improve the effectiveness of selling operations, not very much has been published in detail showing the kind of work which can be done. One of the most interesting accounts of work in this field was given in a paper by Brown, Hulswit and Kettelle, published in *Operations Research*. A brief summary is given here but the complete paper is included in *Marketing Models: Quantitative and Behavioral,* edited by Ralph L. Day.

Background. The company was a large commercial printer worried by its lack of growth despite the buoyancy of business in the territory covered. This was particularly trying because the company standards of workmanship and price were well up to the norms of the industry (the management were sure these should not be altered) and at the same time the company spent more than the average for the industry on sales promotion. It appeared that improving the company's position was dependent on improving its selling effort.

Study. Examination of the market produced the following information which was confirmed by cross-checking where applicable:

Total market $30 million representing 13,000 customers.

Company's share $6 million (20 per cent) from 3,500 customers (24 per cent).

Company total promotional expenditure $500,000, of which $425,000 was salaries, expenses and administration, $75,000 was media advertising.

There were 35 salesmen each making at least 200 sales calls per month; they spent their time equally between regular worthwhile calls, door-to-door canvass and calling immediately on potential customers who had sent in enquiries.

Table 1 shows the breakdown of the market. The questions to be answered were:

"Who are the customers we want?"
"How big are they?"
"What are their buying habits?"
"How do they respond to (total) promotional effort?"

Top section of significant customers(%)	Customers' monthly revenue($)	Percentage of revenue	Number of customers	Total annual revenue ($ million)
1	over 2,870	31·0	130	9·0
5	over 880	56·5	650	16·8
10	over 480	71·0	1,300	20·7
20	over 220	85·5	2,600	24·9
30	over 140	89·5	3,900	26·1
40	over 85	94·0	5,200	27·3
50	over 55	97·0	6,500	28·2

TABLE 1: *Number and size of printing customers*

The market analysis showed that the business was very much concentrated among a small group of large buyers, in fact 20 per cent of the total buyers accounted for over 85 per cent of the total business. This was higher than expected. Furthermore, almost 90 per cent of all buyers favoured one supplier to the extent that they gave more than half of their business to him. This also was contrary to former dogma that buyers always shared out their business as an "insurance policy" against delivery failure.

This led the company to revise its views. The management believed that more personal selling and less expenditure on advertising would produce better results. Further, they believed that they should try to become the biggest supplier of the customers they already had, especially as the 3,500 customers concerned accounted for about 85 per cent of the industry's business (not shown in Table 1). The first three questions were answered. What about the fourth?

Cutting down advertising would free more money for selling effort; concentrating on their own customers and cutting out "enquiry calls" would free selling time, as also would cutting out the "cold canvass" of door-to-door calling. A plan was therefore made taking into account this time and money and the clear importance of concentrating on the large customers with the objective of clarifying whether big buyers would respond to promotional effort.

Eighteen salesmen were selected and, in consultation with the management, each took 36 customers who were then divided into three groups; one would be given a high effort level of 16 hours' attention per month, one a medium effort level of 4 hours' attention per month and the third a low effort level of 1 hour's attention per month. These effort levels included call preparation, actual selling time, entertaining, etc., and the plan was to be operated for three months.

Effort level	Hours/month	Customers/ salesman	Hours/month total
High	16	4	64
Medium	4	8	32
Low	1	24	24
All	0	36	120

TABLE 2: *Intended levels of effort*

The plan was makeshift in that the company did not attempt to select balanced groups or adopt a rigorous selection, since it had to protect its current business. The groups were partially selected on the basis of expected potential, but also on whether or not customers could be expected to absorb the various levels of effort. Generally, the high level group were those customers considered to be of the largest potential and also capable of absorbing the time. The medium group were some smaller customers and some large ones who could not absorb the highest effort. The third group were regular customers whom the company wished to hold plus a few new customers who did not qualify for the higher groups.

Records were kept of actual sales and those sales which might have been expected under the old system. Not surprisingly, the effort intended could not be accurately maintained, but it was kept to a higher level than that previously given. The results were shown in terms of additional effort and response. (A customer "responded" if his turnover with the company increased by a significant proportion of his estimated potential.)

Months since effort increased	RATE OF EFFORT (%)		
	Under 5 hours/month	5 to 9 hours/month	Over 9 hours/month
0	0	10	25
1	0	24	20
2	8	37	0
Cumulative, 3 months	8	53	40

TABLE 3: *Percentage of customers responding versus sales effort*

The groups are those getting less than 5 additional hours of attention, those getting 5–9 hours more attention and those getting over 9 hours *extra* attention per month.

The figures indicated that the 5–9 hours extra effort was the most effective rate. Over 9 hours seemed to be more than the customer could absorb—remembering that the table shows *extra* effort and the normal average was 2 hours per month.

What was clear was that the most profitable subjects were indeed the largest customers. These were rather less likely to respond than the others, but when they did the results were much the most rewarding. From the effort point of view, it seemed that extra hours spent on the largest group were 250 per cent as effective as extra hours spent on customers below the median in terms of revenue increase per unit of effort. Typically, reaction was delayed, then came a sudden jump. The size of this jump *averaged* 25 per cent of customers' estimated potential revenue and two-thirds of the customers had responded by the third month of the experiment.

Whilst it was not suggested that this case was by any means rigorously conducted, it was convincing enough and the detailed statistical support sound enough for the management to recast their sales operation. Each salesman was asked to concentrate on 31 accounts which would take up about 110 hours' work each month; 25 of these were "holding accounts" where the objective was to retain business and 6 were "conversion accounts" where the objective was to convert the business into a major share of the customer's needs. This, it was estimated, would enable the current sales force to expand the business to about $8 million per year after allowing for a normal loss of 5 per cent of customers annually.

This is an interesting study. It is intended merely as an example of what can be done but it may indicate worthwhile areas to investigate in our own operations. Whilst this example shows an application of marketing cost analysis to a problem of selling techniques, an examination of the detail of any area of marketing costs will usually point the way to a potential source of benefit.

Suggested Reading

BATTY, J. *Corporate Planning and Budgetary Control,* Macdonald & Evans, 1970.

CHAPTER 15

The Application of Quantitative Methods to Marketing Strategy

Brand loyalty

A great deal of thought has been devoted by writers on marketing to the use which can and should be made of quantitative methods in seeking to evolve more effective marketing policies. Some of the areas explored are largely conceptual as yet: for example, no one has so far produced a satisfactory formula by which the marketing manager can calculate the optimum size of an advertising campaign—nevertheless much has been done to expose the nature of the factors involved and this alone is worthwhile as a first move towards the eventual solution of a problem of real importance .The paper by A. A. Kuehn, "A Model for Budgeting Advertising", in *Mathematical Models and Methods in Marketing*, marked a considerable advance in the right direction. Elsewhere, much time has been spent in examining the concept of brand loyalty, how this affects the future buying behaviour of consumers, the extent to which it may be possible to measure the loyalty of buyers towards particular branded goods and then how to use this measurement as a guide in formulating marketing strategies.

Brand loyalty is the degree to which buyers of a branded product tend to continue to buy it. Some buyers when they have bought a product once will continue to buy it every time they require such an item thereafter. Others will never buy it again. The majority buy it again sometimes but not always. The actions of most buyers will be governed by their overall view of all the products of which they are aware in any particular field, the availability of these products in the shops which they patronise and the current advertising and promotional activities of the relevant manufacturers and retailers.

There are many practical difficulties in quantifying brand loyalty and then applying the results in formulating and assessing marketing strategies. Where purchase of an item is sufficiently frequent to enable the behaviour of buyers to be followed through a series of purchases, the market tends to be constantly changing as each manufacturer strives to gain an advantage for himself or to combat the moves of a competitor; where purchase is infrequent, the market may be relatively stable but the time needed to cover an adequate number of purchases makes research almost impossible. Let us, however, look at what may eventually be accomplished (attempts are known to have been made but no successful results have yet emerged publicly).

Brand switching analysis

This is one of the more attractive-looking approaches and it consists of an analysis of brand switching based on a development of the work of Bayes, an 18th-century English mathematician, who was one of the originators of the modern theory of probability, and Markov, a Russian mathematician (1856–1922) who developed a theory of prediction based on the assumption of a succession, or chain, of events each one of which stood in a constant relationship with its immediate predecessor.

Before going further let us define one or two other terms:

Brand share is the proportion of the total business in a particular product field which is held by a specified brand.

Brand switching occurs when a buyer, having bought one brand, changes and buys another at the time of his next purchase.

Probability of purchase is the proportional likelihood of a specified purchase being made next time. This is usually indicated as a decimal figure; unity is held to indicate complete certainty that the action will be taken; the sum of all the probabilities of all the possible actions in one particular situation equals 1. For example, if a buyer must buy a product, say cigarettes, when next he goes shopping, and there are only three varieties, A, B and C, which he can buy, then the probabilities of his buying these particular brands may be: A, 0·5; B, 0·3; C, 0·2, thus indicating that there is a 50 per cent probability of his buying A; a 30 per cent probability of his buying B; and a 20 per cent probability of his buying C.

Let us now assume that we have three products and only three families which buy them. An examination of purchases made (as maintained in a diary record by each family) shows the following sequence of purchases:

Time period:	1	2	3	4	5	6	7	8	9	10	11
Family 1	A	A	A	C	C	A	A	A	A	A	A
Family 2	C	B	C	B	B	B	B	B	B	B	A
Family 3	B	C	A	C	A	C	B	C	C	C	C

The total purchases of each product are:

$$
\begin{array}{ll}
A & 12 \\
B & 10 \\
C & 11
\end{array}
$$

If period 1 in the purchasing series in the Table is taken as time "t", the origin of the series, then each family makes ten purchases thereafter. If we can assume:

(a) that the probabilities of switching from one brand to another continue in the same pattern as above;

(b) that these probabilities are determined only by the particular product last purchased;

(c) that there is no change in products, or other stimulation or change in the market situation;

then the following table of purchase relationships can be made out:

Brand purchased on occasion t	Brand purchased on occasion t + 1, i.e. next occasion after t		
	A	B	C
A	7	0	3
B	1	6	3
C	3	3	4

Dividing the number of re-purchases of each product by the total number of purchases by each of our original families after their initial purchase gives the probability (p) that, having initially bought one brand, they will buy that brand again, or if not, which of the other two they will buy. The sequence of purchases in this case does show that if brand B is the last one purchased the probabilities are that the buyer will buy brand A on 1 occasion in 10 (p = 0·1) brand B on 6 occasions in 10 (p = 0·6) and brand C on 3 occasions in 10 (p = 0·3).

This can be shown as a network of transition probabilities.

Network of Transition Probabilities

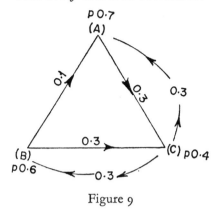

Figure 9

The consumer loyalties are now clearly seen; A and C gain from both the other brands whilst B gains only from C, but A has a higher and C has a lower brand loyalty. This would apparently stem from the product itself as switching does also occur from the other products to C. The assumption in this situation may therefore be that, as a general policy, brand A may be advised to think in terms of marketing action such as promotions, aimed at persuading buyers to switch from other brands to A, provided these do not affect the present brand loyalty based on the present brand image.

Similarly brand C may be in a position where such a policy would be inappropriate since there is a high probability that, even if buyers are persuaded to buy this brand, they will immediately leave the brand for another one next time. Here a policy devoted to creating more loyalty would seem to be the first requirement.

Continuing with our assumptions that the purchasing probabilities remain constant, a forecast of future sales can be derived from the current situation. (Furthermore if the expenditures on the policies decided upon can be estimated, both turnover and profit figures can be forecast too.)

Forecasting sales

If:

$$\text{SAt} = \text{Sales of A at time t}$$
$$\text{SA(t + 1)} = \text{Sales of A at time t + 1}$$
$$\text{pAA} = \text{probability of buying A at t + 1 if bought A at t}$$
$$\text{pBA} = \text{probability of buying A at t + 1 if bought B at t}$$

and similarly SBt and SCt for sales of B and C respectively, then

$$SA(t + 1) = SAt\ pAA + SBt\ pBA + SCt\ pCA$$
$$SB(t + 1) = SAt\ pAB + SBt\ pBB + SCt\ pCB$$
$$SC(t + 1) = SAt\ pAC + SBt\ pBC + SCt\ pCC$$

and

(1) Sales at t_0 = A   12
                 B   10
                 C   11

(2) Sales at t_1 = A $(12 \times 0.7) + (10 \times 0.1) + (11 \times 0.3) = 12.7$
                 B $(12 \times 0.0) + (10 \times 0.6) + (11 \times 0.3) = 9.3$
                 C $(12 \times 0.3) + (10 \times 0.3) + (11 \times 0.4) = 11.0$

(3) Sales at t_2 = A $(12.7 \times 0.7) + (9.3 \times 0.1) + (11 \times 0.3) = 13.12$
                 B $(12.7 \times 0.0) + (9.3 \times 0.6) + (11 \times 0.3) = 8.88$
                 C $(12.7 \times 0.3) + (9.3 \times 0.3) + (11 \times 0.4) = 11.0$

These forecast sales shown can then be tabulated.

Time period	Sales		
	A	B	C
t_0	12·000	10·000	11·000
1	12·700	9·300	11·0
2	13·120	8·880	11·0
3	13·372	8·628	11·0
4	13·523	8·477	11·0
5	13·614	8·386	11·0
6	13·668	8·332	11·0
7	13·701	8·299	11·0
8	13·720	8·280	11·0
9	13·732	8·268	11·0
10	13·739	8·261	11·0
∞	13·750	8·250	11·0

This leads eventually to stability when

$$A = 13.75$$
$$B = 8.25$$
$$C = 11.0$$

    Market analysis of this kind would undoubtedly be of great assistance to the marketing manager but there are great difficulties yet to be overcome in translating this concept into practice. The complexity of calculations is no great problem if electronic data processing facilities are available but the collection of the original data is a formidable task.

We have so far made some quite unreal assumptions—that the products and market should not change and that each purchase is determined only by its immediate predecessor. But in real life there are other troublesome factors. Buyers do not all buy with the same frequency; they do not all buy the same quantity when they buy; the individual buyers may buy the same quantities on different occasions or drop out of the market temporarily or completely. Is it possible to use the idea of analysing buying activity at all in the face of these difficulties?

Two possibilities do, so far, exist. One is to examine the pattern of purchases from a sample of consumers on a continuous panel such as is operated at Attwood Statistics or AGB Research. The other is to run a series of controlled operations in shops, where the price of brand X (the brand under examination) is alternately raised and lowered whilst the prices of all its competitors are kept constant. Such an experiment is described in detail by E. A. Pessemier in *Experimental Methods of Analysing Demand for Branded Consumer Goods*, which is also included in *Marketing Models: Quantitative and Behavioral*, edited by Ralph L. Day.

Here Pessemier describes an investigation of the toilet soap and toothpaste markets in the U.S.A. using this technique of controlled shopping tests in order to investigate the loyalty of buyers to different brands. This loyalty was measured by the degree to which buyers of a brand continued to buy that brand or turned to another, as the price of each brand in turn was maintained in the face of price cuts of different amounts among all competing brands.

Even with this data, the practical use of this technique is at the moment still limited. It is true that future sales could be projected and, if alternative policies and their effects could be costed and calculated respectively, a whole promotional strategy could be postulated and evaluated.

Yet this would be of little value until a means were found of evaluating the probability of brand switching between brands on some more reliable and exhaustive basis than mere last purchase, which is the factor we have assumed to be the only important one in this discussion. Last purchase may well be the most important single factor, of course, but there are numerous others, particularly purchases on previous occasions (from how far back would they be influential?). Changes in competitive products, changes in competitive promotional activity, changes in the availability of products and changes in the economic environment: these are the more important factors but all affect what the buyer will do "next time".

Nevertheless this kind of quantitative approach in itself offers a number of valuable guides to better marketing practice. It shows a good deal about the composition of a common marketing problem. It emphasises the need to examine the gain and loss of new buyers. It indicates which brands may have an incentive towards marketing strategies based on encouraging buyers of other products to try them or, alternatively, which brands would be well advised to try and build up their positions so that buyers continue to buy them and are not wooed away so easily to other brands. Above all it is immediately valuable in showing the marketing manager where lie the gaps in his knowledge not only of his competitors' but also of his own products.

Brand share prediction

So that this should not be considered a merely theoretical digression, let us briefly consider a different approach with somewhat similar objectives developed in the U.K. by Attwood Statistics Ltd. and described in a paper "The Use of Consumer Panels for Brand Share Prediction", given by J. H. Parfitt and B. J. K. Collins at the 1967 conference of The Market Research Society.

Here the investigators have evolved a method of analysing the buying behaviour of people buying either new or established products which takes into consideration buying behaviour after the first period in which the brand under consideration was bought and relating the re-purchases to the first purchase rather than, for example, to the calendar dates. They have also devised a method of evaluating the amounts purchased in order to take into consideration the volume of purchases by buyers of one brand against the amounts of all others in the field bought by those same buyers, and also the amounts of other brands bought by buyers who only bought other brands.

The basic data is taken from the Attwood consumer panel, where housewives record in a diary their actual purchases in a number of product fields. There are three basic concepts:

(a) *Penetration of the brand.* This is the cumulative total of housewives buying the specified brand, shown as a proportion of all the housewives buying in that product field over the period. (Figure 10 shows an example of the penetration of a new brand (T) in the toilet soap field.)

(b) *Repeat purchasing rate.* This is the total of repeat purchases of the specified product made by buyers, subsequent to their first trial, shown as a proportion of *their* total purchases in the field over the period.

For example the buyers of the new toilet soap (T) may over the period buy a total of 100 units of toilet soap of which 25 are units of brand T. Their repeat purchasing rate is thus 25 per cent.

Penetration of Market by Toilet Soap T

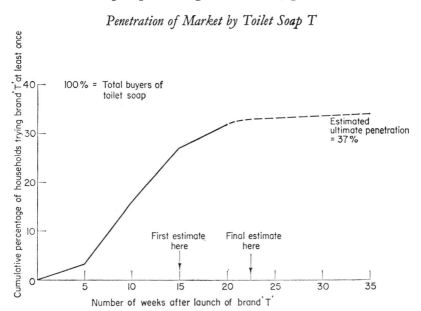

Figure 10

(*c*) *Buying rate index.* This is the relationship between the quantities of all products in a field bought by the buyers of a specified brand compared with the quantities bought by all the other buyers in that field.

There are, for example, heavy, medium and light buyers of most products according to their circumstances. This refinement allows for the possibility that buyers of a specified brand may differ in their usage from the other buyers in that field. The average for all buyers must be 1·0 but heavy buyers may average 1·2 and light buyers only 0·8 units so that the total purchase made per 100 could be:

Heavy users   100 × 1·2 = 120 units
Average users   100 × 1·0 = 100 units
Light users   100 × 0·8 = 80 units

From these three concepts it is clear that:

Penetra-	Repeat	Buying	Ultimate
tion of ×	purchas- ×	rate	= brand share
the brand	ing rate	index	of market

This is illustrated in Figure 11.

Brand Share of Soap Product T

Penetration = 34% ; Buying rate index 1·20 ;
Repeat purchasing rate = 25% ; Estimated brand share = 10·2%

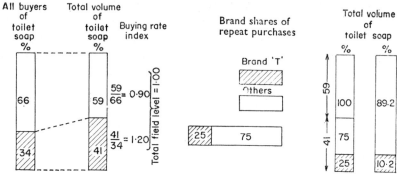

Figure 11

Figure 11 shows the progression of the calculation from the estimated 34 per cent buyers of brand T who would buy altogether 41 per cent of the total toilet soap volume. Their buying rate index is thus 1·20. The repeat purchasing rate is shown as 25 per cent of the total purchases of buyers of brand T. The estimated breakdown of the total market is shown in the right hand columns. 41 per cent of the total volume is bought by buyers of brand T and 25 per cent of this amount is represented by purchases of brand T—10·2 per cent of the whole market.

There are two points of particular importance in this analytical approach. The investigators claim that over a considerable number of similar analyses of consumer products, a pattern emerged which has allowed them to predict quite accurately, from the data available within only a few weeks of the launching of a product, what penetration a brand will ultimately achieve and hence from this calculate the brand's ultimate share of the market. If this can be done for new product launches or for re-launches of altered old products, then the manufacturer will be able to know much earlier than hitherto whether his new product is going to be a success or not.

Secondly, Parfitt and Collins show that in all the cases they have investigated, later entrants into the category of buyers of a brand tend to buy markedly less than earlier entrants and thus have proportionately less influence on the share of the market which the brand achieves. The corollary of this is that if, when a product is launched in the kind of field which this work covers, it does not make good headway in the early days it may never do so. Those later buyers who may be attracted by special promotional offers will not make the radical improvement to market share which a product which initially is a relative failure, will need in order to achieve final success.

Both the theoretical approach and the fieldwork approach described here do tend to indicate what many marketing men know by intuition even if they cannot prove it by quantitative methods. This is that the ultimate future of a brand is dependent basically on its fundamental acceptance by consumers. This is only a way of saying that the brand depends on the brand loyalty of its purchasers, which itself is a reflection of its brand image.

Neither of these approaches offers a theoretical or practical formula for arriving at a means of optimising marketing activities. They do, however, focus attention on relevant factors and possible means of indicating the future of a project. In the latter connection it is interesting to note that the investigators claim that a "Brand share prediction" can be worked out from a test marketing operation to show accurately what share of the total market a new product will probably achieve. It would certainly seem to the author to promise, at least, to indicate at a very early stage where intrinsic product weakness is such as to demand a complete new product approach before the projected brand can have a reasonable hope of success. This alone will make it worthwhile to pursue these techniques.

APPENDIX TO CHAPTER FIFTEEN
Some uses of computers

Computers in marketing

Whilst this is not the place for an exhaustive discussion of computers and their usefulness as a marketing tool we should, in any account of quantitative approaches to marketing, give some indication of their value. Hitherto the use of hunch and intuition in marketing has been largely due to three factors. In the first place marketing managers did not have all the information they would ideally like to have had because it was too expensive in time and money to get the necessary detailed information. Secondly, if the information were obtained, by the time it could be assembled in usable form it was out of date and inapplicable. Thirdly, managers did not know that some desirable information could be obtained at all and thus could not consider it in their assessment of the situation.

A computer is an electronic device for taking a series of factors and sorting, analysing or combining them in simple or complex patterns with great accuracy and at great speed. It cannot however *think*—it can only take data which has been given to it and stored in its "memory" and rearrange this in accordance with a "program" which must also be fed in. An important feature is that the data must be fed in in a form which the machine can handle; this means that the information so put in must be translated on to cards, tapes or discs in a suitable code, usually by a hole punching or a suitable magnetising operation. The data must be clear and unambiguous. It must also be accurate since there is scarcely any operation which can rival a computer in its capacity to produce literally miles of paper nonsense in next to no time if the original data is inaccurate or the program misdirected.

There are many ways in which the marketing man can benefit from the assistance of a computer in both the planning and the control of his operations and comparatively few firms seem yet to have realised the extent to which computers can help in this field. Let us look at a few examples of what can be done.

Sales analysis

Computers are being increasingly used to process orders and produce delivery notes, corresponding invoices, lists of shortages "to follow" and stock remaining. If the invoices are coded to give the information, they can also be sorted by the computer to give analyses of:

(*i*) geographical distribution of products or groups of products;

(*ii*) the distribution of sales among particular industries or different types of customer (e.g. self-service or counter-service shops);

(*iii*) the distribution of sales in total, or for any particular product, by size of the total order or by size of the order for any particular product;

(*iv*) the distribution of sales at special prices against those at normal prices, or against any earlier pattern which has been determined;

(*v*) sales in total, or by product, made by individual salesmen or groups of salesmen;

(*vi*) the profitability of sales made by salesmen (i.e. the actual contribution made in relation to local sales costs).

Sales analyses of this type can, of course, be used for control purposes to see if the operation concerned is running according to plan. If it is not, remedial action can be initiated at once; weaknesses not previously apparent (for example the existence of completely unprofitable activities) can be detected and eliminated; but the whole·object of analysing what has already happened is essentially to give factual information on which to base better plans and improve future operations.

Forecasting

Computers can be a most valuable aid in making sales forecasts. They have already been programmed in a number of instances to show up trends and relationships in internal company activities which have been projected to give very accurate short-term forecasts of future events. So far, however, much less has been achieved in the production of programs incorporating external factors such as rates of interest, general economic activity, competitive company influences and so on. Now that a tool such as the computer is available there can be little doubt but that techniques will be evolved to cope with forecasts further into the future with increasing accuracy, as more experience is gained of what has happened in the past, what the important factors are and what the inter-relationships of these factors are.

Warehouse siting and stock control

One of the most obvious of the uses of a computer to the marketing man is in the siting and control of stocks of a product. Deciding where to maintain warehouses or depots has in the past been substantially a matter of how a company has grown to the stage of needing depots, together with intuitive judgment on the part of those managers concerned at the time. Seldom was a real effort made (often it was not possible) to try and calculate exactly where a warehouse should be situated. The complexity and multiplicity of the factors concerned, and the lack of knowledge of how some of them affected the situation militated against a scientific approach so that sites were chosen on a basis of best judgment as and when a depot or depots seemed to be required.

Now, costs of transport from factory to warehouse, from warehouse to customers, rents, wage rates, space required, all can be worked into a program on a computer to show what effect changes in these factors would have on the optimum site. Thereafter the nearest available position to the optimum site can be taken. Furthermore the computer can be programmed to show the optimum level of stocks for each and all of the products concerned at each site, and the daily deliveries needed there. This, too, is done from an appropriate coding on invoices or delivery notes.

Advertising planning

Computers can also be of great help in developing advertising media schedules. The data to be fed in is the cost of different spaces, the description of the audiences of the possible advertising media, the description of the audience which the advertiser wishes to reach, the frequency with which he would ideally prefer his advertisements to appear, and the appropriation which he has available for the purpose. The computer can then be programmed to work out the best arrangement of his schedule according to the criteria he has adopted. If the information on the current availability of advertising space is also included this too can be taken into account. Alternatively a number of different possible plans can be produced, working on a number of possible situations, each programmed and considered separately.

Yet another use for a computer evaluation is in selecting possible test-marketing areas where the characteristics of the universe are compared with those of a number of possible areas, and either the best fit is demonstrated or the relative variances between the possible test areas is shown in order of magnitude.

The foregoing is not a complete list of the ways in which a computer can be used in marketing operations. Almost any problem can be examined so long as the marketing manager can produce data for either an actual situation, or a simulation model, where the relevant factors and their inter-relationships can be shown. The most profitable mix of products over a range of sales levels and marketing and production costs for each is a typical instance, but the reader must bear in mind that in all these cases the real problem is not to get the computer to work on the data but to get adequate and complete data in the first place, and to keep it up to date. If the manager is personally considering a variable known to be within a range of say eight to ten units the error possible is only two units. If the data given to a computer is in hundreds of thousands and complicated relationships are involved the error may be enormous. If there should also be an unknown factor which is not included in the latter calculation, the result may be an utter nonsense. This sort of nonsense would soon be detected if it were perpetrated by people working manually on a problem, but there is some danger that if the same answer were to come out from a computer "it must be right". Again, a computer cannot think: it depends on the accuracy and validity of the data and the programs fed into it.

Suggested Reading

HUGO, I. ST. J., *Marketing and the Computer,* Pergamon, 1967.

MORRIS & WOODGATE. *Computers in Management,* B.B.C. Publications. (A short, readable, B.B.C. publication.)

MUDDICK, R. G., *Mathematical Models in Marketing,* Intertext, 1971.

CHAPTER 16

Resource Analysis and Long Range Planning

The case for rationalisation

In earlier chapters we have discussed means by which the marketing manager should control his range of products in order to achieve optimum results. We have also discussed the importance of setting sound and clear objectives from the top of the company downwards, and of ensuring that each goal in succession really does help directly towards the attainment of the one above. In order to ensure that the whole operation is on the right track, however, it is clearly necessary that the marketing manager should periodically review the whole situation to determine his company's current position and decide whether any change in objectives is either desirable or necessary.

In very many companies such an examinination will probably show one or more areas where "Pareto's law" appears to apply. This is a principle, based originally on statistical work carried out by Pareto in Italy in the 19th century, which broadly states that 80 per cent of total results can be attributed to 20 per cent of total activity. Drucker found, over a wide range of industrial operations, that this was broadly so; Beeching found that 80 per cent of British Rail costs could be attributed to 20 per cent of the rail network. In the U.K. grocery trade 80 per cent of the turnover is achieved in 45 per cent of the shops and the gap is widening; recently the author was most interested to hear the senior technical research engineer of a highly renowned engineering company state categorically that 80 per cent of his quality problems occurred in a range of 20 per cent of the causes of those problems. There seems a good deal of support for the general principle.

If, therefore, the marketing manager finds similar areas where the vast majority of his costs fall on a small minority of his sales, whilst the great majority of his profits emanate from an equally small (though different) segment of his sales, why should he not concentrate on the most profitable area and withdraw entirely from the other less profitable area? 80 per cent of present sales at 20 per cent of current costs! A happy vision. To settle on this would only seem to be sensible and proper, a rational use of resources and good business for his shareholders. Why not?

Factors preventing complete rationalisation

If we, as manufacturers, concentrate only on those products which it suits us to sell because they are the most profitable, we get into trouble at once with our customers, trade or industrial. Our customers resent this kind of concentration on what suits us—because they cannot do the same. They have to please their own customers (the general public or other industries, are both in the same category here) and therefore have to do what their customers require. Clearly we must do the same; the customer is king and all manufacturers and traders in a free society must, in the ultimate analysis, acknowledge this.

The customer wants service of whatever kind is appropriate to his particular requirement, be it ease of purchase, prompt delivery, a fair price or technical advice. He wants to choose for himself from a range of goods which will satisfy his personal idiosyncrasies and wants, and it is the satisfaction of *his* needs that he aims at, not the convenience of *our* accountants or production men. The restriction of the consumer's choice to suit the manufacturer or trader is a very practical issue and already there are signs of buyer resistance when it is attempted. For example in the search for greater and greater efficiency some grocery supermarkets do not stock certain less popular items such as bay leaves or waterglass because "they aren't worth it". How far this has gone or may go is not at all clear but if housewives really do find that they cannot get the *service* they want from some shops can it be doubted that they will go elsewhere, even if it means to the old-fashioned counter service grocer who "gets what his customers want"? Perhaps he will set up as a specialist supplier right next door and make his fortune!

The argument is a strong one. The customer must be right. Yet competition, the need to develop efficiency, the need of the business, even the needs of the country—require that we should try and improve our operations. We should at least then try to strike a sensible compromise between our own interest and that of the customer and if our assessment of the needs of the customer is right, then the common area of his interest and our own should cover a very high proportion of our own activity. If we do not review our situation and keep very much on our toes we shall not stay in business long for surely our competitors will do just the things we have been discussing and we will cease to be effective.

Resource analysis

One way of looking at basic management indicates that there are three tasks to be achieved. *Firstly* the business must be made and kept efficient and profitable. *Secondly* the real potential for future development must be identified and steps taken to ensure that the company achieves this potential. *Thirdly* the management must examine the business in the light of the changing environment in all its manifestations, physical and psychological, material and human, and make sure that the business is adapting itself or changing itself to meet the changing situation.

Let us, then, examine the company's resources and their deployment. How do resources differ from assets? An asset is what appears in the financial statement and can be realised, that is, sold for money; a resource, on the other hand, is a possession which can be applied to achieving a recognisable objective and which may not in itself be immediately realisable nor even carry a formal value.

Plant and machinery

The company's material physical assets are its factories and the machinery in them. We should go a little further, however, in our context. The assessment of physical resources should include the extent to which the plant is flexible (able to produce variation in products without major modification) and also the present level of loading (utilisation of capacity). If other items can be made or if the capacity is only 70 per cent utilised, the resources, when it comes to re-deploying them, are different from the case of a one-product plant 95 per cent employed to the full.

Organisation and personnel

These cover the management structure, the people composing it, the labour force, the relationship of men and management with the equipment in the factories, and the geographical distribution of these resources in relation to the potential markets. These, too, are present facts but the current organisation may not in fact be keyed to the potential markets because it was devised to suit the markets of some time ago and these may have changed and be still changing.

Finance

Financial strength is vital in relation to the size of the business and the plans for its future. No business can operate without the financial resources to sustain its effort until the results of all the work previously done produce a flow of cash back into the company.

Goodwill

This is a most difficult resource to evaluate. Accountants shudder to see it placed on the balance sheet as an asset and yet it can and should be a very valuable resource. Goodwill is the picture of the company and its products as seen by the market; it is the belief of the customers that the company's operations and its products are sound and that the company is one with which the customers will be pleased to do business, or for which a man will be pleased to work.

Knowledge

This is a separate resource and is different from personnel and organisation. It consists of the corporate know-how and understanding of the market, the products and the relationships of manufacturers and customers. It can literally be the greatest of all resources in a business. How widely is the knowledge spread; is it the minds of only a few men at the top or does it, grade for grade, permeate the whole business? Is it entirely based on techniques, on deep understanding of the technology of a *process*, for example the ways of dealing with oil, or is it based on the understanding of an *industry*, for example the generation and movement of electricity?

Is it based on human attributes? Some businesses have developed a knowledge of how to organise and operate a large decentralised business, such as Unilever in this country, or to run a number of separate businesses on a very light rein, such as Philips in Holland. Some businesses thrive on dealing with the consumer, others on knowing how to cope with the needs of other companies. Some, indeed, have shown a particular flair for being able to deal with people and bring the most unlikely bedfellows together in profitable harmony.

To excel in a particular field means having excellent knowledge and understanding of that field and the appraisal of resources should include the areas of knowledge, what is well done, what is not well done, what the specific knowledge is, how transient it is. Knowledge becomes obsolete like any other resource and finally ceases to have value.

Product leadership

Drucker (in *Managing for Results*), makes a real contribution to a constructive approach to business with the stress he lays on the concept of leadership. He says that a company leads, or is marginal. If it is marginal it will decline as the market changes. Leadership, he emphasises, very seldom spreads over the whole of a company's operations, or all of its products, and the important thing is that leadership is a status conferred by the customer. It is, therefore, a transitory thing depending on the dynamics of the market, how much, how rapidly, it changes. He defines leadership in a product as being a genuine advantage of the product in performance, reliability, price or specific service against its competitors so that it is the one product best fitted for a real customer need. The customer confers leadership on a product by being prepared to pay more for it than for those of its competitors, or by being prepared to wait for it rather than buy an alternative.

Drucker, then, advocates an examination of the company's product range in the light of this basic product philosophy. As a result he believes—and it is a very appealing approach—that there are two groups of product, one a series of clear-cut cases, the other a series of problem cases. Today's and tomorrow's *breadwinners* are leaders or leaders in the making; *productive specialities* are products which greatly assist the development of the company's goodwill; *development products* are those whose potentialities the company has not really grasped.

Examples of all of these exist in the world around us though by the very nature of things they will not stay in their categories for ever. The Volkswagen "Beetle" has been a very obvious breadwinner; quick frozen foods may well be a breadwinner of the future for someone; the Rolls-Royce motor car can almost certainly be classed as a productive speciality (the company is now primarily a manufacturer of aero-engines rather than of automobiles), though once the car was a breadwinner. The sleepers are difficult to see from outside the company, but until recently the idea of container goods transport, which was first tried before the war, might have been so designated and perhaps the Moulton cycle could have been another. Nor is it always possible for a company itself to be sure of its own products. The aim is always to produce a a leader, a breadwinner and the conception of the Vesta range of dehydrated dishes was clearly intended by Batchelors Foods to be a leader from the beginning; but not all projects are so successful.

Drucker's other group are the failures, yesterday's breadwinners, repairable products, unnecessary specialities, unjustifiable specialities and "investments in managerial ego". These again are generally easy to identify. Yesterday's successes abound and the only problem is to know when they have passed the demarcation line. Products which can be altered and given a new lease of life are common enough, especially in the consumables field such as soaps and some foodstuffs. Unnecessary and unjustified specialities are both in abundance in the industrial world where the multiplicity of sizes, types and variations of products from screws to fractional horsepower motors come into this grouping. Investments in managerial ego are seldom admitted but most large concerns have had their crosses to bear in trying to make a racehorse out of a milk float pony, and few companies have the courage shown by Ford (U.S.A.) in admitting the failure of the Edsel car and refusing to make it into an investment in further failure (see *Annals of Business: The Edsel* by John Brooks. Reprinted in *Marketing in Progress,* Ed. Barksdale, 1964). An investment in managerial ego occurs when the management will not let a failure die but keep on trying to push it on an unwilling market.

Change of status. We have touched on the problem of determining when a product has changed its status. There are two simple signs of this, so simple that their significance is not always noted. Firstly, if the sales performance of a product varies significantly, *up or down,* from that expected and there is no visible immediate and clear reason in the market environment, then that product has changed its status. Is it declining, is it yesterday's product or is it in fact proving to be the hoped-for break-through? Secondly, at what stage of its life-cycle is the product? If the cost of getting additional business is becoming more expensive then the marketing manager should accept the warning.

Fixing a "thus far" point is not easy (see page 21). Drucker suggests that if, when expanding sales, the extra cost involved (i.e. marginal cost) rises to 50 per cent of the net gain (i.e. marginal profit), that should be the limit; acceptance of this figure or any other must depend on a full knowledge of the figures, but a limit should be set. Generally a high break-even point can be taken as an indication of malaise, although there are industries, such for example as paper making, newspaper publishing and some chemical operations, where unless plant is kept operating at a very high level of capacity, profits are meagre indeed. This may not be a sign of changing status but it certainly is a sign of danger for the future.

Reappraisal of deployment

Having reviewed the resources and revalued them we should then be able to determine if the resources are well deployed not merely for the present but for the future. Can we make improvements or is the situation satisfactory? This is not merely a case of considering costs figures, profits but also of considering the market and the opportunities awaiting in the market. It is not a matter of *our* market but the *total* market for at any one moment *our* customers may not be those to whom we should be looking in the future.

Again, how far are we concerned with trying to solve some inner problem, some situation which has arisen from what we have come to do now, when we would be far better off devoting our best men, our chief resources to developing a new opportunity for the future? This is not to be taken as constantly looking for pie-in-the-sky but merely a plea that more time should be spent in this direction planning beyond the immediate operation.

All this comes down to a matter of redefining our business. What is it we are in business for? What is the business now and what should it be in the future? Again our approach should begin with the customer and the market.

Looking ahead

Underlying everything is our assessment of the opportunities in the market, what the trends are and what the requirements will be. Then we must select those opportunities which offer the best return for our particular resources in the same way as Drucker describes the development of Rothschilds by the allocation of the brothers to the different European capitals so that each could use to the full his own particular strengths (including keeping the incompetent Kalman in Naples where he could do no harm as there was no business to lose there). Our resources should be focused on our real opportunities and not diverted to other tasks.

We should therefore give the highest priority to the opportunities offering promise of the greatest progress. More than this, we should cut out and abandon weak and unprofitable lines. This we have already considered when discussing the simplification of the range (Chapter 2), but no excuse is needed for reiteration. When it comes to the practice of marketing it has been the author's experience that the decision to stop making a product is one of the most difficult decisions to take. Companies and managers will plan new products, new factories, launch new products. They will take products off the active list and milk them.

But when it comes to closing a product down—what difficulties are raised! In between, there are the marginal cases of products which we shall have to retain but only until such time as we can devise better ones.

Where are these opportunities? In what direction do we go? Do we literally expect that panacea for all marketing ills—market research—to go out and come back with the answers? Scarcely. One starting point is to look at the reasons why the company is held up in various directions. What are the reasons? Are there limiting factors in the market or our handling of the market? Are there unbalanced situations, e.g. have we very high sales costs and are these *really* caused by having too many salesmen? Are we in an industry where a new material is challenging our markets—for example plastic challenging wood or even metal?

Wherever such challenges or lack of balance exist one answer may be to grasp the nettle firmly and deliberately go in the other direction for if the basic limiting factor can be overcome the results can be very considerable indeed. This has been often done not merely by individual companies as when toy manufacturers went into plastics in a big way, but by whole industries, as when the textile manufacturers embraced the new man-made fibres. "If you can't beat them join them" has more than a little sense in it.

A second method may be to examine the existing situation thoroughly and systematically. Most innovation which really deserves the name takes quite a long time to get under way. If the innovation can be seen to have already started a basic change may be en route and we are forewarned. Self-service retailing in this country was seen soon after the war but it was several years before it really got into its stride in the grocery trade, where it has profoundly affected trading methods. It still has scarcely touched other trades but in view of the great differences it has already made in the grocery shops can it be doubted that it will spread with equally widespread effects in other directions?

These two possible starting points alone should point the way to a number of promising areas for exploration. New openings can be made by balancing what is unbalanced. If the selling operation is too large can we not find other products in related or complementary fields rather than cut down the size of the sales force? Unnecessary costs must surely be cut out but are there not new developments which we could embrace and thus retain a well-developed operation which only at present looks top heavy? Too often the view is "it can't be done" yet often it is already being done, though not acknowledged. When there is an argument that we should not manufacture for other companies to sell under their brand name ("own-name labels" as it is called in the retail world) but we are already doing this for one very good customer who is a "special case", we have already made the compromise. This shows it *can* be done. Wherever there is a compromise in existence the doubted action is already being performed.

Foretelling the future is not easy, but in many instances there are indicators and signposts. A great deal of what is going to be the future has already happened or at least has begun to happen. The young housewives of twenty years' time are already alive as young children; the middle-aged parents of teenage children in ten years' time were the newly weds of three or four years ago. Inventions which are the basis of the new methods and products which we shall see in a few years' time have already been made but they have not yet been developed. Container transport, which was only really getting going in 1967, was first tried in 1936. A whole range of products examined by the Economist Intelligence Unit in a report dated July 1966 indicated that from the inception of an idea to the marketing of a finished product on a wide scale, anything from two to ten years might be involved. Sometimes the reasons were the difficulties in overcoming technical problems, sometimes that the market was not yet educated to accept a radical change, sometimes that the inventor had not been able (or did not desire) to develop his idea into a marketing operation. Nevertheless if we can find the true innovation that has not yet been developed we can exploit this time lag and find ourselves out in front of our competitors.

The vital decisions are always simple in concept. What is our business mission to be? What particularly outstanding resources have we in our company? What priorities for products should we lay down? From these come our future plan and with that the dangers Levitt outlines in *Marketing Myopia* disappear—the dangers of being obsolescent in an obsolete industry. The consumer will always be king and we must court him with all our power even though like all kings in history his views and wishes are constantly changing.

Suggested Reading

BROOKS, J. *Annals of Business: The Edsel*, printed in *Marketing in Progress* (Ed. Barksdale), Holt, Rinehart & Winston Ltd., 1964.
DRUCKER, P. F. *Managing for Results*, 2nd edn., Pan, 1967.

CHAPTER 17

A Non-Statistical Approach to Marketing Decision Making

The nature of a decision

Few people like making decisions. Many people have an almost pathological fear of making a decision and taking responsibility for it. Many years ago the author used to wheel his small daughter to a boating pool where every Sunday morning the local model yacht club members exercised their very beautiful craft. He became quite friendly with many of them, for a small child is a wonderful introduction to a new group. One day a middle-aged member, usually full of fun, seemed very upset. It did not take long to find out the reason. This day was one when members were going to race each other. Nothing was at stake, no visitors, no cups, not even a ladder on the club room wall. But he was worried stiff. He had been appointed umpire, by rota, and had never carried out this role before. He admitted to a terrible fear of doing the wrong thing, of having to take responsibility in any way, for in his everyday artisan occupation he knew his job and obeyed orders: he did not have to control any of his fellow workers.

This is not a very unusual situation. Managers, of course, are only a small part of the total work force and they have rather different abilities and characteristics from the majority or they would not be managers. Nevertheless, there seems to be good reason to suppose that many managers dislike taking at least some decisions. When it comes to the margin of their capacity where the importance of the decision is relatively high, their assessment of the risk of being wrong is correspondingly great and they suffer at least some qualms.

Decision making is deciding between two or more possible courses of action. The quality of this decision is in any case dependent on whether the goal is correctly defined, whether all possible courses leading to the achievement of the goal are recognised and whether their outcomes are correctly evaluated. Most of the possible courses not chosen will have some favourable points and the more of these there are, and the nearer the discarded courses are in value to the chosen course, the greater will be the cognitive dissonance which the maker of the decision will feel when he has made it. This may be one reason why making a choice and committing oneself is distasteful to so many. Having to take the responsibility and stand by one's decision despite the fear of the consequences of being wrong is a potent reason for avoiding the situation wherever possible.

However, these factors are unlikely to play a very great part when the decision is relatively simple or the consequences are relatively minor. It is on the margin of the individual's capacity to make good decisions that the decision making becomes really distasteful. Let us then see if there are any signposts which may guide us in the decision making process.

We made the point when discussing long range planning that marketing is concerned with consumers who are people but that marketing practitioners are themselves also fallible people. Whilst more and more scientific and quantitative techniques are becoming available to help the marketing manager, the practice of marketing still remains an art using scientific supports, much in the same way as an architect uses his artistic senses to envisage and design a building, but uses various formulae to ensure that the structure stands firm once it is built. Standards in managerial ability appear to be rising all the time and good practice is apparently becoming better, but there are still very many examples (the reader can surely think of quite a few in his own experience?) of poor practice, sometimes of rank bad practice.

It is a commonplace still to find marketing plans only half conceived: individuals, whole departments, are given no clear view of what they are to do and when to do it. Co-ordination of effort is neglected to the verge of the suicidal. Production departments are not given firm dates for products to be ready, or even of the quantities to be made; transport departments are left hazy about movements of product; salesmen are half-briefed and left without samples to show their customers. These things happen, not necessarily all in one operation, but they should not and need not happen at all.

Decision/planning model

A model is a pattern to follow. To have a model is not to have a golden key, but at least it can and will provide a check list which can be applied to help the decision maker to tackle his work logically and progressively. If this is done, much of the pain and reluctance is taken out of the situation—and as a more careful approach is made, better decisions will be made too.

The following is a verbal model which gives one logical way of going systematically through not merely the making of the decision but the after-work. Follow-up and follow-through are every bit as important as the making of the plan.

Let us, then, put ourselves once more in the marketing manager's chair, where we must consider the following points.

Define the problem

This is one of the simplest possible rules—yet it is forgotten or disregarded in far more cases than should be possible. What *are* we trying to do? The more closely this can be defined the better; it is fine to talk of increasing profits or developing sales but these are not nearly precise enough. "Profits are to be increased by X per cent" could be a better goal, but better still would be "to obtain £X more net profit from product line Z". "Greater sales" can and should be much refined in terms of geographical area and the kind of sales improvement— cash, percentage, physical turnover, more buyers and so on. Should the objective be a conceptual one such as improving the company or brand image, this should be defined as a term and a statement made of the current situation so that a base line against which to measure progress actually exists. Above all else, however, we must ensure that the solution of this particular problem will also help us towards the achievement of the company's main objectives and not merely be an interesting (and possibly irrelevant) exercise. Therefore, *define* the problem.

Make an appreciation of the situation

Having defined the problem, before going any further we should make an orderly study, in detail, of the complete environment of the situation. This should, once more, begin with the customer, who he is, where he is, the patterns of his habits of buying, and his motivations towards buying. Then we should look at the competitive state of the market, who makes up our competitors, their philosophies, strengths

and weaknesses, their products and their relative advantages and disadvantages. We must look at our price levels and pricing policies and
those of our competitors as well and, in particular, see if there is any
pattern of competitive action, how strong it is and whether it is likely
to be different in the future. We should look closely at the nature of
competition in our market, whether it is based on price alone, or on
product improvements, or on advertising techniques and weight. We
should examine carefully the channels of distribution to evaluate their
efficiency, see whether there are any signs of internal changes and reorganisation and whether any alternative channels have been attempted
or should be attempted. This is all market examination and assessment.
We should then examine our own product, its performance, advantages
and disadvantages against its competitors, its image or reputation in
the market. Finally, we should consider our own company's operation
and organisation and how our administrative and production arrangements affect, assist or limit our marketing operations.

Examine the alternative ways of achieving the objective

We have a main objective. The next step is to describe the possible
ways of achieving this. This entails the setting down of the various
alternative courses and what results each will yield; for example, if the
overall objective is to make a defined amount of profit alternative
courses may be: to sell more product at a lower price; to put up the price
and accept a lower level of sales; to sell more product at the present
price by employing a greater sales effort or a greater advertising effort;
and so on. Each alternative course will have its own sub-objective and
we must ensure that in each case the attainment of this sub-goal will
indeed lead towards the attaining of the overall goal. Finally the
alternative courses of action must be sensible ones and not time-wasting
nine-pins merely set up to be knocked down again as being courses
which are not possible or, if possible, will not lead to achieving our
main objective.

Select the most suitable course

This is the actual decision. We will take it after weighing up the
advantages and disadvantages of each of the alternative courses which
we have already uncovered. There is usually a best course but sometimes it is not easy to select it if there are many imponderables and little
quantification for our guidance. No one can help here though advice or
opinion may be sought or offered. The manager has to use his own
judgment and make the final decision.

Define the sub-goals

Once we have decided on the course of action to be taken, we must clearly explain the way in which the chosen course is to be followed. We can do this by breaking down the operation into a series of sub-goals for our immediate assistants to achieve. Here again, as at the beginning of the exercise, the more clearly we define the sub-goals without doing a man's work for him, the better will our subordinates be equipped to go through the procedure themselves at the lower level. Each sub-goal must be described in detail giving the field concerned, the objective and the method of achieving the objective. The whole process is repeated at successive levels of operation and as these descend (according to the size of the business and the number of rungs on the ladder of communication), so the achievement of goals is left less to the discretion and judgment of the man concerned until at the final stage, the goal and the means of achieving it become one and the same—the means *is* the end.

Prepare alternative plans

At this stage, we should provide against—not the unexpected, but the failure of our plan to achieve its end. We must be realistic and remember that this can and does happen. We must lay down clearly the action to be taken if the original plans are forestalled for any reason showing the area in which the original plan failed and the corrective action to be taken. It is important that there should be no doubt as to the criteria of failure, who orders the new plan to be operative and when this is to be ordered. A separate alternative is needed for each failure which we may encounter.

Usually additional information not previously available, such as competitive or consumer reaction, will be a pre-requisite of a decision to adopt a corrective plan; one criterion may be of the type "increase sales by £X but if by date A the increase is not more than £X−Y manager D will put into operation alternative O". In all cases the criteria for action, the date and the initiating manager must be absolutely clear.

Estimate the expected achievement

This is an element often omitted. However uncertain the position is and however difficult the task of doing so we must estimate our expected achievement if we are not merely to drift. To do this we can use judgment, the inspiration of experience, market research, comparisons with other operations which have some affinity and from which some guidance may be drawn, but do it we must.

The nature of the plan

We must make this in detail and all but the most trivial matters must be committed to paper—"writing makyth an exacte man". The plan should show exactly who does what and the author has found it helpful for marketing operations to detail departmental responsibilities in separate appendices, though some practitioners dislike this as it leaves open the possibility of some departments never studying the operation as a whole. *Responsibilities* must be matched by *authorities* and the plan should make equally clear who has the authority to decide what action is to be taken at each stage. All necessary supporting information should also be included.

At this stage, depending on the complexity and importance of the operation and our authority as the decision maker, the next higher authority should be asked to agree and endorse the plan so that it can be put into action.

Communication

We should arrange that all necessary information is passed downwards and also sent back upwards. This latter may involve the use of special sales report pads, or the use of market research surveys, or merely a report on results from those involved in the operation. Whatever it is, we must decide *beforehand* what information other people need and arrange to get it to them, as well as what information we ourselves want back. It is too late once the plan is operating.

The operation, regardless of its scale, should be kept in view during its entire life. We must evaluate it *as we go along* and be prepared to amend it in the light of experience (even if alternative plans are never invoked). We have a new product launch, it goes better than expected. We should clearly take advantage of this, raise our sights and get along —provided we can get adequate production, administration, etc. We have a sales drive and it falls short—we must decide whether to revamp the whole operation, or part of it, and decide what to do about the supply of product coming forward. Finally we must remember two important provisos—one, not to take precipitate action before the information on the situation is adequate; two, to make sure that everyone knows about any changes and their consequences and that all are kept up to date on progress. Co-ordination means consultation and the creation of a sense of belonging, participation and responsibility.

A simple verbal model of this kind can be made for any decision that has to be made. The simpler the situation, the less elaborate the model and vice versa. Having a pattern, progressing step by step taking all the relevant matters into consideration, simplifies even the most difficult decisions. It also gives the decision maker confidence, for the reluctance to make decisions is very much bound up with the fear of doing the wrong thing—and this in turn often develops from hasty action taken without due consideration of the factors involved. Following this model will not make *all* decisions the best possible ones but it will certainly prevent many bad ones being made and improve the proportion of successes—which is the best most of us can do in the long run.

Suggested Reading

ROBINSON, P. J., & LUCK, D. J. *Promotional Decision Making,* McGraw-Hill, 1964.

CHAPTER 18

Is Industrial Marketing Different from Consumer Marketing?

The simplest definition of industrial goods which the author has come across is that given by J. E. Lonsdale in *Selling to Industry*: "Industrial sales are those of goods for running businesses." If we add to it "and institutions", which will then allow us to include hospitals, schools and public authority organisations, then the description seems quite comprehensive.

Why should this side of business be considered markedly different from the other, consumer side? Why does the man in an industrial marketing operation take such delight in saying to his consumer marketing colleagues, "Well, of course you can do that but we couldn't possibly run our business that way!" What way? The speaker could just as easily have been someone in a consumer operation, except that his language might have been rather more vigorous and colourful and job for job he might conceivably have been a few years younger. But why the mystiques? Are there really basic differences of principle and practice between consumer and industrial marketing operations or are the differences purely superficial?

As in most marketing discussions, there is no really easy, simple, all-embracing answer. On the surface, very much indeed is different. The numbers of people employed on the marketing side of a consumer food manufacturing business are usually great in themselves and large in relation to the total number employed in the whole business. The equivalent figures for a large capital goods manufacturer are likely to be much smaller in total and in proportion. Even then there are exceptions on both sides. Let us try and discover some of the likenesses as well as some of the differences and try to see just how different the two operations are.

Again, we must sound a warning note on the very real diversity of operations in each sphere—and the shadowy boundaries between them. We have already mentioned earlier the position of the typewriter as a part industrial, part consumer product. There are many other instances even as simple as that of an overall for use in the home and also in the office. Furthermore, whilst one product may at the same time be both an industrial and a consumer item, it is also quite common for one manufacturing company to make some products which are consumer items and therefore must be marketed through consumer channels, and other products which are industrial items and must be marketed through industrial channels. Either way there is considerable overlapping and many companies operate in both spheres.

Most motor vehicle manufacturers make both cars and commercial vehicles: the cars are both industrial and consumer products but the vans and lorries are essentially industrial products. Tool manufacturers make tools for both industrial and home use and often also make machinery which is entirely industrial, such as large power-driven cutting equipment. Yet fundamentally both industrial and consumer operations are based on the same concept, that marketing aims at providing satisfaction of customer needs at a profit. Thereafter the differing applications of the marketing mix tend to show much operating differences. Let us first, however, go back to the customer.

The industrial buyer

The industrial buyer is not free to please himself what he does. He is an organisation man, working in an organisation and subject to all the pressures and influences of the organisation. He has a job, a function to perform. His success is measured in part by the way people evaluate his performance, in part by the physical evidence of his skill as a buyer in obtaining his company's requirements, in part by his showing his capabilities by putting forward proposals of his own, such as the possibility of using new materials or products which come to his notice.

The professional buyer should have some advantages over the ordinary consumer-buyer as he has the help of a number of quite specific aids in making his buying decisions:

(*i*) *Specification.* Details of performance, design and make-up are frequently available for his guidance, whereas few counterparts occur in consumer buying.

(*ii*) *Delivery*. The requirements of the buyer as to time and place and the ability of the supplier to meet them, must both be matched for business to flow. The industrial buyer may have much more rigid requirements in this direction than the consumer buyer.

(*iii*) *Service*. Whilst this can occasionally reach extraordinary levels of complication, industrial sales service usually includes initial problem-solving (design), installation or erection, and post-installation assistance. Frequently buyers can specify service requirements. Usually suppliers will detail, as a matter of course, their acceptance of such responsibilities as ensuring proper functioning of machinery on installation, instructing operators and giving a warranty over an initial period. This applies much less to the consumer buyer who usually has only the retailer's or manufacturer's offer of after-sales service in limited fields (although most reputable manufacturers give serious attention to genuine complaints of faulty products). In some ways a manufacturer's advertising to the consumer (in so far as it gives information of performance) is a counterpart of industrial pre-sales service; so also is the advice tendered by a retailer in any counter-service shop.

(*iv*) *Price*. The industrial buyer usually has much greater knowledge of prices offered throughout the market than consumer buyers have. He is often in a position where price is not fixed as in a retail shop, but is a bargain struck between buyer and seller according to their respective strengths and needs.

(*v*) *Reputation of supplier*. This is partly a factual area depending on the buyer's actual experience, but is also a compound of hearsay, advertising and the impression made by various representatives. It is a psychological area in the midst of what is usually considered a most prosaic and factual world. All in all, perhaps, the industrial buyer should make more truly rational and logical decisions than the consumer, mostly because he is a skilled professional.

The buying decision is, however, still a matter of choice among alternatives and the guidance which these factors or requirements give to the buyer does not necessarily provide him with a readymade solution. Usually there will be more than one possibility and the position is much influenced by the number of alternative solutions of which the buyer is aware. Here too our behavioural approach helps us to understand the process of buying. The buyer can only make his choice from among the alternatives of which he is aware, i.e. his perception and his cognition widen or confine his range of choice according to the situation, which of course also includes his operational environment, the organisation in which he functions.

Organisational influences on the buyer

There is a well-developed theory about the growth and operation of organisations which also helps towards the understanding of industrial marketing operations. Let us consider some of the salient issues.

Much work in organisations is made into a programme; "routine" is an almost equivalent word. A programme in behavioural language is a "set of responses evoked by an environmental stimulus". It determines the behaviour of some individuals and groups and clearly affects buying activity. An example of a programme is the arrival of the mail in the morning. This starts off a complete routine of opening, sorting and delivering mail to departments and individuals, posting cheques in ledger accounts, sending invoices for checking, and so on, all set in motion by the arrival of bags of mail from the G.P.O. Another programmed activity may concern a standard raw material, say sugar used by a chocolate manufacturer. Sugar is drawn from the warehouse and is used up until the stock gets to a certain figure. At that point the storekeeper informs the buying department, who check current prices, select a supplier, place an order for delivery at a certain date and the delivery is made, checked and paid for—all a routine affair.

The extent to which programmed activity covers the work to be done depends firstly on the perception of those who make up the programmes, whether they see this or that action fitting into a programme which they can devise. If the particular action is not seen in this light then it will not be built into a programme. Secondly, when the occasion arises, those concerned have to decide whether or not a situation fits into any programme which has already been set up. If their perception of it indicates "yes" then the situation is dealt with in the programme. If their perception says "no" then the situation has to be dealt with outside the programmed area. So programmes are much influenced by perception.

Programmes are also affected by the objectives (or goals) of both the organisation and the individuals within them. As higher objectives are split down into lower or sub-objectives in rotation until finally the end aimed at and the means of achieving it become one and the same thing it is of great importance that each objective or goal should directly help the achieving of the next higher one. But as goals are set by individuals this does not always happen. For example the buyer may be trying to prove his own importance or build a personal empire, neither of which goals may help towards the objective of keeping his factory supplied efficiently. The disparity between higher and lower goals is one of the problems in organisational theory but further exploration is outside our current purpose.

A last influence on programmes is the efficiency and layout of the organisation's communications. Information may or may not pass easily; it may or may not pass both ways; at many stages it may be filtered so that it is distorted or only selected portions are transmitted; all this will affect the operation of the programmes. If the buying department does not know that the sugar stock is low, or is told too late, or is told that cocoa not sugar is needed, the programmed activity described earlier cannot take place.

We see then that organisational influences affect the industrial buyer because:

(a) much of what goes on in an organisation is determined by, or affected by, programmes;

(b) both the content of a programme and the way in which it is applied depend very much on individual perceptions;

(c) programmes are much affected by the degree to which those in the organisation adhere to sub-objectives which are congruent with (directly aiding the achievement of) higher objectives;

(d) the efficiency of communications overrides all the rest because if wrong information (or no information) is passed, then the right action, programmed or not, will not be taken.

The study of the industrial buyer in the background of his business environment is certainly a complex subject. He has guide lines, usually far more precise than anything which his consumer counterpart has, and he is a professional with the skills and objectives of a professional. But his expertise is limited by the complexities of the organisation of which he is a part—and in particular by the efficiency of its communications and its control procedures.

The supplier

Industrial marketing is possibly more segmented than consumer marketing in the sense that there is less opportunity to sell products which can be mass-produced. Much industrial marketing is concerned with custom-built equipment or, at best, of modified assemblies using a proportion of common components, and the demand for standard items, of which the requirements can be forecast and stocks built up before the sale, is comparatively small. There are some exceptions, as ever, mostly in the area of component supply, for manufacturers of bolts, brackets, hinges, valves, tubing can frequently adopt mass-production methods, but the scope is still proportionately limited over the whole field.

Market investigation is more difficult in many ways for the industrial supplier (see also page 94). Sampling techniques are always doubtful, for the total number of buyers is limited, and the 80/20 rule so often applies that some at least of the large buyers must be included to ensure an adequate sample. This may prejudice security, although this need not always be so. The researcher will have other headaches too. Who, in the respondent company, is *capable* of answering the questions we wish to ask? The buyer may be the man; equally it could be the Engineer, the Production Manager or even the Managing Director—and it varies from firm to firm. Even then, there are doubts. Are the companies listed the only ones making up "the market"? Could there in fact be other firms (even in other industries) who could use the product (or projected product)? If we don't know, then how can we be sure of our universe or our sample?

Despite the difficulties, much has been achieved in the field of industrial marketing research in recent years, particularly in the obtaining of quantitative information. Yet even when this is not possible, it is usually possible to get qualitative and motivational information, both of which can be of real help in the estimating of future trends and needs. Skilled interviewers can find out a great deal about what firms are doing, what they are considering, planning or investigating. The reasons why some products are selling well and others are not, why firms support some suppliers and fight shy of others: this kind of information is as important to an industrial goods supplier as its counterpart is to his consumer equivalent.

Some special features in industrial marketing

There are a number of special features in industrial marketing, some of which are similar, some very dissimilar to consumer marketing. The following list is abbreviated from Lonsdale (op. cit.).

(*i*) In industrial marketing, purchases are made for more rational reasons. This we have already discussed at some length; the buyer is a professional, he often has a specification for his purchase. He is, however, still subject to the vagaries of both human nature and his own organisation.

(*ii*) Industrial sales are often a multi-person or team activity: frequently the normal representative has to bring in technical help and occasionally more senior people when contracts or large orders are in question.

(*iii*) Industrial sales usually have a technical flavour: it is certainly true that until very recently most industrial goods manufacturers seemed to feel that technical knowledge was more important to their representatives than sales ability. There are now indications that this assumption is being challenged.

(*iv*) In industrial operations there may be a lengthy pre-sales, or at least pre-decision, period of activity: this process often begins with a problem the solving of which leads to technical discussion, specification, prototype, amendment and finally production. Few consumer purchases have an equivalent procedure.

(*v*) Sales service (pre- and post-sales) is more important in industrial marketing than in consumer marketing.

(*vi*) Industrially, the reputation of the seller is a major factor: in the world of consumer goods the brand name rather than the maker's name is often the important one.

(*vii*) The supplier's success is bound up with the success of his customer in industrial operations. In this respect an advertising agency is also a good example of an industrial (services) operation.

(*viii*) Industrial customers may be few in number; there are not many car manufacturers to buy automotive components or newspaper companies to buy high-speed news printing machinery.

(*ix*) Industrial customer firms may be concentrated in particular localities (e.g. makers of cars and cotton or woollen textiles) though there are influences gradually working against this (such as special governmental activity in certain high unemployment areas).

(*x*) The chain of distribution is usually short: manufacturing machinery for example is usually sold by the maker's salesman direct to the user.

(*xi*) The ordering of products may be infrequent: this is particularly true of large capital plant installations.

(*xii*) Stock holding and manufacture before sale is usually limited: although it does occur for standard items such as nuts and bolts and some components, as we have already mentioned.

(*xiii*) Individual orders may be of great value: electricity transformers, gas plants, motorways, ships are some outstanding cases.

(*xiv*) Trading may be reciprocal (that is, each company involved buys from the other): much has been written around this phenomenon but it seems likely that the "blackmail" element of this will have a decreasing effect as each company's marketing operation has a greater influence on the central management of the company.

(*xv*) Publicity and advertising are generally less dominant in industrial marketing: the opportunities of persuading a company to buy an item for which it has not seen a need are more limited; the potential customers are comparatively few and can be more easily visited compared with the consumer equivalents. In a moment, however, we will examine "back pressure" selling which in some ways contradicts this.

(*xvi*) Demand may fluctuate more violently either way in industrial marketing than is the case with consumer goods. Before we can decide whether this is true for, say, consumer durables we must define particular cases. Generally the point is valid. People must eat, or wash, or wear clothes, fairly consistently but companies can and do defer or bring forward the building of new factories or the installation of new machinery according to the state of business, and their expectation of the future.

(*xvii*) The effect of technological change may be felt faster and to a greater extent in industrial marketing. Consumers can carry on with old-fashioned radio or T.V. sets, but a company may go out of business if a competitor revolutionises his product or process and the original company does not. This happened when lorry manufacturers would not take up the original diesel engine but had to follow suit later.

(*xviii*) In industrial operations it may also be true that it takes longer and requires more capital investment to make a major change in direction than in the consumer field. Support for—and exception to— this can be found in many places.

Industrial marketing operations

These are not nearly so different from consumer marketing operations as might be expected. There is still the basic decision on the marketing mix and the importance of the different elements. Advertising, as we have seen, may not be so dominant, sales promotion may be almost non-existent, but sales *pressure* may be quite as high, and if stock cannot always be ready for delivery, before the sale is made, the delivery date itself can be of crucial importance as a sales tool.

In selling, because of the more rational backing and technical needs of the buyer, the most effective argument may frequently be the use of both sides of the case—the advantages, certainly, but also the disadvantages of the product since these will be clear in use when, in any case, the buyer will have learned of the weaker points of the product.

Despite this, there is abundant evidence to support the view that a company sells through a salesman, who is a person, to a buyer who is also a person and that the best results are still gained by selling the benefits to the man (in both his capacities as a buyer and as a person) trying to achieve his own goals.

One very interesting technique now being used by industrial manufacturers is to sell right through beyond his customer to his customer's customer in order to develop a demand from the latter. This is called "back pressure" selling. There are some very notable recent examples of this technique. For instance when the basic production of aluminium ingots looked as if it would be excessive for the market, the manufacturers began advertising to the general public as well as to builders and architects, showing them what advantages would accrue from using aluminium windows, frames, etc. This eventually led to an increased demand for aluminium components from the fabricators, who in turn required more aluminium from the raw materials supplier (the advertiser). Similarly, I.C.I. and Courtaulds have advertised to the general public the usefulness of man-made fibres in clothes, furnishings and carpets in order to develop the purchasing of them so that in turn the raw materials manufacturers (I.C.I. and Courtaulds) could sell more to the various textile manufacturers. This, of course, is very similar in concept to manufacturers' advertising consumer goods direct to the public so that, because of increased consumer demand, they can sell more to the retail trade.

Other facets of industrial marketing are also very similar to their counterparts in consumer operations. We have mentioned market research but another similar area is pricing, where again the environment, product strength and the state of knowledge of both buyer and seller are weighty factors—and most industrial selling is done direct from manufacturer to customer so that the industrial marketing man has the advantage of not having an only partially controlled middleman in between. Both types of marketing require concentration first on the customer's needs; both need to evaluate individual products; both have to watch the market and devise long range strategies.

Whether we see the similarities or the dissimilarities between consumer and industrial marketing predominating depends on our own experience and background. In the principles involved there does seem a great deal of similarity. Whether we see the practices in the same light is a matter for personal judgment. The generally longer time horizons in industrial marketing produce clear differences in the applications of principles, it takes longer to make a sale, the product life-cycle is longer, the general orientation of a particular business is slower to change. Yet men often go from marketing appointments in consumer operations to similar work in industrial operations. Is this because this is the only (present) source of marketing-trained men? Is the lack of a similar migration in the reverse direction a proof that industrially-trained men are not suitable for consumer marketing appointments? There can be no one answer. Rugby football and Association football have much in common, but they are different games and sometimes people trained in the one do very well in the other. Do we see the similarities more than the differences? Is what we seek perhaps a good ball player—or his equivalent, a good marketing man?

Suggested Reading

LONSDALE, J. E. *Selling to Industry*, Business Publications, 1966. (A sales director's view of industrial marketing.)
PATERSON, W. *Industrial Publicity Management,* Business Books, 1968.
ROWE, D., & ALEXANDER, I., *Selling Industrial Products,* Hutchinson, 1965.
WILSON, A. (Ed.) *The Marketing of Industrial Products,* Hutchinson, 1965.

CHAPTER 19

Exporting and International Marketing

The United Kingdom becomes a full member of the European Common Market in January 1973, before these words appear in print. The merits and demerits of this action are not for debate here but it would be entirely wrong for marketing people to ignore the certainty that this event will considerably alter their marketing environment. The change will affect the majority of marketing operations in all of the nine member countries and in many other countries too, and marketing action will have to be adjusted to meet the change. The following table of populations for 1969, from *Supermarket* by T. Boardman is one of the most vivid indicators.

	Estimated population (millions 1969)
U.S.A.	203
U.S.S.R.	240
Common Market (total)	188
U.K.	56
Other applicant countries	12
E.F.T.A. countries not applying	36
Total for present Common Market plus present applicants	256

Within a few years from our entry, tariffs, quotas and other barriers to international trade will be eliminated and there will be a universal schedule of import restrictions (where such exist) between member countries and the world outside. Monetary and fiscal policies will be co-ordinated; free movement within the market will be introduced for services, capital, business enterprise and labour. The new situation will be very different from the past. Firms, indeed whole industries as we now know them, will be operating in a quite different environment. Some of our present protection against foreign invasion of our home market will disappear; some of the continental barriers to our exports will also disappear. How this will affect the individual enterprise can, of course, only be learned by an examination of its situation in detail.

Now for probably the first time in our history, *every* company in the U.K. would be wise to look at markets outside the country. For many these may be the only hope of salvation in the face of shrinking home markets; for others they may provide the prospects of continuing expansion instead of stagnation.

Why export ?

We do not need here to discuss in detail international economics. It must be clear to readers that in a manufacturing and trading country like the U.K. we do not, and cannot, either produce enough food for our own 56 millions or so population nor make all the products we need to support our present living standards, let alone improve them. At the very least some foodstuffs and some raw materials must be imported from overseas. In practice, more than the absolute minimum is brought in because certain imported products (they include consumer and industrial products as well as raw materials) are considered by their buyers to be in some way superior to those made at home. However, all such imports must ultimately be paid for by exports of goods, materials or services from this country.

The need on the part of the country as a whole to have exports to pay for the imports we need is clear. What about the individual company, however? Why should Blank and Co. (Engineers) Ltd. export any (or all) of its products?

In the context of our opening chapter there can be only one answer—that the company by exporting can make a profit and keep in being. No amount of exhortation or learned exposition will outweigh the fundamental importance of this view which proceeds from the same philosophy as that discussed in the section on product strategy and product management in Chaper 2. Products are retained or new ones developed because they contribute towards the overall profitability of the company. No businessman can be expected to become involved in an export trading situation if he is going to lose money consistently on it and have no compensating advantages (occasionally companies may lose money from their immediate export operations but more than recoup this from grants or privileges in other directions). As a rule few firms will export just because the government would like them to do so.

On the other hand there are companies, many of them large and successful, which export the majority of what they make, such as in heavy, or heavy electrical, engineering. In our motor car industry, were it not for their exports the larger groups would certainly make less profit. Even in retail trading the last two or three years has seen a considerable increase in interest in overseas trading and such firms as Tesco, Austin Reed and The House of Fraser are understood to be already well established in Europe and ready to develop further. As in other matters, then, the reasons why a business will or will not become involved in exporting are to be found in an analysis of opportunities to make a profit.

Exporting or international marketing?

When the majority of British firms began to take an interest in overseas markets in years gone by they found that buyers (or their agents) from these markets looked them out and came to them to buy. This was largely because the buyers could not get what they wanted unless they came here for it. Soon manufacturers who did sufficient business established representatives in a number of countries overseas to make it easier both for them and for their customers to maintain contact and develop business. Initially these representatives were often importing agents domiciled in the country concerned but eventually, when the business was big enough, full-time employees whether British or local nationals were maintained overseas to bring to bear the necessary concentration of interest and knowledge—the situation was just as described in Chapter 11 when discussing sales organisation.

In some cases (and the development was paralleled elsewhere in highly developed economies) overseas selling operations expanded until they became very similar to the operations carried out at home. An export manager, based at headquarters, controlled the work of a team of men who were agents and/or full-time representatives and kept in touch by correspondence, cable and personal visits. The largest organisations soon had "area" or "group" organisations with intermediate management, either home-based or situated overseas, as conditions demanded, to supervise the business in markets within countries or groups of countries.

In time, however, the operation sometimes demanded a quite radical change. When there were difficulties in the way of the easy movement of products between countries, such as local governmental action to stimulate local industry by protecting it from overseas competition with tariffs, import quotas and so on, companies found it difficult, if not impossible, to succeed merely by exporting from their home base. They had to establish a complete operation inside the country to which they had previously exported and this development—providing as it did additional employment and increased economic activity—was often welcomed by the country concerned.

This phenomenon was not limited to the less well-developed countries for a number of large firms found that, if they were to expand as they wished, deep penetration of overseas markets was most effectively pursued by being established as both manufacturing and trading organisations within the markets concerned. It is for such reasons that groups such as Unilever and Procter and Gamble, British Leyland and General Motors, Olivetti and Pirelli became established in a number of countries. Sometimes they operated in each as a complete manufacturing and marketing unit; sometimes they assembled and finished products made elsewhere and exported (as in the case of cars) as crated parts for assembly; sometimes they made some parts of their products in one country and sent them to others, because it was more efficient to do so, as Ford does when it exports some car engines from the U.K. to the continent or to the U.S.A.

The overseas centres may be set up with capital from the original home base or partly with locally raised capital. Generally, however, this side of the operation is arranged, some control is maintained from the centre by general direction and the supply of expertise and managerial talent and training. Ultimately the aim is to have a flow-back of profit, though even this may be deferred for many years (especially if there are restrictions in the flow of money) in favour of building up a solid and profitable concern.

This kind of operation is what is generally considered as "international marketing". The company uses its resources of finance, knowledge and organisation to the best advantage throughout the world in order to achieve its own long-term objectives of growth and profitability. It may, of course, not be so helpful to the home country's balance of payments situation. For example, if a company in the U.K. exports £1 million of products, for which £100,000 of raw materials were imported and makes a "net profit" of say £75,000 on the whole, the company has the profit and the balance of payments is in credit to £900,000. If it brings back £100,000 profit from an overseas subsidiary doing £1 million of business and using £100,000 of raw materials obtained outside that country the company's profit position is better. But the home balance of payments has a credit balance of only £100,000 ("invisible exports") instead of the £900,000 before.

In general, nevertheless, it is worth keeping in mind the difference between a straightforward export operation working from the home country and international marketing the latter is the operation of a company simultaneously keeping manufacturing units in a number of countries. Purists will point out that it is also possible for an organisation to have a highly developed marketing operation in an overseas country and yet draw all its products, say, from the home country, and that this is also "international marketing". This is fair comment and Unilever and Olivetti are two groups which have practised this in some markets. Large merchant groups trading, as for example some of the older British Far Eastern trading groups have done, have practised the same kind of marketing without even making any products at all. The general distinction between making in one centre and marketing in a number of centres, as against being established as both makers and marketers in a number of international centres, nevertheless seems to retain its value and we shall recognise this distinction for our present discussions.

International marketing is in itself a very wide subject but the principle involved is essentially simple. The international company is trying to attain its legitimate profit and growth targets, by developing a marketing and manufacturing strategy and deploying its resources in the most effective manner, exactly as a smaller company might do in a simpler context. When marketing is on an international scale international factors must be considered. In particular, as we have seen, restrictions on the movement of goods, money and people have to be allowed for. Perhaps an even more important factor may now be political stability and the risk of overseas establishments being expropriated or subjected to compulsory purchase by the governments of the countries concerned.

This kind of operation is not an American nor yet a British phenomenon. It is largely a feature of size. Given all the complications, for these are never simple situations, the international marketing company is merely trying to optimise the return on its resources by deploying them in different countries, just as a smaller organisation may decide upon the emphasis to be given to each of a few products in a smaller market area but with the same kind of objective, optimum returns over a period of time.

The remainder of our discussion will be concerned with export marketing in the sense of a company established in the U.K. and marketing some, at least, of its products in countries overseas. Much of what we say will still apply *mutatis mutandis* to international marketing.

✷ How different is export marketing?

Marketing in overseas markets is really another form of market segmentation. In order to become involved at all we may assume that the marketer has found some similarity between what he finds the home market wants and what he believes the export market wants. This is true whether he makes cars, clothes or cosmetics: products in some way similar to those he makes at home will be wanted in some overseas market.

There are, however, a number of differences and complicating factors. The precise detail of the product(s) required may vary from what is sold at home and it may vary from country to country. The very distance of the market from home will add to the problem of communication between manufacturer and customer. The transportation of products from factory to user will probably be more difficult and take longer, over longer distances and perhaps with less smooth running transport operations. In turn this will probably mean additional packaging will be needed to protect the product physically (and also from extra risk of pilferage). Each particular market (country in this context) may have quite different methods of documentation and these will almost certainly vary between product group and product group. Furthermore we can expect that the normal risks of commercial intercourse will be increased by an added complexity of the channel of communication, by fluctuating money exchange rates, by the sheer distance and above all by the likelihood of at least two different legal systems being involved and the consequent difficulty and uncertainty of getting an equitable decision in the case of disputed responsibilities.

Across the whole spectrum of possible operations there may not be a great deal of common ground but fortunately the exporter will usually only be concerned with relatively small sectors. Yet it is normally considered sensible when writing about or discussing practical export possibilities to select either a relatively homogeneous product group in a number of overseas markets or a number of product groups in one relatively homogeneous market. To be really down to ground we should confine our attention to one particular product in one particular market. This is, however, a general analysis and not a "do it yourself" kit so we shall consider possible approaches to markets overseas on the assumption that there is no particular individuality which marks out the product from all other product groups and that our marketer is already established in the U.K. and is examining whether or not he should enter an overseas market.

It is our experience that such a company will seldom be in such an unfettered position as to ask "Where shall we export to?" and "What shall we sell there?" and thus have virtually limitless possibilities to consider. Car manufacturers usually make cars or parts of cars; they seldom make chocolate confectionery! Similarly few companies would waste much time considering the legendary selling of refrigerators to Eskimos.

Making a start in export marketing

So we return to one of the original questions asked when considering our basic marketing strategy "What is our business?" and assume that we shall not go beyond that area of opportunity when we try to get extra business abroad. What we shall do is rather to seek diversification by operating in a similar or related product field in another country. We may also assume that our marketing director has already become interested in the possibility of achieving profitable export business from some ministerial exhortation, from gossip with business friends or perhaps from an article in the business press.

Where does he start? How does he start? As in any new marketing project he should start by investigating the market and its possibilities in order to define and locate the opportunities he is looking for. Sound marketing demands a definition of the market and its needs. If there are several possibilities then they must be evaluated and compared in order to select the one most suitable for achieving the company's given objectives (and, always, in relation to the resources available). Thereafter, developing an export strategy is exactly the same as creating one at home except that some of the factors considered and some of the tools available are different from those used at home.

The original idea for an export project, whatever it is, must be clarified and validated. Generally this involves the use of one or more marketing research techniques and, as elsewhere, starting with the cheapest source of information. Almost certainly the two first actions will be to discuss the situation with the marketer's own trade association and with the nearest Board of Trade office. Both of these can and will give not only useful information but sound advice in the application of it. We cannot describe all the ways in which the Board of Trade, in particular, can assist. Suffice it to say that, both in London and in a number of easily accessible regional offices, information collected from trade attachés in every country in the world is made available— free or, at most, for the cost of one or two publications issued by H.M.S.O. at very low prices. The available information is classified by industry and by country and practically all the basic matter one can hope for is there, readily accessible and up to date. This basic material includes populations, standard of living indicators, trading climate and facilities, import and export figures by main industrial classifications usually showing country of origin or destination, tariffs, export or import regulations or restrictions, local legal requirements for packaging, labelling, quality and so on even down to lists of poten- tial agents from whom the potential exporter may choose those to canvass himself. The Board cannot do his work for him but it will give him the unstinted help of knowledgeable, commercially orientated men and women who only ask that their time be not wasted by people who do not have a serious intent or those who profess to wish to tackle a project for which they manifestly have insufficient resources. The Board's officials cannot direct, but their advice (especially over what not to do) is ignored at one's peril.

From these first steps, and the basic information obtained, the would-be exporter should be able to narrow down his approach in terms of product fields and countries; it is exactly the same process as we have already compared to selecting a detailed target and aiming a rifle bullet at it rather than loosing off a round of lead shot "in the general direction". The former is surely the more preferable method.

Once a start has been made it has been our experience that one thing leads to another and the problems become more manageable. For example, there are many government aids and services for export- ing companies. One which must be mentioned is the Export Credits Guarantee Department which is essentially an insurance organisation to protect exporters from at least some of the financial hazards inherent in this business area. There is also now the British Overseas Trade Board which has only been in operation since January 1972. It was formed to co-ordinate the work of many government and non-govern- ment services to exporters and to bring to the notice of companies not only how these services can help them but also what export oppor- tunities appear to be available to them.

In addition there are numerous private organisations which may be of help. There are many export consultants and agencies which special- ise in product groups or groups of countries. These range from people who will advise on products and markets to those who document, package and arrange transhipment of products; the exporter can get help in any or all of these operations as needed. Finally there are a number of sound market research organisations, some of which specialise in industrial or consumer markets or in particular countries. These will handle enquiries ranging from basic market information to product acceptance testing. At least one research group has a consumer panel (Europanel) already operating in eight countries on the continent. The Market Research Society and The Industrial Market Research Society have available lists of member organisations. Marketing Research is one particular business activity where in Europe, if not in the whole world, British expertise is beginning to be recognised as the standard against which to judge all others.

Matching products and markets

What does the market in the importing country want? What are the needs we must meet, the benefits we must supply? We may end up with a number of possible solutions but, though daunting, this is perhaps better than having no answer (and no business). Depending on the particular situation the final answer may range from a product which is physically exactly the same as one we sell at home to another which is within our competence but requires that we set up a new or different production operation to make it; or somewhere in between. The factors determining whether we shall go ahead with this product will be the resources required to make a successful entry, in relation to our total resources, and the degree of risk or uncertainty concerning the making of a satisfactory profit from the operation.

In practice most beginners hope to use exactly the same product(s) as in the home market. This may occasionally happen. More often, perhaps, the degree of modification may not be very considerable. What may kill the project may be to say: "This is what we make and this is what is good enough for Dalekia. The Dalekians will just have to buy it." Usually they will not buy it. Production orientation is a philosophy we ruled out earlier, though it still has not been eradicated from all businesses. It is not, of course, production orientation to see if it is possible to find a match, even a close match, between what some markets want and what we do make, in order not only to have a sound product for the market but also to use up any spare manufacturing capacity we may have and, not least, to reduce manufacturing costs all round.

The needs of the importer

In this discussion we must consider not just the trader involved (whose needs are based on making a profit) but the user customer abroad. These needs fall into a few clear categories and we may perhaps appreciate them more fully by thinking of ourselves as being export customers for countries exporting to us. Why do we buy, let us say, a Swiss watch, an American machine tool (a copy mill perhaps) or a consignment of Scandinavian carton board? What do we expect from buying such products? What worries have we in our minds when we are trying to make up our minds on whether to buy them, or not? If we can answer this kind of question regarding imported products we ourselves buy then certainly the answer to our export problems will be found in the answers to similar questions put to our export customers.

The fundamental reasons for importing are:

(*i*) the satisfaction from buying the product concerned is somehow greater than that obtained from buying similar products made at home. This satisfaction may be either in the physical performance which the product gives, or in the psychological satisfaction stemming from it, or from both;

(*ii*) no products giving equal satisfaction are available from any other source;

(*iii*) no products giving equal satisfaction at comparable prices are available.

This can be restated as that the incentives for buying imports may be in the physical quality of the product, in its product or brand image, in its price or in a mixture of all three.

Similarly, let us consider our worries concerning buying imported products:

(*i*) When the manufacturer is so far away, can we get the service we want both before and after purchase? Can we get repairs done or spare parts supplied quickly enough for our needs?

(*ii*) Can we rely on getting the product when we want it, or at the very least at the time when the supplier says it will be delivered to us? Can we go on getting repeat purchases when we want them?

(*iii*) Will the imported product be packed in the way we are accustomed to have it, in regard to quantity, kind of pack (glass, sealed can, etc.) and so on?

(*iv*) Will the instructions and method of use be measured in cc, such as we are used to, or in fluid ounces which we don't understand?

(*v*) Will the instructions and any accompanying material be in English, which is our native language, or in Spanish, where our only knowledge is what we have picked up on holiday on the Costa Brava?

As before this can be restated as that disincentives against buying imports are in the area of service, speed of service, delivery time, reliability and convenience for local use.

Realistic export strategy

If the would-be exporter is to build up a lasting business in exporting he should approach the operation from the angle of "What would I be likely to want if an exporter came here to do business with me?" and then proceed on the assumption that his own potential customers overseas must be given like courtesy and consideration. Again, it is not enough to try, as so many companies have tried, to get an export order now, when there happens to be surplus capacity in the factory, but still to keep in mind that they hope next year to fill their order book at home and not get tangled up in the complexities of exporting— and, if one or two people overseas want repeat orders, because they happened to like what was sent them, and it isn't very convenient now, then bad luck for them! Stable and profitable business is not likely to come that way.

The exporter already starts with a handicap. Almost certainly in home marketing he has some background, perhaps even a lifetime's experience, of what those in his market are doing and thinking, how far they can be led into new ways, what sacred cows must never be threatened. In first approaching an overseas market he has no such advantage. True, after many years of experience he may acquire the same kind of background but in the early days he must expect to have to get this information by market research methods. What he should never do is to assume that what applies at home also applies in France, India or the U.S.A.

Product design. The product needed may be the same as, similar to, or very different from that sold at home. Yet even slight differences may be very important indeed. There is no sound future in trying to force unsuitable products on the buyer. This is not to say that the buyer always really wants what he *says* he wants. What he requires is something that meets his genuine needs even if the correctness of the decision has to be sold to him. In this connection (and in the following notes on packaging) it is vital that the exporter should not, in ignorance, offend against the culture of his customer's country. White is the colour of mourning in China; at least one cosmetic in the U.K.

has a brand name which is not a polite word to use in a German home. We cannot be too careful in checking the product and its packaging in detail with a qualified adviser from the country to which we intend to send it.

Packaging. We saw earlier that the package has both a physical and a promotional function. It has to separate and contain (where applicable) the appropriate quantity of product and also protect it from physical damage or deterioration until it is used. It usually also provides a medium for conveying information to the user and any intermediate handlers. Both these functions must be efficiently carried out in the changed context of export marketing. The unit package must be suitable for the needs of the user. If the product has had a long and possibly rough journey from factory to user it *must* be protected so that it can survive the rigours of the experience; if this journey also entails passing through extremes of climatic conditions, then the product must be insulated against harmful effects. If the product is of high value to weight and size and is easily disposed of, then it must be protected against the greater danger of pilferage due to its longer time in transit.

Promotional material. One does not expect Eskimos to read Swahili. In turn, *all* promotional material, including the package and container, where applicable, whether it is distributed as part of the product or in any other way, including the normal media of advertising, must be in the language of the buyer. Whilst it may add to the brand image to have directions for use in three or four languages (thus indicating international acceptance) it is most important that the correct impression is conveyed by having the copy translated by really competent professionals, whose mother tongue is to be used on the pack, in order to get the correct idiom and nuance of meaning. Word for word translation "to fit the space" may create a ruinous image. In time we would hope to see enough business to warrant separate packs for each market so that the whole of the available space on them could be used for a fuller exposition of the brand than is possible when three or four languages each repeat the same message.

Service. The service appropriate to a product field may be unique to that field. However, we can scarcely overemphasise the importance *to the exporter* of appreciating that he cannot expect to develop a large and stable business if the service required by his product's user is not supplied. Whether the service is effected from the U.K. (as may happen with large industrial installations) or performed by the local distributor (as in the case of cars) is not usually important; unless the supplier is

reliable, efficient and prepared to supply appropriate service he is better advised not to get involved in the operation at all.

Pricing. As in any marketing operation, pricing plays a large part in
the export marketing mix (see Chapter 9). Again, there are different and
additional factors to take into consideration. Here are some of them:

(*i*) the cost of special export packaging;

(*ii*) the cost of transportation from factory to user including not
merely transit costs but also port or airport fees and clearance dues;

(*iii*) tariffs and import dues;

(*iv*) remuneration of agents and distributors, or the cost of the
exporter's own overseas organisation;

(*v*) warehousing and distributing costs inside the export market
country.

Not all of these charges will necessarily be paid by the exporter,
for there is still a great deal of business done by agents who take over
at the port of exit in the U.K. But, however it is arranged, all these
charges have to be met out of the price finally paid by the user customer
and the exporter, however close or far-away organisationally, must be
satisfied that the user is not asked to pay a price which is so far outside
the bounds of realism that it effectively puts a stop to business.

Costing for export

Companies have been known to take the latest costing of a product
for the home market and then to add to it all the cost of the extra export
activities described above, only to find that at the best possible price
obtainable in the market the high level of côsts ruled out any possibility
of a profit. Why is this kind of action unreasonable? What should be
done if this is not the way to do it?

As before, we must make some assumptions. Let us say, then,
that the company is already operating on a profit-making basis, i.e.
the contributions of the various products have already met the overheads and left a margin for profit; that the costing system is sufficiently
detailed to show selling, promotional and distributive costs separately;
that there is an overseas market able and willing to buy the product;
and finally that an export strategy has been formulated and the necessary organisation set up.

At this stage, the general overheads of the company have been covered and bear no real relevance to the consideration of an export costing. Furthermore, exactly the same applies to those elements of cost
made up by the home sales, sales promotion and distribution activities.
What is very much more to the point is the fact that, if the exporter

can sell to his overseas agent (for example) at a price which covers variable (direct) manufacturing cost, plus whatever extra export changes there may be, and have some margin left over as a contribution to company profits, then the exercise is all worth while as this contribution will be clear gain. In short, the exporter who is operating from a firm home-trade base should operate on a gross margin basis, making sure of course that, at the price he can obtain, he covers both direct manufacturing cost plus all the additional direct costs pertaining to the export operation. If, in fact, export means extra output from the factory which in turn leads to some reduction in the direct costs of both home and export products, then the company will also get an extra bonus for its enterprise.

We should stress once more the importance of working back from price in the market and then seeing whether this leaves an adequate margin above the total of relevant direct costs for the operation to be worthwhile. "Cost plus" as a basis for pricing is no more defensible in exporting than it is in trading at home.

The cost of entering an export market

All we have said regarding sensible ways of approaching export marketing may sound reasonable enough, but this is not to say that it is always simple and easy to do what is needed in real life. The main obstacles are, as always, the difficulties of getting adequate and accurate information at a reasonable cost in a reasonable time. As a result, the practitioner is frequently in a position of having to make his decision with incomplete or inaccurate information. As we have seen, exporting has all the attendant problems of home trading plus a few additional complications of its own.

One of the most pressing of these is the initial cost of effecting a successful entry into an export market. This may be slight in relation to the potential gain, or it may be heavy; it may be small absolutely in relation to the company's resources, or it may be large. The first thing is to get this cost into perspective in absolute terms and in proportion to the potential gain in relation to the company's size and the resources it is prepared to commit to the exercise. This kind of assessment is in no way different in character from any similar exercise in any other form of market diversification; for the export beginner-company it may, however, seem to be more difficult because some of the factors are less familiar.

What does the initial entry cost consist of? The following are the main items:

(*i*) The cost of altering the product physically to make it suitable for the new market. This may vary from nil, if the product is exactly as sold at home, to a considerable figure, if a complete new project has to be mounted, with a complex R. & D. development programme and no hope of using the resultant product in any other market which might share the costs.

(*ii*) Additional production costs. Here we should include the cost of new plant or altering existing plant or production methods. We should also include the cost of the "lost opportunities" if production of this export product means that production for any other market is curtailed for lack of capacity, etc.

(*iii*) Repackaging costs. These should include all the costs involved in designing or altering packaging to suit the export market including, where applicable, not merely alterations to the pack but extra crating, etc., which might be necessary for additional protection whilst in transit and also the cost of buying an economical first run of packaging material which may have to be thrown out if the total volume hoped for is not achieved.

(*iv*) Preliminary marketing costs. These include such items as marketing research, visits to the market by executives and similar costs incurred in the preliminary investigations.

(*v*) Marketing export organisation costs. These are the costs of setting up a ·marketing operation including selling and promotional costs, promotional material and activities (including advertising and P. R.) and the cost of taking on and maintaining any extra staff at home or abroad and the cost of maintaining them for a minimum period even if the operation is closed down.

All these costs should be estimated, totalled and considered as a kind of quasi fixed cost of the operation (packaging material and such like items must not of course be included in both the direct element and the fixed element). This fixed cost has then to be met from the contribution made by the exported item until a break-even point is reached and a real contribution made to the total company operation in the same way as is described in Chapter 14.

Organisation for exporting

Let us underline yet again the basic presumption that we have a company which really is serious about developing an export operation. Given this, what kind of organisation will it need to carry out the work? Once more the solution is largely dependent upon the size of the operation and the complexity of the particular product market.

Almost certainly most companies in the initial stages of developing export markets will hope to keep the entry costs down for any particular market and probably proceed from one market to another stage by stage so as not to overstretch their administrative and other facilities. In the early stages we would then expect to find the General Sales Manager or Sales Director giving some of his own time to the new operation but probably deputing one of his assistants as export manager. In order to avoid the uneconomic use of representatives in the early stages he will probably appoint one or more agents in the markets concerned and rely upon encouraging them to carry out all the promotional work needed and also to provide whatever customer service is required.

At the other end of the scale, in a large well-developed market, the company may need in an established operation, a fully fledged export division to market all its relevant products overseas and led by a senior manager reporting directly to the marketing director. Within this division there may be brand or product managers, and sales managers, with a fully fledged sales team and distribution organisation with depots or warehouses quite similar to that used at home. It is impossible to generalise except to say that the tendency has been for firms to start in a relatively small way and create a bigger organisation as this becomes needed and that in its most sophisticated form it is difficult to see very much difference between a full-scale overseas marketing set-up and the organisation overseas of an international marketing company, or even of the company in its own homeland.

The same applies to organising advertising, sales promotion and public relations. The home advertising department working with the company's advertising agency may be able to manage competently with perhaps some help from the countries concerned in checking translations of promotional material. The advertising agency may indeed have its own branches (or at least associated agencies) in many of the countries concerned. This is becoming increasingly true of Europe and North America and quite often the original interest in an export market comes from suggestions made by the company's (international) advertising agency when the latter is developing its own internal strategy for growth. The extent to which this happens will depend on the degree to which the agency's familiarity with its client's home markets will help in the client's export business together with the agency's understanding of the export market itself and its familiarity with, and physical capacity to handle, advertising media there.

Consortia

Finally we should touch on one other variation of an organisation for export which has achieved some significance in late years, particularly among smaller or medium-sized companies in engineering—it has a counterpart in the more formal organisations of the larger companies concerned, at the heavy end, with building nuclear power stations. The consortium is a group of non-competing companies which come together and set up a common export marketing organisation which operates on behalf of all the members, and is paid for by them in some agreed proportion. The reasons behind using consortia are two. Firstly, the provision of full-time competent people at a cheaper rate because their services are shared; secondly, that the member companies are usually recruited because their products are complementary and not competitive and that very often either a complete "package deal" (e.g. pressure vessels and pumps and piping rather than any one of these) can be sold or the consortium, having learned of a particular requirement, can pursue the matter and bring in the other members to supply other products not originally mentioned.

Unfortunately, the very reasons which bring companies together in consortia are the very reasons for the consortia breaking up later. The group is formed when risk and uncertainty is highest and knowledge and certainty lowest. When operations have developed well and prosperity is enjoyed, some members of the groups may tend to disagree about such matters as sharing costs and over whose opinion should prevail when there are alternative possible courses to follow. Consortia are formed when companies feel unsure of their ability to go it alone; they break up when companies feel strong enough to go their own way. There are exceptions.

Interest in exporting and the importance of exporting have been greatly stimulated by the entry of the United Kingdom into the Common Market. It seems certain that many companies will soon be considering countries in Europe as market segments just as they have considered the different regions of the home market in the past. The brutal fact also is that if this view does not prevail many companies may be overtaken by events and go out of business.

This is nothing new. It is simply another illustration of the constant change in the marketing environment. The more successful marketing managers will adapt to it—indeed speed up the change by their own reaction. The only real danger seems to be that some companies may still try to play at overseas marketing and hope to make successful sporadic forays abroad when it suits their own purposes. Action based on a serious and genuine attempt to assess what the customer wants and thinks offers a far greater probability of success.

Suggested Reading

RYANS, J. R., JUN., & BAKER, J. C. *World Marketing: a Multinational Approach,* Wiley, 1967.
DEVERELL, C. S. *Marketing Management for Europe,* Butterworth, 1969.
FRAIN, J. *Export Salesmanship,* U.C.T.A., 1970.
NEILLANDS, R., & DESCHAMPSNEUFS, H. *Exporting,* Pan, 1969.
Services for British Exporters, B.O.T. Export Handbook, H.M.S.O., 1972.

Index